LEVIATHAN
Parts I and II

THOMAS HOBBES

With an introduction by
HERBERT W. SCHNEIDER

· ·

The Library of Liberal Arts

published by

THE BOBBS-MERRILL COMPANY, INC.
INDIANAPOLIS · NEW YORK

Thomas Hobbes: 1588-1679

LEVIATHAN was originally published in 1651

. . . .

CONTENTS
· · · · · · · · · · · · · · · · ·

PART TWO: OF COMMONWEALTH

EDITOR'S INTRODUCTION

The *Leviathan* is a classic of English literature. Its author was an accomplished classicist at an early age and an assistant to Francis Bacon while he was writing his *Essays*. Hobbes's style shows the influence of both the ancient classics and Bacon; it also reflects the light in the merry eyes of a wit and the dead earnest of a philosopher. The work begins with the technicalities of psychology and ends with a fierce religious invective against "the kingdom of darkness." It was recognized at once as a powerful tract for the times and also as a permanent contribution to moral philosophy.

As a philosophical composition, the *Leviathan* is noteworthy for three major achievements: (1) it contains a rational construction of natural law as the basis of positive law, in preference to common law; (2) it provides a representative theory of absolute authority as a modern substitute for the divine right theory; (3) it is the first comprehensive exposition of bourgeois ethics. But in the plan of its author it was also the culmination of a systematic trilogy: (1) on physical bodies; (2) on human nature; and (3) on bodies politic. The sovereign body politic or commonwealth, according to the *Leviathan,* is an "artificial animal" and a "mortal God" constructed by the covenants of men in the interests of security, justice, and peace. To the generation of this mortal God or "great Leviathan," says Hobbes in Chapter XVII, "we owe under the Immortal God our peace and defense."

The first two parts of the *Leviathan,* included in this edition, expound the secular doctrine of commonwealth in terms of reason; the other two parts expound the religious doctrine of a holy commonwealth in terms of revelation and divine law. In 1651, when the work was first published, the religious parts were for immediate application to the crisis in which Cromwell found himself. Since then, the secular system of the first two books has won increasing respect. To Hobbes himself, however, both parts, the general theory and the religious application, were taken with utmost seriousness and both express Hobbes's intense devotion to his country and to his faith.

Thomas Hobbes, son of an incompetent vicar, was born near Malmesbury in Gloucestershire during the general alarm over the approaching Spanish Armada in 1588. He attended Magdalen Hall, Oxford, a college in which Puritanism was dominant and where he probably also came under Ockhamite influence. Here he learned to despise Aristotelian scholasticism and to search among the sciences for a better method. The Puritans were then the leaders in the new physical sciences and it was natural that Hobbes in his Oxford environment should, like his contemporary on the Continent, René Descartes, turn his back on Jesuit texts and on Aristotelianism and look in the direction of Galileo. He was fortunate to be appointed tutor to a young earl whom he accompanied in 1610 to the Continent. During his travels he devoted himself to translating Thucydides, learning geometry and optics, and working on a theory of sensation as a form of motion. In 1634, he was able to settle down in Paris, where he soon became a member of the circle around the Abbé Mersenne and made the acquaintance of Gassendi and Descartes and a group of other prominent scientists. He made a pilgrimage to Galileo in Italy. In 1637, he returned to England intending to expand his *Little Treatise* on sensation (inspired largely by Harvey's discovery of the circulation of the blood) into a more general work on bodily motions, to which he gave the title *De Corpore*. But the political crisis of 1640 forced him to turn his attention to politics. He circulated among friends his *Elements of Law* (1640) in which he worked out a theory of undivided sovereignty without divine right. Such a doctrine, though mediating theoretically, was popular with neither party in the civil war. Fearing imprisonment by one or the other party, especially by the growing enemies of absolutism, he left hurriedly for Paris, where he remained until 1651. During this time, in 1646, he became a tutor to the exiled Prince of Wales, the future Charles II. But after the publication of *De Cive* (1642) and of the expanded English version, the *Leviathan,* in 1651, Hobbes became known on the Continent as a rabid Protestant and he lost favor among the royalist exiles. He was therefore greatly relieved when it became safe in 1651, under Cromwell, for him to return to England.

The *Leviathan* appeared in London at a critical juncture in Cromwell's career when, after his victory over the royalists at Worcester, he was strong enough to defy the Rump Parliament and usher in the Protectorate. This trend of affairs was much to Hobbes's liking. He had remained religiously an independent, taking communion with the Church of England privately but refusing to associate publicly with Anglicans because they were "seditious." He was outspoken in his contempt for Presbyterians and Catholics. His *De Cive,* published on the Continent, had followed immediately on John Milton's publication in England (1641) of his tract, *Of Reformation Touching Church-Discipline in England,* and Parts II and III of the *Leviathan* could readily be interpreted as an ideology for Cromwell. For the argument was based on Calvinist psychology, on the Puritan doctrine of covenant, and on Cromwell's creation of a "Christian Commonwealth"—a covenanted absolutism under God. But hardly had Hobbes imagined himself to have found a sovereign in harmony with his doctrines when Cromwell's authority began to crumble and civil war again threatened. In 1660, Charles II and Hobbes accepted each other somewhat grudgingly. Charles called Hobbes "the Bear" and Hobbes was disappointed in witnessing the temporary restoration of the divine right monarchy of the Stuarts. In the Latin edition of the *Leviathan* (1668) he made a few politic changes,[1] proclaimed himself a loyal subject of His Majesty, and settled down in retirement with a small pension.

He died in 1679 "glad to find a hole to creep out of the world at."[2] During his retirement he engaged in several fruitless disputes on scientific questions; he imagined himself to be a better mathematician than he really was. He wrote an important *Dialogue between a Philosopher and a student of the Common Laws of England.* This dialogue, published posthumously, became the immediate inspiration for the revival of

[1] None of these changes affected the argument of Parts I and II.
[2] Aubrey's *Life of Hobbes* (1813).

Hobbes's philosophy by the Austinian school of analytic juris-
prudence early in the nineteenth century in defense of the
"omnicompetence" of Parliament and of statute law in the face
of opposition by the courts which defended the constitution on
the basis of common law. To this revival is also due Sir William
Molesworth's edition (1839-45) of the sixteen volumes of
Hobbes's complete works.

Despite his intellectual aggressiveness and his contentious
style, Hobbes was a sober, pious person, who never broke with
the Church of England though he had decided Puritan leanings. His opposition to Arminianism and to freewill doctrine
indicates his Calvinist leanings and his departures from Anglican theology. Because of his independence he was accused by
both Roman Catholics and Anglican High Churchmen of
atheism, which was a stock charge brought against anticlericals.
But he was certainly neither an atheist nor a materialist. He
believed in the essentials of the Christian revelation and in the
doctrine of personal salvation. He wrote that he would never
deny, even at a sovereign's bidding if ever a sovereign were
foolish enough to ask it, that "Christ died for my sins." Believing that all beings are "bodies," he conceived of the "body
politic" as an organism, and he thought that God must have a
body composed of some "ethereal" substance. Hence he believed in "spiritual bodies" and distinguished sharply between
corporeality and materiality. The treatment of covenant theology in Part III of *Leviathan* is thoroughly Puritan, and in
general Part II should be regarded as a secularized version of
the English Puritans' theory of a commonwealth.

Hobbes himself said that the *Leviathan* lays the foundations
for "the science of natural justice." He regarded the science of
justice to be the culmination of the science of consequences.
It is not a "mechanical science," as has often been maintained
erroneously, but it is thoroughly natural and rational. He never
departed from the conception of philosophy which he formu-
lated early in his career:

> By philosophy is understood the knowledge acquired by
> reasoning from the manner of the generation of anything to
> the properties, or from the properties to some possible way of

~~generation of the same; to the end to be able to produce, as far as matter and human force permit, such effects as human life requires.~~[3]

This "natural science of justice" has three major branches, as was suggested above; and these three branches it is necessary to explain briefly.

1) *The rational construction of law.* Hobbes is content to ~~interpret a law as an authoritative comman~~d, whether human or divine. But ~~each command must be justified~~, and ~~the justification of statute law consists in showing that it is merely an application of natural law. The government, in other words, is responsible morally to the principles of "natural justi~~ce," and any violation of these principles will sooner or later be punished by God in his exercise of power in his "kingdom by nature." Hobbes formulates nineteen laws of nature with considerable care, endeavoring to prove in each case that it follows from the general maxims of right reason or prudence. These rules are discovered by analyzing the consequences of their absence in the "state of nature," where they govern merely *in foro interno,* in conscience, but not externally, since they are not observed and enforced. In other words, ~~Hobbes's political rationalism is utilitarian.~~ This is the first attempt to construct a systematic utilitarian rationalization of natural law. Thus, conceiving ~~natural law to be the moral basis and norm for statute law,~~ Hobbes does not need to appeal to custom, precedent, or common law as the source of justice. There need be no "sense" of justice in human nature, for the *science* of justice is the only reliable guide for law.

But in order to make this science possible there must be a science of the consequences of human passions. It is with this science that the *Leviathan* begins. This is a branch of the Galilean science of motion. Human motions or motives must be studied not as the scholastics studied them, as "passions" or "affects," but rather as active forces or motions, in terms of their consequences. Thus, beginning with the traditional list of passions, Hobbes tries to prove that their general consequence is to create in each individual, as he pursues his natural "rights"

[3] Beginning of Ch. XLVI of the *Leviathan,* which chapter is included as an introduction in this edition. See Note on the Text, p. xvii.

or self-government in the freedom of the state of nature, "a perpetual and restless desire of power after power that ceases only in death" (Ch. XI). The consequence of this lust for power is universal competition—the "war of all against all"—and the consequence of this competition is that human life in a state of nature would be "solitary, poor, nasty, brutish and short" (Ch. XIII). From such a state man is rescued by three forces in human nature: fear, hope, and reason. It is reason that "suggests convenient articles of peace" or natural laws (Ch. XIII).

2) *A representative theory of absolute authority.* Hobbes's myth of "Leviathan," of the artificial creation of a social organism or collective person, is his way of escaping the traditional assumption that authority always comes from above. According to this theory, an authority is an agent or person authorized, the legal bearer of another's person. The unity of a commonwealth is created when a group of men covenant to appoint a single "body" or will as the common bearer of the person of each. Thus a government becomes the representative or authoritative person of all the members of the "body politic" and in virtue of having such unity of authorized will or person the commonwealth establishes sovereignty. This theory had already been worked out as a theory of church government by the "covenant theologians" of the Puritans; it remained for Hobbes to give it rational form and apply it to states. As a theory of church government it was an attack on the theory of episcopal authority through apostolic succession; as a secular theory of authority it was a substitute for divine right. It was the entering wedge for the theory of representative government, though Hobbes himself had no intention to use it as a theory of self-government or democracy. On the contrary, it was his attempt to justify absolutism by "natural justice."

3) *Bourgeois ethics.* The moral bonds on which Hobbes builds commonwealth are those of contractual obligation. The first law of nature, according to Hobbes, is: Seek peace or else security. The second is: Be willing to enter into "a mutual transferring of right, which men call *contract*." And the majority of the other laws of nature define the conditions under which contractual ties can operate peacefully and successfully.

The commonwealth is clearly not a feudal order, but a civil society. The idea of sovereignty is dragged in from feudal times, but otherwise Hobbes constructs his political ethics for modern, urban, commercial communities. This becomes evident especially when one reads the details of civil law as Hobbes formulates them in Chapters XXVI to XXIX. He has a lawyer's interest in establishing legal principles for regulating the economic life of a community. In his formulation of both foreign and domestic policies he reflects the concerns of the bourgeoisie and the politics of Cromwell. In short, Hobbes was not a speculative philosopher imagining a theoretical social contract. He constructed a vivid ideology for the spirit of contract in general. He was fully aware of the growing need for a peaceful, contractual, stable, equitable regulation of corporate enterprises and competitive commerce. He was looking ahead to the general moral reconstruction of society which was evidently needed if the commonwealth was ever to emerge from civil war into a state of "nutrition and procreation," which state, he maintained, depends on "the right distribution of the commodities of sea and land" (Ch. XXIV).

The science of natural justice is the only science necessary for sovereigns. . . . No other philosopher hitherto has put into order and sufficiently or probably proved all the theorems of moral doctrine that men may learn thereby how to govern and how to obey (Ch. XXXI).

I cannot think it will be condemned at this time either by the public judge of doctrine, or by any that desire the continuance of public peace. And in this hope I return to my interrupted speculations of bodies natural, wherein, if God give me health to finish it, I hope the novelty will as much please, as in the doctrine of this artificial body it uses to offend. For such truth as opposes no man's profit, nor pleasure, is to all men welcome. ("Conclusion" of the *Leviathan*.)

HERBERT W. SCHNEIDER

SELECTED BIBLIOGRAPHY

THE PRINCIPAL WRITINGS OF HOBBES

1630-37? *A Short Tract on First Principles* (also referred to as *The Little Treatise*). First published in 1889 by F. Tönnies as an appendix to his edition of *The Elements of Law.*

1640 *The Elements of Law.* First published in England in 1650 as two treatises: *On Human Nature* and *De Corpore Politico* (both in English). A corrected edition in one volume was published by F. Tönnies, Cambridge, 1889.

1640-41 *Correspondence with Descartes and Objections to his Meditations.* First published by Molesworth in Vol. V of the Collected Latin Works, 1845.

1642 *De Cive.* Written in Latin, published in Paris, 1642. Translated by Hobbes and published in England, 1651, under the title, *Philosophical Rudiments concerning Government and Society.* Revised edition by Sterling P. Lamprecht, New York, 1949.

1641-44? *Tractatus Opticus* (in Latin). Published by Mersenne in his *Optique* as Book VII, 1644.

1646 *Of Liberty and Necessity.* First published 1654 and related to the controversy with Bishop Bramhall, 1656.

1651 *Leviathan, or the Matter, Form and Power of a Commonwealth, ecclesiastical and civil.* London, 1651. A Latin version, with considerable variations, prepared by Hobbes, was published in 1668.

1655 *De Corpore* (in Latin). First published in 1655, but may have been completed as early as 1645.

1658 *De Homine* (in Latin). This is a reworking of the first part of *The Elements of Law.* Published 1658.

1660 *Behemoth or the Long Parliament.* London, 1679.

1666 *A Dialogue between a Philosopher and a Student of Common Laws of England.* Published posthumously, 1681.

Sir William Molesworth published the Complete Works: the English Works, in 11 volumes, 1839. The Latin Works, in 5 volumes, 1845.

SELECTED RECENT WORKS ON HOBBES

Laird, John. *Hobbes*. London, 1934. xii, 324 pp.

Brandt, Frithjof. *Thomas Hobbes' Mechanical Conception of Nature*. London, 1928. 399 pp. Translation from the Danish.

Strauss, Leo. *The Political Philosophy of Hobbes, Its Basis and Genesis*. Oxford, 1936. xx, 172 pp.

Peters, Richard. *Hobbes*. London, 1956. 272 pp. (Penguin Book).

Warrender, Howard. *The Political Philosophy of Hobbes; His Theory of Obligation*. Oxford, 1957. 346 pp.

Tönnies, Ferdinand. *Hobbes, Leben und Lehre*. Stuttgart, 1896. xiii, 232 pp. 3d ed., 1925.

Polin, Raymond. *Politique et Philosophie chez Thomas Hobbes*. Paris, 1953. xx, 267 pp.

NOTE ON THE TEXT

The present reprint of the first two parts of *Leviathan* follows the standard text. It has been carefully compared with the first edition of 1651, and grateful acknowledgment is made to the Philosophy Department of Columbia University for its cooperation in making the priceless copy available for this purpose. For the first time in an American edition, the present volume retains the marginal notes of the original edition. Within the limits set by Hobbes's style, spelling, capitalization, and punctuation have been revised to conform to present-day American usage. A number of footnotes have been added by the Editor and the publisher's editorial staff. A special effort has been made to identify the numerous biblical references.

The present edition also contains, in addition to Parts One and Two, Chapter 46, "Of Darkness from Vain Philosophy and Fabulous Traditions," and the concluding chapter, "A Review and Conclusion." Chapter 46 has been placed at the beginning of the text as an introduction, and a word of explanation is due the reader for this arrangement. This chapter is known to be an early essay of Hobbes, though the original title and date of composition are unknown. It represents his "discourse on method," comparable to the more famous *Discours* by his contemporary, René Descartes. In it he summarized the kind of critique of scholasticism and of the scholastic Aristotle which was current in the Oxford of his day, and at the beginning he put a fine formulation of his conception of scientific method, according to the school of Galileo. The title which he assigned to it when he incorporated it in the last Book of the *Leviathan* was obviously suggested by the title of that book, "The Kingdom of Darkness." The substance of the essay, however, makes it an excellent, programmatic expression of the spirit of revolt in Hobbes and in the age to which the *Leviathan* belonged.

H. W. S.

LEVIATHAN

OR

THE MATTER, FORM, AND POWER
OF A COMMONWEALTH
ECCLESIASTICAL AND CIVIL

To My Most Honored Friend
MR. FRANCIS GODOLPHIN
of Godolphin

Honored Sir,

Your most worthy brother, Mr. Sidney Godolphin, when he lived, was pleased to think my studies something, and otherwise to oblige me, as you know, with real testimonies of his good opinion, great in themselves, and the greater for the worthiness of his person. For there is not any virtue that disposes a man, either to the service of God, or to the service of his country, to civil society, or private friendship, that did not manifestly appear in his conversation, not as acquired by necessity, or affected upon occasion, but inherent, and shining in a generous constitution of his nature. Therefore, in honor and gratitude to him, and with devotion to yourself, I humbly dedicate unto you this my discourse of Commonwealth. I know not how the world will receive it, nor how it may reflect on those that shall seem to favor it. For in a way beset with those that contend, on one side, for too great liberty and, on the other side, for too much authority, 'tis hard to pass between the points of both unwounded. But yet, methinks, the endeavor to advance the civil power should not be by the civil power condemned; nor private men, by reprehending it, declare they think that power too great. Besides, I speak not of the men, but, in the abstract, of the seat of power (like to those simple and unpartial creatures in the Roman Capitol that with their noise defended those within it, not because they were they, but there), offending none, I think, but those without, or such within, if there be any such, as favor them. That which perhaps may most offend are certain texts of Holy Scripture, alleged by me to other purpose than ordinarily they use to be by others. But I have done it with due submission,

1

and also, in order to my subject, necessarily; for they are the
outworks of the enemy, from whence they impugn the civil
power. If notwithstanding this, you find my labor generally de-
cried, you may be pleased to excuse yourself and say, I am a
man that love my own opinions, and think all true I say, that I
honored your brother, and honor you, and have presumed on
that, to assume the title, without your knowledge of being, as
I am,

Sir,

Your most humble,

and obedient Servant,

THOMAS HOBBES.

Paris, April $\frac{15}{25}$ 1651.

OF DARKNESS FROM VAIN PHILOSOPHY
AND FABULOUS TRADITIONS[1]

What philosophy is. By philosophy is understood *the knowledge acquired by reasoning from the manner of the generation of anything to the properties, or from the properties to some possible way of generation of the same; to the end to be able to produce, as far as matter and human force permit, such effects as human life requires.* So the geometrician from the construction of figures finds out many properties thereof, and from the properties new ways of their construction, by reasoning; to the end to be able to measure land and water, and for infinite other uses. So the astronomer, from the rising, setting, and moving of the sun and stars in divers parts of the heavens, finds out the causes of day and night and of the different seasons of the year, whereby he keeps an account of time; and the like of other sciences.

Prudence no part of philosophy. By which definition it is evident that we are not to account as any part thereof that original knowledge called experience in which consists prudence, because it is not attained by reasoning but found as well in brute beasts as in man, and is but a memory of successions of events in times past, wherein the omission of every little circumstance altering the effect frustrates the expectation of the most prudent; whereas nothing is produced by reasoning aright but general, eternal, and immutable truth.

No false doctrine is part of philosophy: Nor are we therefore to give that name to any false conclusions, for he that reasons aright in words he understands can never conclude an error;

No more is revelation supernatural: Nor to that which any man knows by supernatural revelation, because it is not acquired by reasoning;

Nor that which is gotten by reasoning from the authority

[1] [This is ch. 46 from Part IV. It is placed here at the beginning of this edition of the *Leviathan* for reasons explained in the Note on the Text, p. xvii.]

3

Nor learning taken upon credit of authors. of books, because it is not by reasoning from the cause to the effect nor from the effect to the cause, and is not knowledge, but faith.

Of the beginnings and progress of philosophy. The faculty of reasoning being consequent to the use of speech, it was not possible but that there should have been some general truths found out by reasoning as ancient almost as language itself. The savages of America are not without some good moral sentences; also they have a little arithmetic, to add and divide in numbers not too great; but they are not, therefore, philosophers. For as there were plants of corn and wine in small quantity dispersed in the fields and woods before men knew their virtue or made use of them for their nourishment or planted them apart in fields and vineyards, in which time they fed on acorns and drank water, so also there have been divers true, general, and profitable speculations from the beginning as being the natural plants of human reason. But they were at first but few in number; men lived upon gross experience; there was no method—that is to say, no sowing nor planting of knowledge by itself apart from the weeds and common plants of error and conjecture. And the cause of it being the want of leisure from procuring the necessities of life and defending themselves against their neighbors, it was impossible, till the erecting of great commonwealths, it should be otherwise. *Leisure* is the mother of *philosophy*, and *Commonwealth* the mother of *peace* and *leisure*. Where first were great and flourishing *cities,* there was first the study of *philosophy*. The *Gymnosophists* of India, the *Magi* of Persia, and the *Priests* of Chaldea and Egypt are counted the most ancient philosophers; and those countries were the most ancient of kingdoms. *Philosophy* was not risen to the Grecians and other people of the west whose *commonwealths,* no greater perhaps than Lucca or Geneva, had never *peace* but when their fears of one another were equal, nor the *leisure* to observe anything but one another. At length, when war had united many of these Grecian lesser cities into fewer and greater, then began *seven men,* of several parts of Greece, to get the reputation of being *wise*—some of them for *moral* and *politic* sentences, and others for the learning of the Chaldeans and Egyptians, which was *astronomy* and *geometry*.² But we hear not yet of any *schools* of *philosophy*.

Of the schools of philosophy among the Athenians. After the Athenians, by the overthrow of the Persian armies, had gotten the dominion of the sea and thereby of all the islands and maritime cities of the Archipelago as well of Asia as Europe, and were grown wealthy, they that had no employment neither at home nor abroad had little else to employ themselves in but either (as St. Luke says, Acts 17: 21) *in telling and hearing news* or in discoursing of *philosophy* publicly to the youth of the city. Every master took some place for that purpose. Plato, in certain public walks called *Academia*, from one *Academus;* Aristotle in the walk of the temple of Pan, called *Lyceum;* others in the *Stoa,* or covered walk, wherein the merchants' goods were brought to land; others in other places where they spent the time of their leisure in teaching or in disputing of their opinions; and some in any place where they could get the youth of the city together to hear them talk. And this was it which Carneades also did at Rome when he was ambassador, which caused Cato to advise the senate to dispatch him quickly for fear of corrupting the manners of the young men that delighted to hear him speak, as they thought, fine things.³

From this it was that the place where any of them taught and disputed was called *schola,* which in their tongue signifies *leisure;* and their disputations, *diatribae,* that is to say, *passing of the time.* Also the philosophers themselves had the name of their sects, some of them from these their schools: for they that followed Plato's doctrine were called *Academics;* the followers of Aristotle *Peripatetics,* from the walk he taught in; and those

2 [The "seven wise men"—Solon, Chilon, Pittacus, Bias, Periander (or Epimenides), Cleobulus, and Thales—lived in the 6th century B.C.]

3 [Carneades (214-129 B.C.), a Greek philosopher, was the leading skeptic of his day. His public lectures at Rome in 155 while a member of an Athenian embassy made a profound impression. As a public official and senator, the severe Marcus Porcius Cato (234-149 B.C.) endeavored to preserve the old Roman virtues against the growing love of luxury and the spread of Greek culture. His hostility to Carneades was aroused by the philosopher's undermining of traditional values.]

that Zeno taught *Stoics*, from the *Stoa*—as if we should denominate men from *Moor-fields*, from *Paul's Church*, and from the *Exchange*, because they meet there often to prate and loiter.

Nevertheless, men were so much taken with this custom that in time it spread itself over all Europe and the best part of Africa, so as there were schools publicly erected and maintained for lectures and disputations almost in every commonwealth.

Of the schools of the Jews.
There were also schools, anciently, both before and after the time of our Saviour, among the Jews; but they were schools of their law. For though they were called synagogues—that is to say, congregations of the people—yet, inasmuch as the law was every Sabbath day read, expounded, and disputed in them, they differed not in nature but in name only from public schools, and were not only in Jerusalem but in every city of the Gentiles where the Jews inhabited. There was such a school at Damascus, whereinto Paul entered to persecute. There were others at Antioch, Iconium, and Thessalonica, whereinto he entered to dispute; and such was the synagogue of the *Libertines, Cyrenians, Alexandrians, Cilicians,* and those of Asia—that is to say, the school of *Libertines* and of *Jews* that were strangers in Jerusalem; and of this school they were that disputed (Acts 6: 9) with St. Stephen.

The school of the Grecians unprofitable.
But what has been the utility of those schools? What science is there at this day acquired by their readings and disputings? That we have of geometry, which is the mother of all natural science, we are not indebted for it to the schools. Plato, that was the best philosopher of the Greeks, forbade entrance into his school to all that were not already in some measure geometricians. There were many that studied that science to the great advantage of mankind, but there is no mention of their schools, nor was there any sect of geometricians, nor did they then pass under the name of philosophers. The natural philosophy of those schools was rather a dream than science, and set forth in senseless and insignificant language, which cannot be avoided by those that will teach philosophy without having first attained great knowledge in geometry. For nature works by motion, the ways and degrees whereof cannot be known without the knowledge of the proportions and properties of lines and figures. Their moral philosophy is but a description of their

own passions. For the rule of manners, without civil government, is the law of nature; and in it, the law civil that determines what is *honest* and *dishonest*, what is *just* and *unjust*, and generally what is *good* and *evil*. Whereas they make the rules of *good* and *bad* by their own *liking* and *disliking;* by which means, in so great diversity of taste, there is nothing generally agreed on, but everyone does, as far as he dares, whatsoever seems good in his own eyes, to the subversion of commonwealth. Their *logic*, which should be the method of reasoning, is nothing else but captions of words and inventions how to puzzle such as should go about to pose them. To conclude, there is nothing so absurd that the old philosophers, as Cicero says (who was one of them), have not some of them maintained. And I believe that scarce anything can be more absurdly said in natural philosophy than that which now is called *Aristotle's Metaphysics;* nor more repugnant to government than much of that he has said in his *Politics;* nor more ignorantly than a great part of his *Ethics.*

The schools of the Jews unprofitable. The school of the Jews was originally a school of the law of Moses, who commanded (Deut. 31: 10) that at the end of every seventh year, at the Feast of the Tabernacles, it should be read to all the people, that they might hear and learn it. Therefore the reading of the law, which was in use after the captivity every Sabbath day, ought to have had no other end but the acquainting of the people with the Commandments which they were to obey, and to expound unto them the writings of the prophets. But it is manifest, by the many reprehensions of them by our Saviour, that they corrupted the text of the law with their false commentaries and vain traditions, and so little understood the prophets that they did neither acknowledge Christ nor the works he did, of which the prophets prophesied. So that by their lectures and disputations in their synagogues they turned the doctrine of their law into a fantastical kind of philosophy concerning the incomprehensible nature of God and of spirits, which they compounded of the vain philosophy and theology of the Grecians, mingled with their own fancies drawn from the obscurer places of the Scripture, and which might most easily be wrested to their purpose; and from the fabulous traditions of their ancestors.

University,
what it is.

That which is now called a *university* is a joining together, and an incorporation under one government, of many public schools in one and the same town or city. In which the principal schools were ordained for the three professions—that is to say, of the Roman religion, of the Roman law, and of the art of medicine. And for the study of philosophy, it has no otherwise place than as a handmaid to the Roman religion; and since the authority of Aristotle is only current there, that study is not properly philosophy (the nature whereof depends not on authors) but *Aristotelity.* And for geometry, till of very late times it had no place at all, as being subservient to nothing but rigid truth. And if any man by the ingenuity of his own nature had attained to any degree of perfection therein, he was commonly thought a magician and his art diabolical.

Errors brought into
religion from Aris-
totle's metaphysics.

Now to descend to the particular tenets of vain philosophy derived to the universities and thence into the Church, partly from Aristotle, partly from blindness of understanding, I shall first consider their principles. There is a certain *philosophia prima* on which all other philosophy ought to depend, and consists principally in right limiting of the significations of such appellations or names as are of all others the most universal; which limitations serve to avoid ambiguity and equivocation in reasoning, and are commonly called definitions: such as are the definitions of body, time, place, matter, form, essence, subject, substance, accident, power, act, finite, infinite, quantity, quality, motion, action, passion, and divers others necessary to the explaining of a man's conceptions concerning the nature and generation of bodies. The explication—that is, the settling of the meaning—of which, and the like terms, is commonly in the Schools called *metaphysics*, as being a part of the philosophy of Aristotle which has that for title. But it is in another sense, for there it signifies as much as *books written or placed after his natural philosophy;* but the Schools take them for *books of supernatural philosophy,* for the word *metaphysics* will bear both these senses. And indeed that which is there written is for the most part so far from the possibility of being understood, and so repugnant to natural reason, that whosoever thinks there is anything to be understood by it must needs think it supernatural.

Errors concerning abstract essences. From these metaphysics, which are mingled with the Scripture to make School divinity, we are told there be in the world certain essences separated from bodies, which they call *abstract essences* and *substantial forms.* For the interpreting of which jargon there is need of somewhat more than ordinary attention in this place. Also I ask pardon of those that are not used to this kind of discourse for applying myself to those that are. The world (I mean not the earth only, that denominates the lovers of it *worldly men,* but the *universe,* that is, the whole mass of all things that are) is corporeal—that is to say, body—and has the dimensions of magnitude, namely, length, breadth, and depth; also every part of body is likewise body and has the like dimensions; and consequently every part of the universe is body, and that which is not body is no part of the universe; and because the universe is all, that which is no part of it is *nothing,* and consequently *nowhere.* Nor does it follow from hence that spirits are *nothing,* for they have dimensions and are therefore really *bodies,* though that name in common speech be given to such bodies only as are visible or palpable—that is, that have some degree of opacity. But for spirits, they call them incorporeal, which is a name of more honor and may therefore with more piety be attributed to God himself, in whom we consider not what attribute expresses best his nature, which is incomprehensible, but what best expresses our desire to honor him.

To know now upon what grounds they say there be *essences abstract* or *substantial forms,* we are to consider what those words do properly signify. The use of words is to register to ourselves and make manifest to others the thoughts and conceptions of our minds. Of which words, some are the names of the things conceived: as the names of all sorts of bodies that work upon the senses and leave an impression in the imagination. Others are the names of the imaginations themselves; that is to say, of those ideas or mental images we have of all things we see or remember. And others again are names of names or of different sorts of speech: as *universal, plural, singular* are the names of names; and *definition, affirmation, negation, true, false, syl-*

logism, interrogation, promise, covenant are the names of certain forms of speech. Others serve to show the consequence or repugnance of one name to another, as when one says *a man is a body* he intends that the name of *body* is necessarily consequent to the name of *man,* as being but several names of the same thing, *man;* which consequence is signified by coupling them together with the word *is.* And as we use the verb *is,* so the Latins use their verb *est,* and the Greeks their ἐστι through all its declinations. Whether all other nations of the world have in their several languages a word that answers to it or not, I cannot tell; but I am sure they have not need of it. For the placing of two names in order may serve to signify their consequence, if it were the custom (for custom is it that gives words their force), as well as the words *is* or *be* or *are* and the like.

And if it were so that there were a language without any verb answerable to *est* or *is* or *be,* yet the men that used it would be not a jot the less capable of inferring, concluding, and of all kind of reasoning than were the Greeks and Latins. But what then would become of these terms of *entity, essence, essential, essentiality* that are derived from it, and of many more that [4] depend on these, applied as most commonly they are? They are therefore no names of things, but signs by which we make known that we conceive the consequence of one name or attribute to another: as when we say *a man is a living body* we mean not that the *man* is one thing, the *living body* another, and the *is* or *being* a third, but that the *man* and the *living body* is the same thing; because the consequence, *if he be a man, he is a living body,* is a true consequence, signified by that word *is.* Therefore, *to be a body, to walk, to be speaking, to live, to see,* and the like infinitives, also *corporeity, walking, speaking, life, sight,* and the like that signify just the same, are the names of *nothing,* as I have elsewhere more amply expressed.[5]

But to what purpose, may some man say, is such subtlety in a work of this nature where I pretend to nothing but what is necessary to the doctrine of government and obedience? It is to this purpose: that men may no longer suffer themselves to be abused by them that by this doctrine of *separated essences,* built

4 [The original has "than."]
5 [Cf. Chapter IV, "Of Speech."]

on the vain philosophy of Aristotle, would fright them from obeying the laws of their country with empty names as men fright birds from the corn with an empty doublet, a hat, and a crooked stick. For it is upon this ground that when a man is dead and buried they say his soul—that is, his life—can walk separated from his body, and is seen by night among the graves. Upon the same ground they say that the figure and color and taste of a piece of bread has a being there where they say there is no bread. And upon the same ground they say that faith and wisdom and other virtues are sometimes *poured* into a man, sometimes *blown* into him from Heaven, as if the virtuous and their virtues could be asunder; and a great many other things that serve to lessen the dependence of subjects on the sovereign power of their country. For who will endeavor to obey the laws if he expect obedience to be poured or blown into him? Or who will not obey a priest, that can make God, rather than his sovereign—nay, than God himself? Or who that is in fear of ghosts will not bear great respect to those that can make the holy water that drives them from him? And this shall suffice for an example of the errors which are brought into the Church from the *entities* and *essences* of Aristotle, which it may be he knew to be false philosophy, but wrote it as a thing consonant to and corroborative of their religion, and fearing the fate of Socrates.

Being once fallen into this error of *separated essences,* they are thereby necessarily involved in many other absurdities that follow it. For seeing they will have these forms to be real, they are obliged to assign them *some place.* But because they hold them incorporeal, without all dimension of quantity, and all men know that place is dimension and not to be filled but by that which is corporeal, they are driven to uphold their credit with a distinction that they are not indeed anywhere *circumscriptive* but *definitive*—which terms, being mere words and in this occasion insignificant, pass only in Latin, that the vanity of them may be concealed. For the circumscription of a thing is nothing else but the determination or defining of its place, and so both the terms of the distinction are the same. And in particular, of the essence of a man, which, they say, is his soul, they affirm it to be all of it in his little finger and all of it in every part, how small soever, of his body, and yet no more soul in the whole body than in any one of those parts. Can any man think that God is served with such absurdities? And yet all this is necessary to believe to those that will believe the existence of an incorporeal soul separated from the body.

And when they come to give account how an incorporeal substance can be capable of pain and be tormented in the fire of hell or purgatory, they have nothing at all to answer but that it cannot be known how fire can burn souls.

Again, whereas motion is change of place, and incorporeal substances are not capable of place, they are troubled to make it seem possible how a soul can go hence, without the body, to heaven, hell, or purgatory; and how the ghosts of men, and I may add of their clothes which they appear in, can walk by night in churches, churchyards, and other places of sepulture. To which I know not what they can answer, unless they will say they walk *definitivè*, not *circumscriptivè*, or *spiritually*, not *temporally;* for such egregious distinctions are equally applicable to any difficulty whatsoever.

Nunc-stans. For the meaning of *eternity*, they will not have it to be an endless succession of time; for then they should not be able to render a reason how God's will and preordaining of things to come should not be before his prescience of the same as the efficient cause before the effect or agent before the action, nor of many other their bold opinions concerning the incomprehensible nature of God. But they will teach us that eternity is the standing still of the present time, a *nunc-stans,* as the Schools call it; which neither they nor any else understand, no more than they would a *hic-stans* for an infinite greatness of place.

One body in many places, and many bodies in one place at once. And whereas men divide a body in their thought by numbering parts of it, and in numbering those parts number also the parts of the place it filled, it cannot be but in making many parts we make also many places of those parts, whereby there cannot be conceived in the mind of any man more or fewer parts than there are places for; yet they will have us believe that by the almighty power of God one body may be at one and the same time in many places, and many bodies at one and the same time in one place—as if it were an acknowledgment of the Divine Power to say that which is is not, or that which has been has not been. And these are but a small part of the incongruities they are forced to from their disputing philosophically instead of admiring and adoring of the divine and incomprehensible nature, whose attributes cannot signify what he is but ought to signify our desire to honor him with the best appellations we can think on. But they that venture to reason of his nature from these attributes of honor, losing their understanding in the very first attempt, fall from one inconvenience into another without end and without number, in the same manner as when a man ignorant of the ceremonies of court, coming into the presence of a greater person than he is used to speak to and stumbling at his entrance, to save himself from falling lets slip his cloak, to recover his cloak lets fall his hat, and with one disorder after another discovers his astonishment and rusticity.

Absurdities in natural philosophy, as gravity the cause of heaviness. Then for *physics*—that is, the knowledge of the subordinate and secondary causes of natural events—they render none at all but empty words. If you desire to know why some kind of bodies sink naturally downwards toward the earth and others go naturally from it, the Schools will tell you out of Aristotle that the bodies that sink downwards are *heavy,* and that this heaviness is it that causes them to descend. But if you ask what they mean by *heaviness,* they will define it to be an endeavor to go to the center of the earth. So that the cause why things sink downward is an endeavor to be below—which is as much as to say that bodies descend or ascend because they do. Or they will tell you the center of the earth is the place of rest and conservation for heavy things, and therefore they endeavor to be there— as if stones and metals had a desire or could discern the place they would be at as man does, or loved rest as man does not, or that a piece of glass were less safe in the window than falling into the street.

Quantity put into body already made. If we would know why the same body seems greater, without adding to it, one time than another, they say when it seems less it is *condensed,* when greater *rarefied.* What is that *condensed* and *rarefied?* Condensed is when there is in the very same matter less quantity than before, and rarefied, when more. As if there could be matter that had not some determined quantity, when quantity is nothing else but the determination of matter—that is to say, of body—by which we say one body is greater or lesser than another by thus or thus much. Or as if a body were made without any quantity at all, and that afterwards more or less were put into it according as it is intended the body should be more or less dense.

Pouring in of souls. For the cause of the soul of man, they say *creatur infundendo* and *creando infunditur*— that is, *it is created by pouring it in* and *poured*

Ubiquity of apparition. *in by creation.* For the cause of sense, a ubiquity of *species*—that is, of the *shows* or *apparitions* of objects, which, when they be apparitions to the eye, is *sight;* when to the ear, *hearing;* to the palate, *taste;* to the nostril, *smelling;* and to the rest of the body, *feeling.*

Will, the cause of willing. For cause of the will to do any particular action, which is called *volitio,* they assign the faculty—that is to say, the capacity in general— that men have to will sometimes one thing, sometimes another, which is called *voluntas,* making the *power* the cause of the *act.* As if one should assign for cause of the good or evil acts of men their ability to do them.

Ignorance an occult cause. And in many occasions they put for cause of natural events their own ignorance, but disguised in other words: as when they say fortune is the cause of things contingent—that is, of things whereof they know no cause—and as when they attribute many effects to *occult qualities*—that is, qualities not known to them and therefore also, as they think, to no man else. And to *sympathy, antipathy, antiperistasis, specifical qualities,* and other like terms which signify neither the agent that produces them nor the operation by which they are produced.

If such *metaphysics* and *physics* as this be not *vain philosophy,* there was never any, nor needed St. Paul to give us warning to avoid it.[6]

One makes the things incongruent, another the incongruity. And for their moral and civil philosophy, it has the same or greater absurdities. If a man do an action of injustice—that is to say, an action contrary to the law—God they say is the prime cause of the law and also the prime cause of that and all

6 [Col. 2: 8.]

other actions, but no cause at all of the injustice, which is the inconformity of the action to the law. This is vain philosophy. A man might as well say that one man makes both a straight line and a crooked, and another makes their incongruity. And such is the philosophy of all men that resolve of their conclusions before they know their premises, pretending to comprehend that which is incomprehensible; and of attributes of honor to make attributes of nature, as this distinction was made to maintain the doctrine of free will—that is, of a will of man not subject to the will of God.

Aristotle and other heathen philosophers define good and evil by the appetite of men; and well enough, as long as we consider them governed every one by his own law, for in the condition of men that have no other law but their own appetites there can be no general rule of good and evil actions. But in a commonwealth this measure is false: not the appetite of private men but the law, which is the will and appetite of the state, is the measure. And yet is this doctrine still practiced, and men judge the goodness or wickedness of their own and of other men's actions, and of the actions of the commonwealth itself, by their own passions; and no man calls good or evil but that which is so in his own eyes, without any regard at all to the public laws, except only monks and friars that are bound by vow to that simple obedience to their superior to which every subject ought to think himself bound by the law of nature to the civil sovereign. And this private measure of good is a doctrine not only vain but also pernicious to the public state.

Private appetite the rule of public good.

And that lawful marriage is unchastity. It is also vain and false philosophy to say the work of marriage is repugnant to chastity or continence, and by consequence to make them moral vices; as they do that pretend chastity and continence for the ground of denying marriage to the clergy. For they confess it is no more but a constitution of the Church that requires in those holy orders that continually attend the altar and administration of the eucharist a continual abstinence from women under the name of continual chastity, continence, and purity. Therefore they call the lawful use of wives want of chastity and continence, and so make marriage a sin or at least a thing so impure and unclean as to render a man unfit for the altar. If the law were made because the use of wives is incontinence and contrary to chastity, then all marriage is vice; if because it is a thing too impure and unclean for a man consecrated to God, much more should other natural, necessary, and daily works which all men do render men unworthy to be priests because they are more unclean.

But the secret foundation of this prohibition of marriage of priests is not likely to have been laid so slightly as upon such errors in moral philosophy, nor yet upon the preference of single life to the estate of matrimony which proceeded from the wisdom of St. Paul, who perceived how inconvenient a thing it was for those that in those times of persecution were preachers of the gospel and forced to fly from one country to another to be clogged with the care of wife and children; but upon the design of the Popes and priests of aftertimes to make themselves the clergy—that is to say, sole heirs of the kingdom of God in this world—to which it was necessary to take from them the use of marriage, because our Saviour says that at the coming of his kingdom the children of God *shall neither marry, nor be given in marriage, but shall be as the angels in heaven* [7]—that is to say, spiritual. Seeing then they had taken on them the name of spiritual, to have allowed themselves, when there was no need, the propriety of wives had been an incongruity.

And that all government but popular is tyranny. From Aristotle's civil philosophy they have learned to call all manner of commonwealths but the popular (such as was at that time the state of Athens) tyranny. All kings they called tyrants, and the aristocracy of the thirty governors set up there by the Lacedemonians that subdued them, the thirty tyrants.[8] As also to call the condition of the people under the democracy *liberty*. A *tyrant* originally signified no more simply but a *monarch*. But when afterwards in most parts of Greece that kind of

[7] [Mark 12: 25.]

[8] [At the end of the Peloponnesian War (404 B.C.) the Athenian oligarchs, with the aid of the victorious Spartans, established a committee of thirty men ostensibly to write a new constitution for Athens. The thirty, however, seized complete power and, by execution and confiscation, proceeded to crush the democratic faction. They were deposed by moderate oligarchs in 403.]

government was abolished, the name began to signify, not only the thing it did before, but with it the hatred which the popular states bore toward it. As also the name of king became odious after the deposing of the kings in Rome, as being a thing natural to all men to conceive some great fault to be signified in any attribute that is given in despite and to a great enemy. And when the same men shall be displeased with those that have the administration of the democracy or aristocracy, they are not to seek for disgraceful names to express their anger in, but call readily the one *anarchy,* and the other *oligarchy* or the *tyranny of a few.* And that which offends the people is no other thing but that they are governed, not as every one of them would himself, but as the public representant, be it one man or an assembly of men, thinks fit—that is, by an arbitrary government; for which they give evil names to their superiors, never knowing till perhaps a little after a civil war that without such arbitrary government such war must be perpetual, and that it is men and arms, not words and promises, that make the force and power of the laws.

That not men, but law governs. And therefore this is another error of Aristotle's politics, that in a well-ordered commonwealth not men should govern, but the laws. What man that has his natural senses, though he can neither write nor read, does not find himself governed by them he fears and believes can kill or hurt him when he obeys not? Or that believes the law can hurt him—that is, words and paper—without the hands and swords of men? And this is of the number of pernicious errors, for they induce men as oft as they like not their governors to adhere to those that call them tyrants, and to think it lawful to raise war against them; and yet they are many times cherished from the pulpit by the clergy.

Laws over the conscience. There is another error in their civil philosophy, which they never learned of Aristotle nor Cicero nor any other of the heathen: to extend the power of the law, which is the rule of actions only, to the very thoughts and consciences of men by examination and *inquisition* of what they hold, notwithstanding the conformity of their speech and actions. By which men are either punished for answering the truth of their thoughts or constrained to an-

swer an untruth for fear of punishment. It is true that the civil
magistrate, intending to employ a minister in the charge of
teaching, may inquire of him if he be content to preach such
and such doctrines, and in case of refusal may deny him the employment. But to force him to accuse himself of opinions when
his actions are not by law forbidden is against the law of nature,
and especially in them who teach that a man shall be damned
to eternal and extreme torments if he die in a false opinion concerning an article of the Christian faith. For who is there, that
knowing there is so great danger in an error, whom the natural
care of himself compels not to hazard his soul upon his own
judgment rather than that of any other man that is uncon-
cerned in his damnation?

For a private man without the authority of the commonwealth—that is to say, without permission from
the representant thereof—to interpret the law
by his own spirit is another error in the politics,
but not drawn from Aristotle nor from any other of the heathen
philosophers. For none of them deny but that in the power of
making laws is comprehended also the power of explaining
them when there is need. And are not the Scriptures, in all
places where they are law, made law by the authority of the
commonwealth and, consequently, a part of the civil law?

*Private interpreta-
tion of law.*

Of the same kind it is also when any but the sovereign re-
strains in any man that power which the commonwealth has
not restrained, as they do that impropriate the preaching of the
gospel to one certain order of men where the laws have left it
free. If the state give me leave to preach or teach—that is, if it
forbid me not—no man can forbid me. If I find myself among
the idolaters of America, shall I that am a Christian, though not
in orders, think it a sin to preach Jesus Christ till I have received orders from Rome? Or when I have preached, shall not I
answer their doubts and expound the Scriptures to them—that
is, shall I not teach? But for this may some say, as also for administering to them the sacraments, the necessity shall be esteemed for a sufficient mission, which is true; but this is true
also, that for whatsoever a dispensation is due for the necessity,
for the same there needs no dispensation when there is no law
that forbids it. Therefore to deny these functions to those to

whom the civil sovereign has not denied them is a taking away of a lawful liberty, which is contrary to the doctrine of civil government.

Language of School divines. More examples of vain philosophy brought into religion by the doctors of School divinity might be produced, but other men may if they please observe them of themselves. I shall only add this, that the writings of School divines are nothing else for the most part but insignificant trains of strange and barbarous words, or words otherwise used than in the common use of the Latin tongue such as would pose Cicero and Varro and all the grammarians of ancient Rome. Which if any man would see proved, let him, as I have said once before, see whether he can translate any School divine into any of the modern tongues, as French, English, or any other copious language, for that which cannot in most of these be made intelligible is not intelligible in the Latin. Which insignificancy of language, though I cannot note it for false philosophy, yet it has a quality not only to hide the truth but also to make men think they have it and desist from further search.

Errors from tradition. Lastly, for the errors brought in from false or uncertain history, what is all the legend of fictitious miracles in the lives of the saints, and all the histories of apparitions and ghosts alleged by the doctors of the Roman Church to make good their doctrines of hell and purgatory, the power of exorcism, and other doctrines which have no warrant, neither in reason nor Scripture, as also all those traditions which they call the unwritten word of God; but old wives' fables? Whereof, though they find dispersed somewhat in the writings of the ancient fathers, yet those fathers were men that might too easily believe false reports, and the producing of their opinions for testimony of the truth of what they believed has no other force with them that, according to the counsel of St. John (I John 4: 1), examine spirits than in all things that concern the power of the Roman Church (the abuse whereof either they suspected not or had benefit by it) to discredit their testimony in respect of too rash belief of reports; which the most sincere men, without great knowledge of natural causes, such as the fathers were, are commonly the most subject to. For naturally the best men are the least suspicious of fraudulent purposes. Gregory the Pope and St. Bernard have somewhat of apparitions of ghosts that said they were in purgatory, and so has our Bede, but nowhere, I believe, but by report from others.[9] But if they or any other relate any such stories of their own knowledge, they shall not thereby confirm the more such vain reports but discover their own infirmity or fraud.

With the introduction of false, we may join also the suppression of true philosophy by such men as neither by lawful authority nor sufficient study are competent judges of the truth.

Suppression of reason. Our own navigations make manifest, and all men learned in human sciences now acknowledge, there are antipodes; and every day it appears more and more that years and days are determined by motions of the earth. Nevertheless, men that have in their writings but supposed such doctrine, as an occasion to lay open the reasons for and against it, have been punished for it by authority ecclesiastical. But what reason is there for it? Is it because such opinions are contrary to true religion? That cannot be, if they be true. Let therefore the truth be first examined by competent judges, or confuted by them that pretend to know the contrary. Is it because they be contrary to the religion established? Let them be silenced by the laws of those to whom the teachers of them are subject—that is, by the laws civil. For disobedience may lawfully be punished in them that against the laws teach even true philosophy. Is it because they tend to disorder in government as countenancing rebellion or sedition? Then let them be silenced and the teachers punished by virtue of his power to whom the care of the public quiet is committed, which is the authority civil. For whatsoever power ecclesiastics take upon themselves (in any place where they are subject to the state) in their own right, though they call it God's right, is but usurpation.

[9] [Reference is to Gregory VIII, pope Oct.-Dec., 1187. St. Bernard of Clairvaux (1090-1153), a mystic and the outstanding representative of medieval monasticism, played an important part in church affairs, most notably in preaching the Second Crusade. A Northumbrian monk and priest, Bede (672-735) has been called the Father of English History by virtue of his chief work, the *Ecclesiastical History of the English Nation.*]

OF MAN

THE INTRODUCTION

Nature, the art whereby God has made and governs the world, is by the *art* of man, as in many other things, so in this also imitated—that it can make an artificial animal. For seeing life is but a motion of limbs, the beginning whereof is in some principal part within, why may we not say that all *automata* (engines that move themselves by springs and wheels as does a watch) have an artificial life? For what is the *heart* but a *spring,* and the *nerves* but so many *strings,* and the *joints* but so many *wheels* giving motion to the whole body such as was intended by the artificer? *Art* goes yet further, imitating that rational and most excellent work of nature, *man.* For by art is created that great LEVIATHAN called a COMMONWEALTH or STATE—in Latin, CIVITAS—which is but an artificial man, though of greater stature and strength than the natural, for whose protection and defense it was intended; and in which the *sovereignty* is an artificial *soul,* as giving life and motion to the whole body; the *magistrates* and other *officers* of judicature and execution, artificial *joints; reward* and *punishment,* by which, fastened to the seat of the sovereignty, every joint and member is moved to perform his duty, are the *nerves,* that do the same in the body natural; the *wealth* and *riches* of all the particular members are the *strength; salus populi,* the *people's safety, its business; counselors,* by whom all things needful for it to know are suggested unto it, are the *memory; equity* and *laws,* an artificial *reason* and *will; concord, health; sedition, sickness;* and *civil war, death.* Lastly, the *pacts* and *covenants* by which the parts of this body politic were at first made, set together, and united resemble that *fiat,* or the *let us make man,* pronounced by God in the creation.

To describe the nature of this artificial man, I will consider First, the *matter* thereof, and the *artificer,* both which is *man.* Secondly, *how* and by what *covenants* it is made, what are the *rights* and just *power* or *authority* of a *sovereign,* and what it is that *preserves* and *dissolves* it. Thirdly, what is a *Christian commonwealth.* Lastly, what is the *kingdom of darkness.*[1]

1 [The present edition contains only the first and second parts.]

Concerning the first, there is a saying much usurped of late that *wisdom* is acquired, not by reading of *books*, but of *men*. Consequently whereunto, those persons that for the most part can give no other proof of being wise take great delight to show what they think they have read in men by uncharitable censures of one another behind their backs. But there is another saying not of late understood by which they might learn truly to read one another if they would take the pains: that is, *nosce teipsum, read thyself*, which was not meant, as it is now used, to countenance either the barbarous state of men in power toward their inferiors or to encourage men of low degree to a saucy behavior toward their betters, but to teach us that, for the similitude of the thoughts and passions of one man to the thoughts and passions of another, whosoever looks into himself and considers what he does when he does *think, opine, reason, hope, fear*, etc., and upon what grounds, he shall thereby read and know what are the thoughts and passions of all other men upon the like occasions. I say the similitude of *passions*, which are the same in all men: *desire, fear, hope*, etc.; not the similitude of the *objects* of the passions, which are the things *desired, feared, hoped*, etc., for these the constitution individual and particular education do so vary, and they are so easy to be kept from our knowledge, that the characters of man's heart, blotted and confounded as they are with dissembling, lying, counterfeiting, and erroneous doctrines, are legible only to him that searches hearts. And though by men's actions we do discover their design sometimes, yet to do it without comparing them with our own, and distinguishing all circumstances by which the case may come to be altered, is to decipher without a key and be for the most part deceived by too much trust or by too much diffidence, as he that reads is himself a good or evil man.

But let one man read another by his actions never so perfectly, it serves him only with his acquaintance, which are but few. He that is to govern a whole nation must read in himself, not this or that particular man, but mankind; which, though it be hard to do, harder than to learn any language or science, yet when I shall have set down my own reading orderly and perspicuously, the pains left another will be only to consider if he also find not the same in himself. For this kind of doctrine admits no other demonstration.

PART ONE: OF MAN

CHAPTER ONE

OF SENSE

Concerning the thoughts of man, I will consider them first singly and afterwards in train or dependence upon one another. Singly, they are every one a *representation* or *appearance* of some quality or other accident of a body without us which is commonly called an *object*. Which object works on the eyes, ears, and other parts of a man's body, and by diversity of working produces diversity of appearances.

The original of them all is that which we call SENSE, for there is no conception in a man's mind which has not at first, totally or by parts, been begotten upon the organs of sense. The rest are derived from that original.

To know the natural cause of sense is not very necessary to the business now in hand, and I have elsewhere written of the same at large.[1] Nevertheless, to fill each part of my present method, I will briefly deliver the same in this place.

The cause of sense is the external body or object which presses the organ proper to each sense, either immediately as in the taste and touch, or mediately as in seeing, hearing, and smelling; which pressure, by the mediation of the nerves and other strings and membranes of the body continued inward to the brain and heart, causes there a resistance or counter-pressure or endeavor of the heart to deliver itself, which endeavor, because *outward,* seems to be some matter without. And this *seeming* or *fancy* is that which men call *sense,* and consists, as to the eye, in a *light* or *color figured;* to the ear, in a *sound;* to the nostril, in an *odor;* to the tongue and palate, in a *savor;* and to

1 [In *The Elements of Law* (1650) and later in *De corpore* (1655) and *De homine* (1658).]

25

the rest of the body, in *heat, cold, hardness, softness,* and such other qualities as we discern by *feeling.* All which qualities, called *sensible,* are in the object that causes them but so many several motions of the matter by which it presses our [2] organs diversely. Neither in us that are pressed are they anything else but divers motions, for motion produces nothing but motion. But their appearance to us is fancy, the same waking that dreaming. And as pressing, rubbing, or striking the eye makes us fancy a light, and pressing the ear produces a din, so do the bodies also we see or hear produce the same by their strong, though unobserved, action. For if those colors and sounds were in the bodies or objects that cause them, they could not be severed from them as by glasses, and in echoes by reflection, we see they are, where we know the thing we see is in one place, the appearance in another. And though at some certain distance the real and very object seem invested with the fancy it begets in us, yet still the object is one thing, the image or fancy is another. So that sense, in all cases, is nothing else but original fancy, caused, as I have said, by the pressure—that is, by the motion—of external things upon our eyes, ears, and other organs thereunto ordained.

But the philosophy schools through all the universities of Christendom, grounded upon certain texts of Aristotle, teach another doctrine, and say, for the cause of *vision,* that the thing seen sends forth on every side a *visible species*—in English, a *visible show, apparition,* or *aspect,* or *a being seen*—the receiving whereof into the eye is *seeing.* And for the cause of *hearing,* that the thing heard sends forth an *audible species*—that is, an *audible aspect* or *audible being seen*—which, entering at the ear, makes *hearing.* Nay, for the cause of *understanding* also they say the thing understood sends forth an *intelligible species* —that is, an *intelligible being seen*—which, coming into the understanding, makes us understand. I say not this as disproving the use of universities; but because I am to speak hereafter of their office in a commonwealth, I must let you see on all occasions by the way what things would be amended in them, among which the frequency of insignificant speech is one.

[2] [The edition of 1651 has "out."]

CHAPTER TWO

OF IMAGINATION

That when a thing lies still, unless somewhat else stir it, it will lie still forever is a truth that no man doubts of. But that when a thing is in motion it will eternally be in motion unless somewhat else stay it, though the reason be the same—namely, that nothing can change itself—is not so easily assented to. For men measure not only other men but all other things by themselves, and, because they find themselves subject after motion to pain and lassitude, think everything else grows weary of motion and seeks repose of its own accord, little considering whether it be not some other motion wherein that desire of rest they find in themselves consists. From hence it is that the schools say heavy bodies fall downward out of an appetite to rest and to conserve their nature in that place which is most proper for them, ascribing appetite and knowledge of what is good for their conservation, which is more than man has, to things inanimate, absurdly.

When a body is once in motion, it moves, unless something else hinder it, eternally; and whatsoever hinders it cannot in an instant, but in time and by degrees, quite extinguish it; and as we see in the water, though the wind cease, the waves give not over rolling for a long time after, so also it happens in that motion which is made in the internal parts of a man then when he sees, dreams, etc. For after the object is removed or the eye shut, we still retain an image of the thing seen, though more obscure than when we see it. And this is it the Latins call *imagination* from the image made in seeing, and apply the same, though improperly, to all the other senses. But the Greeks call it *fancy,* which signifies *appearance* and is as proper to one sense as to another. IMAGINATION, therefore, is nothing but *decaying sense* and is found in men and many other living creatures as well sleeping as waking.

The decay of sense in men waking is not the decay of the motion made in sense but an obscuring of it in such manner as the light of the sun obscures the light of the stars, which stars do no less exercise their virtue by which they are visible in the day than in the night. But because among many strokes which our eyes, ears, and other organs receive from external bodies the predominant only is sensible, therefore, the light of the sun being predominant, we are not affected with the action of the stars. And any object being removed from our eyes, though the impression it made in us remain, yet other objects more present succeeding and working on us, the imagination of the past is obscured and made weak, as the voice of a man is in the noise of the day. From whence it follows that the longer the time is after the sight or sense of any object, the weaker is the imagination. For the continual change of man's body destroys in time the parts which in sense were moved, so that distance of time and of place has one and the same effect in us. For as at a great distance of place that which we look at appears dim and without distinction of the smaller parts, and as voices grow weak and inarticulate, so also, after great distance of time, our imagination of the past is weak and we lose, for example, of cities we have seen many particular streets, and of actions many particular circumstances. This *decaying sense,* when we would express the thing itself—I mean *fancy* itself—we call *imagination,* as I said before; but when we would express the decay and signify that the sense is fading, old, and past, it is called *memory.* So that imagination and memory are but one thing, which for divers considerations has divers names.

Memory.   Much memory, or memory of many things, is called *experience.* Again, imagination being only of those things which have been formerly perceived by sense, either all at once or by parts at several times, the former, which is the imagining the whole object as it was presented to the sense, is *simple* imagination, as when one imagines a man or horse which he has seen before. The other is *compounded,* as when, from the sight of a man at one time and of a horse at another, we conceive in our mind a centaur. So when a man compounds the image of his own person with the image of the actions of another man, as when a man imagines himself a Hercules or an Alexander [1]—which happens often to them that are

1 [Hercules (Greek, Heracles), a hero of Greek mythology, won a reputation for strength and courage by his performance of the twelve Labors. Alexander III of Macedonia, "the Great" (356-323 B.C.), destroyed the Persian empire and erected an empire of his own extending from Greece to India.]

much taken with reading of romances—it is a compound imagination and properly but a fiction of the mind. There be also other imaginations that rise in men, though waking, from the great impression made in sense: as from gazing upon the sun, the impression leaves an image of the sun before our eyes a long time after; and from being long and vehemently attent upon geometrical figures, a man shall in the dark, though awake, have the images of lines and angles before his eyes; which kind of fancy has no particular name, as being a thing that does not commonly fall into men's discourse.

Dreams. The imaginations of them that sleep are those we call *dreams*. And these also, as all other imaginations, have been before, either totally or by parcels, in the sense. And because in sense the brain and nerves, which are the necessary organs of sense, are so benumbed in sleep as not easily to be moved by the action of external objects, there can happen in sleep no imagination and therefore no dream but what proceeds from the agitation of the inward parts of man's body; which inward parts, for the connection they have with the brain and other organs, when they be distempered do keep the same in motion; whereby the imaginations there formerly made appear as if a man were waking, saving that the organs of sense being now benumbed so as there is no new object which can master and obscure them with a more vigorous impression, a dream must needs be more clear, in this silence of sense, than our waking thoughts. And hence it comes to pass that it is a hard matter, and by many thought impossible, to distinguish exactly between sense and dreaming. For my part, when I consider that in dreams I do not often nor constantly think of the same persons, places, objects, and actions that I do waking, nor remember so long a train of coherent thoughts dreaming as at other times; and because waking I often observe the absurdity of dreams, but never dream of the absurdities of my waking thoughts—I am well satisfied that, being awake, I know I dream not, though when I dream I think myself awake.

And seeing dreams are caused by the distemper of some of the inward parts of the body, divers distempers must needs cause different dreams. And hence it is that lying cold breeds dreams of fear and raises the thought and image of some fearful object, the motion from the brain to the inner parts and from the inner parts to the brain being reciprocal; and that as anger causes heat in some parts of the body when we are awake, so when we sleep the overheating of the same parts causes anger and raises up in the brain the imagination of an enemy. In the same manner as natural kindness, when we are awake, causes desire, and desire makes heat in certain other parts of the body, so also too much heat in those parts while we sleep raises in the brain an imagination of some kindness shown. In sum, our dreams are the reverse of our waking imaginations, the motion when we are awake beginning at one end and when we dream at another.

Apparitions or visions.

The most difficult discerning of a man's dream from his waking thoughts is then when by some accident we observe not that we have slept, which is easy to happen to a man full of fearful thoughts and whose conscience is much troubled and that sleeps without the circumstances of going to bed or putting off his clothes, as one that nods in a chair. For he that takes pains and industriously lays himself to sleep, in case any uncouth and exorbitant fancy come unto him, cannot easily think it other than a dream. We read of Marcus Brutus (one that had his life given him by Julius Caesar and was also his favorite, and notwithstanding murdered him), how at Philippi, the night before he gave battle to Augustus Caesar, he saw a fearful apparition, which is commonly related by historians as a vision but, considering the circumstances, one may easily judge to have been but a short dream.[2] For sitting in his tent, pensive and troubled with the horror of his rash act, it was not hard for him, slumbering in the cold, to dream of that which most affrighted him; which fear, as by degrees it made him wake, so also it must needs make the apparition by degrees to vanish; and having no assurance that he slept, he could have no cause to think it a dream or anything but a vision. And this is no very rare accident; for even they that be perfectly awake, if they be timorous and superstitious, possessed with fearful tales, and alone in the dark, are subject to the like fancies and believe they see spirits and dead

2 [Brutus and other Roman senators, fearing the power of the dictator Caesar, slew him on the floor of the senate in 44 B.C. Caesar was avenged by Mark Antony, who defeated the conspirators Brutus and Cassius at the battle of Philippi (42 B.C.). Brutus committed suicide after his defeat. The incident of Brutus' vision is treated in Shakespeare's *Julius Caesar*.]

men's ghosts walking in churchyards; whereas it is either their fancy only or else the knavery of such persons as make use of such superstitious fear to pass disguised in the night to places they would not be known to haunt.

From this ignorance of how to distinguish dreams and other strong fancies from vision and sense did arise the greatest part of the religion of the gentiles in time past that worshiped satyrs, fauns, nymphs, and the like, and nowadays the opinion that rude people have of fairies, ghosts, and goblins and of the power of witches. For as for witches, I think not that their witchcraft is any real power, but yet that they are justly punished for the false belief they have that they can do such mischief joined with their purpose to do it if they can, their trade being nearer to a new religion than to a craft or science. And for fairies and walking ghosts, the opinion of them has, I think, been on purpose either taught or not confuted to keep in credit the use of exorcism, of crosses, of holy water, and other such inventions of ghostly men. Nevertheless, there is no doubt but God can make unnatural apparitions; but that he does it so often as men need to fear such things more than they fear the stay or change of the course of nature, which he also can stay and change, is no point of Christian faith. But evil men, under pretext that God can do anything, are so bold as to say anything when it serves their turn, though they think it untrue; it is the part of a wise man to believe them no farther than right reason makes that which they say appear credible. If this superstitious fear of spirits were taken away, and with it prognostics from dreams, false prophecies, and many other things depending thereon by which crafty, ambitious persons abuse the simple people, men would be much more fitted than they are for civil obedience.

And this ought to be the work of the schools, but they rather nourish such doctrine. For, not knowing what imagination or the senses are, what they receive they teach: some saying that imaginations rise of themselves and have no cause, others that they rise most commonly from the will and that good thoughts are blown (inspired) into a man by God and evil thoughts by the devil, or that good thoughts are poured (infused) into a man by God and evil ones by the devil. Some say the senses receive the species of things and deliver them to the common sense, and the common sense delivers them over to the fancy, and the fancy

to the memory, and the memory to the judgment, like handing
of things from one to another, with many words making nothing understood.

Understanding.   The imagination that is raised in man, or any
                         other creature endowed with the faculty of im-
agining, by words or other voluntary signs is that we generally
call *understanding* and is common to man and beast. For a dog
by custom will understand the call or the rating of his master,
and so will many other beasts. That understanding which is peculiar to man is the understanding not only his will but his conceptions and thoughts by the sequel and contexture of the
names of things into affirmations, negations, and other forms of
speech; and of this kind of understanding I shall speak hereafter.

CHAPTER THREE

OF THE CONSEQUENCE OR TRAIN OF IMAGINATIONS

By *consequence* or TRAIN of thoughts, I understand that succession of one thought to another which is called, to distinguish
it from discourse in words, *mental discourse.*

When a man thinks on anything whatsoever, his next
thought after is not altogether so casual as it seems to be. Not
every thought to every thought succeeds indifferently. But as we
have no imagination whereof we have not formerly had sense,
in whole or in parts, so we have no transition from one imagination to another whereof we never had the like before in our
senses. The reason whereof is this. All fancies are motions
within us, relics of those made in the sense; and those motions
that immediately succeeded one another in the sense continue
also together after sense; insomuch as the former coming again
to take place and be predominant, the latter follows by coherence of the matter moved, in such manner as water upon a
plane table is drawn which way any one part of it is guided by
the finger. But because in sense to one and the same thing per-

ceived sometimes one thing, sometimes another succeeds, it comes to pass in time that in the imagining of anything there is no certainty what we shall imagine next; only this is certain: it shall be something that succeeded the same before at one time or another.

Train of thoughts unguided.

This train of thoughts, or mental discourse, is of two sorts. The first is *unguided, without design and inconstant,* wherein there is no passionate thought to govern and direct those that follow to itself as the end and scope of some desire or other passion—in which case the thoughts are said to *wander,* and seem impertinent one to another as in a dream. Such are commonly the thoughts of men that are not only without company but also without care of anything, though even then their thoughts are as busy as at other times but without harmony—as the sound which a lute out of tune would yield to any man, or in tune to one that could not play. And yet in this wild ranging of the mind, a man may ofttimes perceive the way of it and the dependence of one thought upon another. For in a discourse of our present civil war,[1] what could seem more impertinent than to ask, as one did, what was the value of a Roman penny? Yet the coherence to me was manifest enough. For the thought of the war introduced the thought of the delivering up the king to his enemies; the thought of that brought in the thought of the delivering up of Christ; and that again the thought of the thirty pence, which was the price of that treason; and thence easily followed that malicious question—and all this in a moment of time, for thought is quick.

Train of thoughts regulated.

The second is more constant, as being *regulated by some desire and design.* For the impression made by such things as we desire or fear is strong and permanent, or, if it cease for a time, of quick return; so strong it is sometimes as to hinder and break our sleep. From desire arises the thought of some means we have seen produce the like of that which we aim at; and from the thought of that, the thought of means to that mean; and so continually till we come to some beginning within our own power. And because the end, by the greatness of the impression, comes often to mind, in case our thoughts begin to wander they are

1 [Cf. Editor's Introduction, pp. vii ff.]

quickly again reduced into the way; which, observed by one of
the seven wise men, made him give men this precept, which is
now worn out: *Respice finem* [2]—that is to say, in all your actions
look often upon what you would have as the thing that directs
all your thoughts in the way to attain it.

The train of regulated thoughts is of two kinds: one, when of
an effect imagined we seek the causes or means that produce it,
and this is common to man and beast. The other is when, imagining anything whatsoever, we seek all the possible effects
that can by it be produced—that is to say, we imagine what we
can do with it when we have it. Of which I have not at any time
seen any sign but in man only, for this is a curiosity hardly incident to the nature of any living creature that has no other passion but sensual, such as are hunger, thirst, lust, and anger. In
sum, the discourse of the mind, when it is governed by design, is
nothing but *seeking* or the faculty of invention—which the
Latins called *sagacitas* and *solertia,* a hunting out of the causes
of some effect, present or past, or of the effects of some present
or past cause. Sometimes a man seeks what he has lost; and from
that place and time wherein he misses it his mind runs back,
from place to place and time to time, to find where and when he
had it—that is to say, to find some certain and limited time and
place in which to begin a method of seeking. Again, from
thence his thoughts run over the same places and times to find
what action or other occasion might make him lose it. This
we call *remembrance* or calling to mind; the
Remembrance. Latins call it *reminiscentia,* as it were a *re-
conning* of our former actions.

Sometimes a man knows a place determinate, within the compass whereof he is to seek; and then his thoughts run over all
the parts thereof, in the same manner as one would sweep a
room to find a jewel, or as a spaniel ranges the field till he find a
scent, or as a man should run over the alphabet to start a rhyme.
Prudence. Sometimes a man desires to know the event of
an action; and then he thinks of some like action past and the events thereof one after another, supposing
like events will follow like actions. As he that foresees what will
become of a criminal re-cons what he has seen follow on the like

2 ["Consider the end." For the seven wise men, see p. 5, n. 2.]

crime before, having this order of thoughts: the crime, the officer, the prison, the judge, and the gallows. Which kind of thoughts is called *foresight*, and *prudence* or *providence*, and sometimes *wisdom*, though such conjecture, through the difficulty of observing all circumstances, be very fallacious. But this is certain: by how much one man has more experience of things past than another, by so much also he is more prudent, and his expectations the seldomer fail him. The *present* only has a being in nature; things *past* have a being in the memory only; but things *to come* have no being at all, the *future* being but a fiction of the mind applying the sequels of actions past to the actions that are present, which with most certainty is done by him that has most experience, but not with certainty enough. And though it be called prudence when the event answers our expectation, yet in its own nature it is but presumption. For the foresight of things to come, which is providence, belongs only to him by whose will they are to come. From him only, and supernaturally, proceeds prophecy. The best prophet naturally is the best guesser, and the best guesser he that is most versed and studied in the matters he guesses at, for he has most *signs* to guess by.

Signs.   A *sign* is the evident antecedent of the consequent, and, contrarily, the consequent of the antecedent when the like consequences have been observed before; and the oftener they have been observed, the less uncertain is the sign. And therefore he that has most experience in any kind of business has most signs whereby to guess at the future time and consequently is the most prudent; and so much more prudent than he that is new in that kind of business as not to be equaled by any advantage of natural and extemporary wit —though perhaps many young men think the contrary.

Nevertheless it is not prudence that distinguishes man from beast. There be beasts that at a year old observe more, and pursue that which is for their good more prudently, than a child can do at ten.

Conjecture of the time past.   As prudence is a *presumption* of the *future*, contracted from the *experience* of time *past*, so there is a presumption of things past taken from other things, not future but past also. For he that has seen by what courses and degrees a flourishing state has first come into civil war and then to ruin, upon the sight of the ruins of any other state will guess the like war and the like courses have been there also. But this conjecture has the same uncertainty almost with the conjecture of the future, both being grounded only upon experience.

There is no other act of man's mind that I can remember, naturally planted in him, so as to need no other thing to the exercise of it but to be born a man and live with the use of his five senses. Those other faculties of which I shall speak by and by, and which seem proper to man only, are acquired and increased by study and industry, and of most men learned by instruction and discipline, and proceed all from the invention of words and speech. For besides sense and thoughts and the train of thoughts, the mind of man has no other motion; though by the help of speech and method the same faculties may be improved to such a height as to distinguish men from all other living creatures.

Whatsoever we imagine is *finite*. Therefore there is no idea or conception of anything we call *infinite*. No man can have in his mind an image of infinite magnitude nor conceive infinite swiftness, infinite time, or infinite force, or infinite power. When we say anything is infinite, we signify only that we are not able to conceive the ends and bounds of the things named, having no conception of the thing but of our own inability. And therefore the name of God is used, not to make us conceive him—for he is incomprehensible, and his greatness and power are unconceivable—but that we may honor him. Also because whatsoever, as I said before, we conceive has been perceived first by sense, either all at once or by parts, a man can have no thought representing anything not subject to sense. No man, therefore, can conceive anything but he must conceive it in some place and endowed with some determinate magnitude and which may be divided into parts, nor that anything is all in this place and all in another place at the same time, nor that two or more things can be in one and the same place at once; for none of these things ever have nor can be incident to sense, but are absurd speeches taken upon credit, without any signification at all, from deceived philosophers and deceived or deceiving Schoolmen.

CHAPTER FOUR

OF SPEECH

Original of speech. The invention of *printing,* though ingenious, compared with the invention of *letters* is no great matter. But who was the first that found the use of letters is not known. He that first brought them into Greece, men say, was Cadmus, the son of Agenor, king of Phoenicia. A profitable invention for continuing the memory of time past and the conjunction of mankind, dispersed into so many and distant regions of the earth; and withal difficult, as proceeding from a watchful observation of the divers motions of the tongue, palate, lips, and other organs of speech, whereby to make as many differences of characters to remember them. But the most noble and profitable invention of all other was that of SPEECH, consisting of *names* or *appellations* and their connection, whereby men register their thoughts, recall them when they are past, and also declare them one to another for mutual utility and conversation; without which there had been among men neither commonwealth nor society nor contract nor peace, no more than among lions, bears, and wolves. The first author of *speech* was God himself, that instructed Adam how to name such creatures as he presented to his sight, for the Scripture goes no further in this matter.[1] But this was sufficient to direct him to add more names as the experience and use of the creatures should give him occasion, and to join them in such manner by degrees as to make himself understood; and so by succession of time so much language might be gotten as he had found use for, though not so copious as an orator or philosopher has need of, for I do not find anything in the Scripture out of which, directly or by consequence, can be gathered that Adam was taught the names of all figures, numbers, measures, colors, sounds, fancies, relations —much less the names of words and speech, as *general, special, affirmative, negative, interrogative, optative, infinitive,* all which are useful, and least of all of *entity, intentionality, quiddity,* and other insignificant words of the school.

1 [Gen. 2:19-20.]

But all this language gotten and augmented by Adam and his posterity was again lost at the Tower of Babel, when, by the hand of God, every man was stricken for his rebellion with an oblivion of his former language.[2] And being hereby forced to disperse themselves into several parts of the world, it must needs be that the diversity of tongues that now is proceeded by degrees from them in such manner as need, the mother of all inventions, taught them, and in tract of time grew everywhere more copious.

The use of speech. The general use of speech is to transfer our mental discourse into verbal, or the train of our thoughts into a train of words; and that for two commodities, whereof one is the registering of the consequences of our thoughts, which, being apt to slip out of our memory and put us to a new labor, may again be recalled by such words as they were marked by. So that the first use of names is to serve for *marks* or *notes* of remembrance. Another is when many use the same words to signify, by their connection and order, one to another, what they conceive or think of each matter, and also what they desire, fear, or have any other passion for. And for this use they are called *signs.* Special uses of speech are these: First, to register what by cogitation we find to be the cause of anything, present or past, and what we find things present or past may produce or effect—which, in sum, is acquiring of arts. Secondly, to show to others that knowledge which we have attained—which is to counsel and teach one another. Thirdly, to make known to others our wills and purposes, that we may have the mutual help of one another. Fourthly, to please and delight ourselves and others by playing with our words, for pleasure or ornament, innocently.

Abuses of speech. To these uses there are also four correspondent abuses. First, when men register their thoughts wrong by the inconstancy of the signification of their words, by which they register for their conception that which they never conceived, and so deceive themselves. Secondly, when they use words metaphorically—that is, in other senses than that they are ordained for—and thereby deceive others. Thirdly, by words when they declare that to be their will which is not. Fourthly,

2 [Gen. 11:1-9.]

when they use them to grieve one another, for, seeing nature has armed living creatures, some with teeth, some with horns, and some with hands, to grieve an enemy, it is but an abuse of speech to grieve him with the tongue, unless it be one whom we are obliged to govern, and then it is not to grieve but to correct and amend.

The manner how speech serves to the remembrance of the consequence of causes and effects consists in the imposing of *names* and the *connection* of them.

Names, proper and common. Of names, some are *proper* and singular to one only thing, as *Peter, John, this man, this tree;* and some are *common* to many things, *man, horse, tree,* every of which, though but one name, is neverthe-less the name of divers particular things, in respect of all which *Universal.* together it is called a *universal,* there being nothing in the world universal but names, for the things named are every one of them individual and singu-lar.

One universal name is imposed on many things for their si-militude in some quality or other accident; and whereas a proper name brings to mind one thing only, universals recall any one of those many.

And of names universal, some are of more and some of less ex-tent, the larger comprehending the less large; and some again of equal extent, comprehending each other reciprocally. As for example: the name *body* is of larger signification than the word *man* and comprehends it; and the names *man* and *rational* are of equal extent, comprehending mutually one another. But here we must take notice that by a name is not always under-stood, as in grammar, one only word, but sometimes by circum-locution many words together. For all these words, *he that in his actions observes the laws of his country,* make but one name, equivalent to this one word—*just.*

By this imposition of names, some of larger, some of stricter signification, we turn the reckoning of the consequences of things imagined in the mind into a reckoning of the conse-quences of appellations. For example: a man that has no use of speech at all, such as is born and remains perfectly deaf and dumb, if he set before his eyes a triangle and by it two right

angles such as are the corners of a square figure, he may, by
meditation, compare and find that the three angles of that triangle are equal to those two right angles that stand by it. But if
another triangle be shown him, different in shape from the
former, he cannot know, without a new labor, whether the
three angles of that also be equal to the same. But he that has
the use of words, when he observes that such equality was consequent, not to the length of the sides nor to any other particular thing in his triangle, but only to this, that the sides were
straight and the angles three, and that that was all for which he
named it a triangle, will boldly conclude universally that such
equality of angles is in all triangles whatsoever, and register his
invention in these general terms: *every triangle has its three
angles equal to two right angles.* And thus the consequence
found in one particular comes to be registered and remembered
as a universal rule, and discharges our mental reckoning of time
and place, and delivers us from all labor of the mind saving the
first, and makes that which was found true *here* and *now* to be
true in *all times* and *places*.

But the use of words in registering our thoughts is in nothing
so evident as in numbering. A natural fool that could never
learn by heart the order of numeral words, as *one, two,* and
three, may observe every stroke of the clock, and nod to it, or
say *one, one, one,* but can never know what hour it strikes. And
it seems there was a time when those names of number were not
in use, and men were fain to apply their fingers of one or both
hands to those things they desired to keep account of; and that
thence it proceeded that now our numeral words are but ten in
any nation, and in some but five, and then they begin again.
And he that can tell ten, if he recite them out of order will lose
himself and not know when he has done. Much less will he be
able to add and subtract and perform all other operations of
arithmetic. So that without words there is no possibility of reckoning of numbers, much less of magnitudes, of swiftness, of
force, and other things the reckonings whereof are necessary to
the being or well-being of mankind.

When two names are joined together into a consequence or
affirmation, as thus: *a man is a living creature,* or thus: *if he be
a man, he is a living creature,* if the latter name, *living creature,*

signify all that the former name *man* signifies, then the affirmation or consequence is *true;* otherwise *false.* For *true* and *false* are attributes of speech, not of things. And where speech is not, there is neither *truth* nor *falsehood; error* there may be, as when we expect that which shall not be or suspect what has not been, but in neither case can a man be charged with untruth.

Necessity of definitions. Seeing then that truth consists in the right ordering of names in our affirmations, a man that seeks precise truth had need to remember what every name he uses stands for and to place it accordingly, or else he will find himself entangled in words as a bird in lime twigs, the more he struggles the more belimed. And therefore in geometry, which is the only science that it has pleased God hitherto to bestow on mankind, men begin at settling the significations of their words, which settling of significations they call *definitions* and place them in the beginning of their reckoning.

By this it appears how necessary it is for any man that aspires to true knowledge to examine the definitions of former authors, and either to correct them where they are negligently set down or to make them himself. For the errors of definitions multiply themselves according as the reckoning proceeds, and lead men into absurdities which at last they see but cannot avoid without reckoning anew from the beginning, in which lies the foundation of their errors. From whence it happens that they which trust to books do as they that cast up many little sums into a greater, without considering whether those little sums were rightly cast up or not; and at last finding the error visible, and not mistrusting their first grounds, know not which way to clear themselves, but spend time in fluttering over their books as birds that, entering by the chimney and finding themselves enclosed in a chamber, flutter at the false light of a glass window for want of wit to consider which way they came in. So that in the right definition of names lies the first use of speech, which is the acquisition of science; and in wrong or no definitions lies the first abuse, from which proceed all false and senseless tenets which make those men that take their instruction from the authority of books, and not from their own meditation, to be as much below the condition of ignorant men as men endowed

with true science are above it. For between true science and erroneous doctrines, ignorance is in the middle. Natural sense
and imagination are not subject to absurdity. Nature itself cannot err; and as men abound in copiousness of language, so they
become more wise or more mad than ordinary. Nor is it possible
without letters for any man to become either excellently wise
or, unless his memory be hurt by disease or ill constitution of
organs, excellently foolish. For words are wise men's counters,
they do but reckon by them; but they are the money of fools
that value them by the authority of an Aristotle, a Cicero, or a
Thomas [Aquinas], or any other doctor whatsoever, if but a
man.

Subject to names.   *Subject to names* is whatsoever can enter into
or be considered in an account, and be added
one to another to make a sum, or subtracted one from another
and leave a remainder. The Latins called accounts of money
rationes, and accounting *ratiocinatio;* and that which we in
bills or books of account call *items,* they call *nomina*—that is,
names; and thence it seems to proceed that they extended the
word *ratio* to the faculty of reckoning in all other things. The
Greeks have but one word, λόγος,[3] for both *speech* and *reason*—
not that they thought there was no speech without reason, but
no reasoning without speech—and the act of reasoning they
called *syllogism,* which signifies summing up of the consequences of one saying to another. And because the same thing
may enter into account for divers accidents, their names are, to
show that diversity, diversely wrested and diversified. This diversity of names may be reduced to four general heads.

First, a thing may enter into account for *matter* or *body,* as
living, sensible, rational, hot, cold, moved, quiet, with all which
names the word *matter* or *body* is understood, all such being
names of matter.

Secondly, it may enter into account or be considered for some
accident or quality which we conceive to be in it, as for *being
moved,* for *being so long,* for *being hot,* etc.; and then, of the
name of the thing itself, by a little change or wresting, we make
a name for that accident which we consider; and for *living* put
into the account *life;* for *moved, motion;* for *hot, heat;* for *long,*

3 [*Logos.*]

length, and the like; and all such names are the names of the accidents and properties by which one matter and body is distinguished from another. These are called *names abstract,* because severed, not from matter, but from the account of matter.

Thirdly, we bring into account the properties of our own bodies, whereby we make such distinction as, when anything is seen by us, we reckon not the thing itself but the sight, the color, the idea of it in the fancy; and when anything is heard, we reckon it not, but the hearing or sound only, which is our fancy or conception of it by the ear; and such are names of fancies.

Fourthly, we bring into account, consider, and give names to *names* themselves, and to *speeches,* for *general, universal, special, equivocal* are names of names. And *affirmation, interrogation, commandment, narration, syllogism, sermon, oration,* and many other such are names of speeches. And this is all the variety of names *positive,* which are put to mark

Use of names positive.

somewhat which is in nature or may be feigned by the mind of man: as bodies that are or may be conceived to be; or, of bodies, the properties that are or may be feigned to be; or words and speech.

There be also other names, called *negative,*

Negative names, with their uses.

which are notes to signify that a word is not the name of the thing in question, as these words: *nothing, no man, infinite, indocible, three want four,* and the like, which are nevertheless of use in reckoning or in correcting of reckoning, and call to mind our past cogitations, though they be not names of anything because they make us refuse to admit of names not rightly used.

All other names are but insignificant sounds,

Words insignificant.

and those of two sorts. One, when they are new and yet their meaning not explained by definition, whereof there have been abundance coined by Schoolmen and puzzled philosophers.

Another, when men make a name of two names whose significations are contradictory and inconsistent, as this name: an *incorporeal body* or, which is all one, an *incorporeal substance,* and a great number more. For whensoever any affirmation is false, the two names of which it is composed, put together and made one, signify nothing at all. For example, if it be a false affirmation to say *a quadrangle is round,* the word *round quad-rangle* signifies nothing but is a mere sound. So likewise, if it be false to say that virtue can be poured, or blown up and down, the words *inpoured virtue, inblown virtue* are as absurd and insignificant as a *round quadrangle.* And therefore you shall hardly meet with a senseless and insignificant word that is not made up of some Latin or Greek names. A Frenchman seldom hears our Saviour called by the name of *parole,* but by the name of *verbe* often; yet *verbe* and *parole* differ no more but that one is Latin, the other French.

Understanding. When a man, upon the hearing of any speech, has those thoughts which the words of that speech and their connection were ordained and constituted to signify, then he is said to understand it, *understanding* being nothing else but conception caused by speech. And therefore if speech be peculiar to man, as for aught I know it is, then is understanding peculiar to him also. And therefore of absurd and false affirmations, in case they be universal, there can be no understanding, though many think they understand them [4] when they do but repeat the words softly or con them in their mind.

What kinds of speeches signify the appetites, aversions, and passions of man's mind, and of their use and abuse, I shall speak when I have spoken of the passions. [Ch. VI, pp. 51 ff.]

Inconstant names. The names of such things as affect us—that is, which please and displease us—because all men be not alike affected with the same thing nor the same man at all times, are in the common discourses of men of *inconstant* signification. For seeing all names are imposed to signify our conceptions, and all our affections are but conceptions, when we conceive the same things differently we can hardly avoid different naming of them. For though the nature of that we conceive be the same, yet the diversity of our reception of it, in respect of different constitutions of body and prejudices of opinion, gives everything a tincture of our different passions. And therefore in reasoning a man must take heed of words which, besides the signification of what we imagine of their nature, have a signification also of the nature, disposition, and interest of the speaker: such as are the names of virtues and vices, for one man

4 [The edition of 1651 has "then."]

calls *wisdom* what another calls *fear,* and one *cruelty* what another *justice,* one *prodigality* what another *magnanimity,* and one *gravity* what another *stupidity,* etc. And therefore such names can never be true grounds of any ratiocination. No more can metaphors and tropes of speech; but these are less dangerous, because they profess their inconstancy, which the other do not.

CHAPTER FIVE

OF REASON AND SCIENCE

Reason, what it is. When a man *reasons,* he does nothing else but conceive a sum total from *addition* of parcels, or conceive a remainder from *subtraction* of one sum from another; which, if it be done by words, is conceiving of the consequence of the names of all the parts to the name of the whole, or from the names of the whole and one part to the name of the other part. And though in some things, as in numbers, besides adding and subtracting men name other operations, as *multiplying* and *dividing,* yet they are the same; for multiplication is but adding together of things equal, and division but subtracting of one thing as often as we can. These operations are not incident to numbers only, but to all manner of things that can be added together and taken one out of another. For as arithmeticians teach to add and subtract in *numbers,* so the geometricians teach the same in *lines, figures* solid and superficial, *angles, proportions, times,* degrees of *swiftness, force, power,* and the like; the logicians teach the same in *consequences of words,* adding together two *names* to make an *affirmation,* and two *affirmations* to make a *syllogism,* and many *syllogisms* to make a *demonstration;* and from the *sum* or *conclusion* of a *syllogism* they subtract one *proposition* to find the other. Writers of politics add together *pactions* to find men's *duties,* and lawyers *laws* and *facts* to find what is *right* and *wrong* in the actions of private men. In sum, in what matter soever there is place for *addition* and *subtraction,* there also is place for *reason;* and where these have no place, there *reason* has nothing at all to do.

Reason defined.   Out of all which we may define—that is to say, determine—what that is which is meant by this word *reason* when we reckon it among the faculties of the mind. For REASON, in this sense, is nothing but *reckoning*—that is, adding and subtracting—of the consequences of general names agreed upon for the *marking* and *signifying* of our thoughts; I say *marking* them when we reckon by ourselves, and *signifying* when we demonstrate or approve our reckonings to other men.

Right reason, where.   And as in arithmetic unpracticed men must, and professors themselves may often, err and cast up false, so also in any other subject of reasoning the ablest, most attentive, and most practiced men may deceive themselves and infer false conclusions; not but that reason itself is always right reason, as well as arithmetic is a certain and infallible art, but no one man's reason, nor the reason of any one number of men, makes the certainty, no more than an account is therefore well cast up because a great many men have unanimously approved it. And therefore as when there is a controversy in an account the parties must by their own accord set up, for right reason, the reason of some arbitrator or judge, to whose sentence they will both stand, or their controversy must either come to blows or be undecided for want of a right reason constituted by nature, so is it also in all debates of what kind soever. And when men that think themselves wiser than all others clamor and demand right reason for judge, yet seek no more but that things should be determined by no other men's reason but their own, it is as intolerable in the society of men as it is in play after trump is turned to use for trump on every occasion that suit whereof they have most in their hand. For they do nothing else that will have every of their passions, as it comes to bear sway in them, to be taken for right reason, and that in their own controversies, betraying their want of right reason by the claim they lay to it.

The use of reason.   The use and end of reason is not the finding of the sum and truth of one or a few consequences remote from the first definitions and settled significations of names, but to begin at these and proceed from one consequence to another. For there can be no certainty of the last conclusion without a certainty of all those affirmations and negations on which it was grounded and inferred. As when a master of a family, in taking an account, casts up the sums of all the bills of expense into one sum, and not regarding how each bill is summed up by those that give them in account nor what it is he pays for, he advantages himself no more than if he allowed the account in gross, trusting to every of the accountants' skill and honesty; so also in reasoning of all other things he that takes up conclusions on the trust of authors, and does not fetch them from the first items in every reckoning, which are the significations of names settled by definitions, loses his labor; and does not know anything, but only believes.

Of error and absurdity.   When a man reckons without the use of words, which may be done in particular things, as when upon the sight of any one thing we conjecture what was likely to have preceded or is likely to follow upon it, if that which he thought likely to follow follows not, or that which he thought likely to have preceded it has not preceded it, this is called *error,* to which even the most prudent men are subject. But when we reason in words of general signification and fall upon a general inference which is false, though it be commonly called *error,* it is indeed an *absurdity* or senseless speech. For error is but a deception in presuming that somewhat is past or to come of which, though it were not past, or not to come, yet there was no impossibility discoverable. But when we make a general assertion, unless it be a true one, the possibility of it is inconceivable. And words whereby we conceive nothing but the sound are those we call *absurd, insignificant,* and *nonsense.* And therefore if a man should talk to me of a *round quadrangle,* or *accidents of bread in cheese,* or *immaterial substances,* or of *a free subject, a free will,* or any *free* but free from being hindered by opposition, I should not say he were in an error but that his words were without meaning—that is to say, absurd.

I have said before, in the second chapter, that a man did excel all other animals in this faculty: that when he conceived anything whatsoever, he was apt to inquire the consequences of it and what effects he could do with it. And now I add this other degree of the same excellence: that he can by words reduce the consequences he finds to general rules, called *theorems* or *aphorisms*—that is, he can reason or reckon not only in number but in all other things whereof one may be added unto or subtracted from another.

But this privilege is allayed by another, and that is, by the privilege of absurdity, to which no living creature is subject but man only. And of men, those are of all most subject to it that profess philosophy. For it is most true that Cicero says of them somewhere that there can be nothing so absurd but may be found in the books of philosophers. And the reason is manifest. For there is not one of them that begins his ratiocination from the definitions or explications of the names they are to use, which is a method that has been used only in geometry, whose conclusions have thereby been made indisputable.

Causes of absurdity. 1. The first cause of absurd conclusions I ascribe to the want of method in that they begin not their ratiocination from definitions—that is, from settled significations of their words—as if they could cast account without knowing the value of the numeral words *one, two,* and *three.*

And whereas all bodies enter into account upon divers considerations, which I have mentioned in the precedent chapter, these considerations being diversely named, divers absurdities proceed from the confusion and unfit connection of their names into assertions. And therefore,

2. The second cause of absurd assertions I ascribe to the giving of names of *bodies* to *accidents,* or of *accidents* to *bodies:* as they do that say *faith is infused* or *inspired* when nothing can be *poured* or *breathed* into anything but body; and that *extension* is *body;* that *phantasms* are *spirits,* etc.

3. The third I ascribe to the giving of the names of the *accidents of bodies without us* to the *accidents* of our *own bodies:* as they do that say the *color is in the body, the sound is in the air,* etc.

4. The fourth, to the giving of the names of *bodies* to *names* or *speeches:* as they do that say that *there be things universal,* that a *living creature is genus* or a *general thing,* etc.

5. The fifth, to the giving of the names of *accidents* to *names* and *speeches:* as they do that say *the nature of a thing is its definition, a man's command is his will,* and the like.

6. The sixth, to the use of metaphors, tropes, and other rhe-

torical figures instead of words proper. For though it be lawful
to say, for example, in common speech *the way goes or leads
hither or thither, the proverb says this or that,* whereas ways
cannot go nor proverbs speak, yet in reckoning and seeking of
truth such speeches are not to be admitted.

7. The seventh, to names that signify nothing but are taken
up and learned by rote from the schools: as *hypostatical, tran-
substantiate, consubstantiate, eternal-now,* and the like canting
of Schoolmen.

To him that can avoid these things it is not easy to fall into
any absurdity, unless it be by the length of an account, wherein
he may perhaps forget what went before. For all men by nature
reason alike and well when they have good principles. For who
is so stupid as both to mistake in geometry and also to persist in
it when another detects his error to him?

Science.   By this it appears that reason is not, as sense
and memory, born with us, nor gotten by ex-
perience only, as prudence is, but attained by industry: first in
apt imposing of names, and secondly by getting a good and
orderly method in proceeding from the elements, which are
names, to assertions made by connection of one of them to another, and so to syllogisms, which are the connections of one
assertion to another, till we come to a knowledge of all the consequences of names appertaining to the subject in hand; and
that is it men call SCIENCE. And whereas sense and memory are
but knowledge of fact, which is a thing past and irrevocable,
science is the knowledge of consequences and dependence of
one fact upon another, by which out of that we can presently do
we know how to do something else when we will, or the like
another time; because when we see how anything comes about,
upon what causes and by what manner, when the like causes
come into our power we see how to make it produce the like
effects.

Children, therefore, are not endowed with reason at all till
they have attained the use of speech, but are called reasonable
creatures for the possibility apparent of having the use of reason in time to come. And the most part of men, though they
have the use of reasoning a little way, as in numbering to some
degree, yet it serves them to little use in common life, in which

they govern themselves, some better, some worse, according to their differences of experience, quickness of memory, and inclinations to several ends, but specially according to good or evil fortune and the errors of one another. For as for *science* or certain rules of their actions, they are so far from it that they know not what it is. Geometry they have thought conjuring; but for other sciences, they who have not been taught the beginnings and some progress in them, that they may see how they be acquired and generated, are in this point like children that, having no thought of generation, are made believe by the women that their brothers and sisters are not born but found in the garden.

But yet they that have no *science* are in better and nobler condition with their natural prudence than men that, by misreasoning or by trusting them that reason wrong, fall upon false and absurd general rules. For ignorance of causes and of rules does not set men so far out of their way as relying on false rules and taking for causes of what they aspire to those that are not so, but rather causes of the contrary.

To conclude, the light of human minds is perspicuous words, but by exact definitions first snuffed and purged from ambiguity; *reason* is the *pace*; increase of *science*, the *way*; and the benefit of mankind, the *end*. And, on the contrary, metaphors and senseless and ambiguous words are like *ignes fatui*; [1] and reasoning upon them is wandering among innumerable absurdities; and their end, contention and sedition, or contempt.

Prudence and sapience, with their difference. As much experience is *prudence*, so is much science *sapience*. For though we usually have one name of wisdom for them both, yet the Latins did always distinguish between *prudentia* and *sapientia*, ascribing the former to experience, the latter to science. But to make their difference appear more clearly, let us suppose one man endowed with an excellent natural use and dexterity in handling his arms, and another to have added to that dexterity an acquired science of where he can offend or be offended by his adversary in every possible posture or guard; the ability of the former would be to the ability of the latter as prudence to sapience: both useful, but the latter infallible. But they that, trusting only to the authority of books,

[1] [Will-o'-the-wisps.]

follow the blind blindly are like him that, trusting to the false rules of a master of fence, ventures presumptuously upon an adversary that either kills or disgraces him.

Signs of science. The signs of science are some certain and infallible, some uncertain. Certain, when he that pretends the science of anything can teach the same—that is to say, demonstrate the truth thereof perspicuously to another; uncertain, when only some particular events answer to his pretense, and upon many occasions prove so as he says they must. Signs of prudence are all uncertain, because to observe by experience and remember all circumstances that may alter the success is impossible. But in any business whereof a man has not infallible science to proceed by, to forsake his own natural judgment and be guided by general sentences read in authors and subject to many exceptions is a sign of folly and generally scorned by the name of pedantry. And even of those men themselves that in councils of the commonwealth love to show their reading of politics and history, very few do it in their domestic affairs where their particular interest is concerned, having prudence enough for their private affairs; but in public they study more the reputation of their own wit than the success of another's business.

CHAPTER SIX

OF THE INTERIOR BEGINNINGS OF VOLUN-
TARY MOTIONS COMMONLY CALLED THE
PASSIONS, AND THE SPEECHES BY
WHICH THEY ARE EXPRESSED

Motion, vital and animal. There be in animals two sorts of *motions* peculiar to them: one called *vital*, begun in generation and continued without interruption through their whole life—such as are the *course of the blood*, the *pulse*, the *breathing*, the *concoction, nutrition, excretion*, etc.—to which motions there needs no help of imagination; the other is *animal motion*, otherwise called *voluntary motion*—as to go, to *speak*, to *move* any of our limbs in such manner as is first fancied in our minds. That sense is motion in the organs and interior parts of man's body caused by the action of the things we see, hear, etc., and that fancy is but the relics of the same motion remaining after sense, has been already said in the first and second chapters. And because *going, speaking,* and the like voluntary motions depend always upon a precedent thought of *whither, which way,* and *what,* it is evident that the imagination is the first internal beginning of all voluntary motion. And although unstudied men do not conceive any motion at all to be there where the thing moved is invisible or the space it is moved in is, for the shortness of it, insensible, yet that does not hinder but that such motions are. For let a space be never so little, that which is moved over a greater space, whereof that little one is part, must first be moved over that. These small beginnings of motion within the body of man, before they appear in walking, speaking, striking, and other visible actions, are commonly called ENDEAVOR.

Endeavor.

Appetite. Desire.

This endeavor, when it is toward something which causes it, is called APPETITE or DESIRE, the latter being the general name and the other oftentimes restrained to signify the desire of food, namely *hunger* and *thirst.* And when the endeavor is fromward something, it is generally called AVERSION. These words, *appetite* and *aversion,* we have from the Latins; and they both of them signify the motions, one of approaching, the other of retiring. So also do the Greek words for the same, which are ὁρμὴ and ἀφορμὴ. For nature itself does often press upon men those truths which afterwards, when they look for somewhat beyond nature, they stumble at. For the Schools find in mere appetite to go or move no actual motion at all; but because some motion they must acknowledge, they call it metaphorical motion, which is but an absurd speech, for though words may be called metaphorical, bodies and motions cannot.

Hunger. Thirst.

Aversion.

Love. Hate.

That which men desire they are also said to LOVE, and to HATE those things for which they have aversion. So that desire and love are the same thing, save that by desire we always signify the absence of the object, by love most commonly the presence of the same. So also by aversion we signify the absence, and by hate the presence of the object.

Of appetites and aversions, some are born with men, as appetite of food, appetite of excretion, and exoneration, which may also and more properly be called aversions from somewhat they feel in their bodies; and some other appetites, not many. The rest, which are appetites of particular things, proceed from experience and trial of their effects upon themselves or other men. For of things we know not at all, or believe not to be, we can have no further desire than to taste and try. But aversion we have for things, not only which we know have hurt us, but also that we do not know whether they will hurt us or not.

Contempt. Those things which we neither desire nor hate we are said to *contemn*, CONTEMPT being nothing else but an immobility or contumacy of the heart in resisting the action of certain things; and proceeding from that the heart is already moved otherwise by other more potent objects or from want of experience of them.

And because the constitution of a man's body is in continual mutation, it is impossible that all the same things should always cause in him the same appetites and aversions; much less can all men consent in the desire of almost any one and the same object.

Good. Evil. But whatsoever is the object of any man's appetite or desire, that is it which he for his part calls *good*; and the object of his hate and aversion, *evil*; and of his contempt, *vile* and *inconsiderable*. For these words of good, evil, and contemptible are ever used with relation to the person that uses them, there being nothing simply and absolutely so, nor any common rule of good and evil to be taken from the nature of the objects themselves—but from the person of the man, where there is no commonwealth, or, in a commonwealth, from the person that represents it, or from an arbitrator or judge whom men disagreeing shall by consent set up and make his sentence the rule thereof.

Pulchrum. Turpe. The Latin tongue has two words whose significations approach to those of good and evil but are not precisely the same, and those are *pulchrum* and *turpe*. Whereof the former signifies that which by some apparent signs promises good, and the latter that which promises evil.

But in our tongue we have not so general names to express them by. But for *pulchrum* we say in some things *fair*, in others *beautiful* or *handsome* or *gallant* or *honorable* or *comely* or *amiable;* and for *turpe, foul, deformed, ugly, base, nauseous,* and the like as the subject shall require; all which words, in their proper places, signify nothing else but the *mien* or countenance that promises good and evil. So that of good there be three kinds: good in the promise, that is *pulchrum;* good in effect, as the end desired, which is called *jucundum, delightful;*

Delightful. Profit- and good as the means, which is called *utile,*
able. Unpleasant.
Unprofitable. *profitable;* and as many of evil: for *evil* in promise is that they call *turpe;* evil in effect and end is *molestum, unpleasant, troublesome;* and evil in the means, *inutile, unprofitable, hurtful.*

As in sense that which is really within us is, as I have said before, only motion caused by the action of external objects, but in appearance to the sight light and color, to the ear sound, to the nostril odor, etc., so when the action of the same object is continued from the eyes, ears, and other organs to the heart, the real effect there is nothing but motion or endeavor, which consists in appetite or aversion to or from the ob-

Delight. ject moving. But the appearance or sense of
Displeasure. that motion is that we either call *delight* or *trouble of mind.*

Pleasure. This motion, which is called appetite, and for the appearance of it *delight* and *pleasure,* seems to be a corroboration of vital motion and a help thereunto; and therefore such things as caused delight were not improperly called *jucunda, à juvando,* from helping or fortifying,
Offense. and the contrary, *molesta, offensive,* from hindering and troubling the motion vital.

Pleasure, therefore, or *delight* is the appearance or sense of good; and *molestation* or *displeasure* the appearance or sense of evil. And consequently all appetite, desire, and love is accompanied with some delight more or less, and all hatred and aversion with more or less displeasure and offense.

Of pleasures or delights, some arise from the sense of an ob-
Pleasures of sense. ject present, and those may be called *pleasures of sense*—the word *sensual,* as it is used by those only that condemn them, having no place till there be laws. Of

this kind are all onerations and exonerations of the body, as also all that is pleasant in the *sight, hearing, smell, taste,* or *touch.* Others arise from the expectation that proceeds from foresight of the end or consequence of things, whether those things in the sense please or displease. And these are *pleasures of the mind* of him that draws those consequences, and are generally called JOY. In the like manner, displeasures are some in the sense, and called PAIN; others in the expectation of consequences, and are called GRIEF.

Pleasures of the mind.

Joy.

Pain.

Grief.

These simple passions called *appetite, desire, love, aversion, hate, joy,* and *grief* have their names for divers considerations diversified. As first, when they one succeed another, they are diversely called from the opinion men have of the likelihood of attaining what they desire. Secondly, from the object loved or hated. Thirdly, from the consideration of many of them together. Fourthly, from the alteration or succession itself.

Hope.

Despair.

Fear.

For *appetite* with an opinion of attaining is called HOPE. The same without such opinion, DESPAIR. *Aversion* with opinion of HURT from the object, FEAR.

Courage.

The same with hope of avoiding that hurt by resistance, COURAGE.

Anger.

Sudden *courage,* ANGER.

Confidence.

Constant *hope,* CONFIDENCE of ourselves.

Diffidence.

Constant *despair,* DIFFIDENCE of ourselves.

Indignation.

Anger for great hurt done to another when we conceive the same to be done by injury, INDIGNATION.

Benevolence.

Good nature.

Desire of good to another, BENEVOLENCE, GOOD WILL, CHARITY. If to man generally, GOOD NATURE.

Covetousness.

Desire of riches, COVETOUSNESS, a name used always in signification of blame because men contending for them are displeased with one another attaining them, though the desire in itself be to be blamed or allowed according to the means by which these riches are sought.

Ambition.

Desire of office or precedence, AMBITION, a name used also in the worse sense for the reason before mentioned.

Desire of things that conduce but a little to our ends, and fear of things that are but of little hindrance, PUSILLANIMITY.

Pusillanimity.

Contempt of little helps and hindrances, MAGNANIMITY.

Magnanimity.

Magnanimity in danger of death or wounds, VALOR, FORTITUDE.

Valor.

Magnanimity in the use of riches, LIBERALITY.

Liberality.

Pusillanimity in the same, WRETCHEDNESS, MISERABLENESS, or PARSIMONY, as it is liked or disliked.

Miserableness.

Love of persons for society, KINDNESS.

Kindness.

Love of persons for pleasing the sense only, NATURAL LUST.

Natural lust.

Love of the same acquired from rumination, that is, imagination of pleasure past, LUXURY.

Luxury.

Love of one singularly, with desire to be singularly beloved, THE PASSION OF LOVE. The same with fear that the love is not mutual, JEALOUSY.

The passion of love.

Jealousy.

Desire, by doing hurt to another, to make him condemn some fact of his own, REVENGEFULNESS.

Revengefulness.

Desire to know why and how, CURIOSITY, such as is in no living creature but *man;* so that man is distinguished, not only by his reason, but also by this singular passion from other *animals,* in whom the appetite of food and other pleasures of sense, by predominance, take away the care of knowing causes, which is a lust of the mind that, by a perseverance of delight in the continual and indefatigable generation of knowledge, exceeds the short vehemence of any carnal pleasure.

Curiosity.

Fear of power invisible, feigned by the mind or imagined from tales publicly allowed, RELIGION; not allowed, SUPERSTITION. And when the power imagined is truly such as we imagine, TRUE RELIGION.

Religion.

Superstition.

True religion.

Fear without the apprehension of why or what, PANIC TERROR, called so from the fables that make Pan the author of them; whereas in truth there is always in him that so fears, first, some apprehension of the cause,

Panic terror.

though the rest run away by example, everyone supposing his fellow to know why. And therefore this passion happens to none but in a throng or multitude of people.

Admiration.   *Joy* from apprehension of novelty, ADMIRATION, proper to man because it excites the appetite of knowing the cause.

Joy arising from imagination of a man's own power and ability is that exultation of the mind which is called GLORYING,

Glory.   which, if grounded upon the experience of his own former actions, is the same with *confidence,* but if grounded on the flattery of others, or only sup-

Vainglory.   posed by himself for delight in the consequences of it, is called VAINGLORY, which name is properly given because a well-grounded *confidence* begets attempt, whereas the supposing of power does not and is therefore rightly called *vain.*

Dejection.   *Grief* from opinion of want of power is called DEJECTION of mind.

The *vainglory* which consists in the feigning or supposing of abilities in ourselves which we know are not is most incident to young men, and nourished by the histories or fictions of gallant persons; and is corrected oftentimes by age and employment.

Sudden glory.   *Sudden glory* is the passion which makes those *grimaces* called LAUGHTER, and is caused either

Laughter.   by some sudden act of their own that pleases them or by the apprehension of some deformed thing in another, by comparison whereof they suddenly applaud themselves. And it is incident most to them that are conscious of the fewest abilities in themselves, who are forced to keep themselves in their own favor by observing the imperfections of other men. And therefore much laughter at the defects of others is a sign of pusillanimity. For of great minds, one of the proper works is to help and free others from scorn and compare themselves only with the most able.

Sudden dejection.   On the contrary, *sudden dejection* is the passion that causes WEEPING, and is caused by such

Weeping.   accidents as suddenly take away some vehement hope or some prop of their power; and they are most subject to it that rely principally on helps external, such as are women and children. Therefore some weep for the loss of friends, others for their unkindness, others for the sudden stop made to their thoughts of revenge by reconciliation. But in all cases, both laughter and weeping are sudden motions, custom taking them both away. For no man laughs at old jests or weeps for an old calamity.

Shame.   *Grief* for the discovery of some defect of ability is SHAME, or the passion that discovers itself in *Blushing.*   BLUSHING, and consists in the apprehension of something dishonorable; and in young men is a sign of the love of good reputation and commendable; in old men it is a sign of the same, but, because it comes too late, not commendable.

Impudence.   The *contempt* of good reputation is called IM-PUDENCE.

Pity.   *Grief* for the calamity of another is PITY, and arises from the imagination that the like calamity may befall himself, and therefore is called also COMPASSION, and in the phrase of this present time a FELLOW-FEELING: and therefore for calamity arriving from great wickedness, the best men have the least pity; and for the same calamity, those hate pity that think themselves least obnoxious to the same.

Cruelty.   *Contempt* or little sense of the calamity of others is that which men call CRUELTY, pro-ceeding from security of their own fortune. For that any man should take pleasure in other men's great harms, without other end of his own, I do not conceive it possible.

Grief for the success of a competitor in wealth, honor, or other good, if it be joined with endeavor to enforce our own *Emulation.*   abilities to equal or exceed him, is called EMU-LATION, but joined with endeavor to supplant *Envy.*   or hinder a competitor, ENVY.

When in the mind of man appetites and aversions, hopes and fears concerning one and the same thing arise alternately, and divers good and evil consequences of the doing or omitting the thing propounded come successively into our thoughts, so that sometimes we have an appetite to it, sometimes an aversion from it, sometimes hope to be able to do it, sometimes despair or fear to attempt it—the whole sum of desires, aversions, hopes, and fears continued till the thing be either done or thought impossible is that we call DELIBERATION.

Deliberation.

Therefore of things past there is no *deliberation,* because manifestly impossible to be changed; nor of things known to be impossible, or thought so, because men know or think such deliberation vain. But of things impossible which we think possible, we may deliberate, not knowing it is in vain. And it is called *deliberation* because it is a putting an end to the *liberty* we had of doing or omitting according to our own appetite or aversion.

This alternate succession of appetites, aversions, hopes, and fears is no less in other living creatures than in man, and therefore beasts also deliberate.

Every *deliberation* is then said to *end* when that whereof they deliberate is either done or thought impossible, because till then we retain the liberty of doing or omitting according to our appetite or aversion.

In *deliberation,* the last appetite or aversion immediately adhering to the action or to the omission thereof

The will.

is that we call the WILL—the act, not the faculty, of *willing.* And beasts that have *deliberation* must necessarily also have *will.* The definition of the *will* given commonly by the Schools, that it is a *rational appetite,* is not good. For if it were, then could there be no voluntary act against reason. For a *voluntary act* is that which proceeds from the *will,* and no other. But if instead of a rational appetite we shall say an appetite resulting from a precedent deliberation, then the definition is the same that I have given here. *Will, therefore, is the last appetite in deliberating.* And though we say in common discourse a man had a will once to do a thing that nevertheless he forbore to do, yet that is properly but an inclination which makes no action voluntary, because the action depends not of it but of the last inclination or appetite. For if the intervenient appetites make any action voluntary, then by the same reason all intervenient aversions should make the same action involuntary; and so one and the same action should be both voluntary and involuntary.

By this it is manifest that not only actions that have their beginning from covetousness, ambition, lust, or other appetites to the thing propounded, but also those that have their beginning from aversion or fear of those consequences that follow the omission, are *voluntary actions*.

Forms of speech, in passion. The forms of speech by which the passions are expressed are partly the same and partly different from those by which we express our thoughts. And first, generally all passions may be expressed *indicatively*, as *I love, I fear, I joy, I deliberate, I will, I command;* but some of them have particular expressions by themselves, which nevertheless are not affirmations unless it be when they serve to make other inferences besides that of the passion they proceed from. Deliberation is expressed *subjunctively,* which is a speech proper to signify suppositions with their consequences, as *if this be done, then this will follow;* and differs not from the language of reasoning, save that reasoning is in general words, but deliberation for the most part is of particulars. The language of desire and aversion is *imperative,* as *do this, forbear that;* which, when the party is obliged to do or forbear, is *command,* otherwise *prayer* or else *counsel.* The language of vainglory, of indignation, pity, and revengefulness, *optative;* but of the desire to know there is a peculiar expression called *interrogative,* as *what is it, when shall it, how is it done,* and *why so?* Other language of the passions I find none, for cursing, swearing, reviling, and the like do not signify as speech but as the actions of a tongue accustomed.

These forms of speech, I say, are expressions or voluntary significations of our passions; but certain signs they be not, because they may be used arbitrarily whether they that use them have such passions or not. The best signs of passions present are either in the countenance, motions of the body, actions, and ends or aims which we otherwise know the man to have.

And because in deliberation the appetites and aversions are raised by foresight of the good and evil consequences and sequels of the action whereof we deliberate, the good or evil effect thereof depends on the foresight of a long chain of consequences, of which very seldom any man is able to see to the end. But for so far as a man sees, if the good in those consequences be greater than the evil, the whole chain is that which writers call

*Good and evil
apparent.*

apparent or *seeming good.* And contrarily, when the evil exceeds the good the whole is *apparent* or *seeming evil,* so that he who has by experience or reason the greatest and surest prospect of consequences deliberates best himself and is able when he will to give the best counsel unto others.

Felicity.

Continual success in obtaining those things which a man from time to time desires—that is to say, continual prospering—is that men call FELICITY; I mean the felicity of this life. For there is no such thing as perpetual tranquillity of mind while we live here, because life itself is but motion and can never be without desire, nor without fear, no more than without sense. What kind of felicity God has ordained to them that devoutly honor him, a man shall no sooner know than enjoy, being joys that now are as incomprehensible as the word of Schoolmen, *beatifical vision,* is unintelligible.

Praise.

Magnification.

Μακαρισμός.

The form of speech whereby men signify their opinion of the goodness of anything is PRAISE. That whereby they signify the power and greatness of anything is MAGNIFYING. And that whereby they signify the opinion they have of a man's felicity is by the Greeks called *μακαρισμός,* for which we have no name in our tongue. And thus much is sufficient for the present purpose to have been said of the PASSIONS.

CHAPTER SEVEN

OF THE ENDS OR RESOLUTIONS OF DISCOURSE

Of all *discourse* governed by desire of knowledge there is at last an *end,* either by attaining or by giving over. And in the chain of discourse, wheresoever it be interrupted, there is an end for that time.

If the discourse be merely mental, it consists of thoughts that the thing will be and will not be, or that it has been and has not been, alternately. So that wheresoever you break off the chain of a man's discourse, you leave him in a presumption of *it will be* or *it will not be*, or *it has been* or *has not been*. All which is *opinion*. And that which is alternate appetite, in deliberating concerning good and evil, the same is alternate opinion in the inquiry of the truth of *past* and *future*. And as the last appetite in deliberation is called the *will*, so the last opinion in search of the truth of past and future is called the JUDG-

Judgment, or sentence final. MENT or *resolute* and *final sentence* of him that discourses. And as the whole chain of appetites alternate in the question of good or bad is called *deliberation*, so the whole chain of opinions alternate in the

Doubt. question of true or false is called DOUBT.

No discourse whatsoever can end in absolute knowledge of fact, past or to come. For as for the knowledge of fact, it is originally sense, and ever after memory. And for the knowledge of consequence, which I have said before is called science, it is not absolute but conditional. No man can know by discourse that this or that is, has been, or will be, which is to know absolutely, but only that if this be, that is; if this has been, that has been; if this shall be, that shall be—which is to know conditionally, and that not the consequence of one thing to another, but of one name of a thing to another name of the same thing.

And therefore when the discourse is put into speech and begins with the definitions of words, and proceeds by connection of the same into general affirmations, and of these again into syllogisms, the end or last sum is called the conclusion; and the thought of the mind by it signified is that conditional knowledge, or knowledge of the consequence of words, which is com-

Science. monly called SCIENCE. But if the first ground of such discourse be not definitions, or if the definitions be not rightly joined together into syllogisms, then the end or conclusion is again OPINION, namely of

Opinion. the truth of somewhat said, though sometimes in absurd and senseless words without possibility of being understood. When two or more men know of one and the same

Conscious. fact, they are said to be CONSCIOUS of it one to another, which is as much as to know it together. And because such are fittest witnesses of the facts of one another or of a third, it was and ever will be reputed a very evil

act for any man to speak against his *conscience,* or to corrupt or force another so to do, insomuch that the plea of conscience has been always hearkened unto very diligently in all times. Afterwards, men made use of the same word metaphorically for the knowledge of their own secret facts and secret thoughts; and therefore it is rhetorically said that the conscience is a thousand witnesses. And last of all, men vehemently in love with their own new opinions, though never so absurd, and obstinately bent to maintain them, gave those their opinions also that reverenced name of conscience, as if they would have it seem unlawful to change or speak against them, and so pretend to know they are true when they know at most but that they think so.

When a man's discourse begins not at definitions, it begins either at some other contemplation of his own—and then it is still called opinion—or it begins at some saying of another, of whose ability to know the truth and of whose honesty in not deceiving he doubts not; and then the discourse is not so much concerning the thing as the person, and the resolution is called

Belief. Faith.   BELIEF and FAITH: *faith in* the man, *belief* both *of* the man and *of* the truth of what he says. So that in belief are two opinions: one of the saying of the man, the other of his virtue. To *have faith in,* or *trust to,* or *believe a man* signify the same thing—namely, an opinion of the veracity of the man—but to *believe what is said* signifies only an opinion of the truth of the saying. But we are to observe that this phrase, *I believe in,* as also the Latin *credo in* and the Greek πιστεύω ἔις, are never used but in the writings of divines. Instead of them, in other writings are put *I believe him, I trust him, I have faith in him, I rely on him;* and in Latin *credo illi, fido illi;* and in Greek, πιστεύω αὐτῷ; and that this singularity of the ecclesiastic use of the word has raised many disputes about the right object of the Christian faith.

But by *believing in,* as it is in the creed, is meant, not trust in the person, but confession and acknowledgment of the doctrine. For not only Christians, but all manner of men do so believe in God as to hold all for truth they hear him say, whether they understand it or not, which is all the faith and trust can possibly be had in any person whatsoever; but they do not all believe the doctrine of the creed.

From whence we may infer that when we believe any saying

whatsoever it be, to be true from arguments taken, not from the thing itself or from the principles of natural reason, but from the authority and good opinion we have of him that has said it, then is the speaker or person we believe in or trust in, and whose word we take, the object of our faith; and the honor done in believing is done to him only. And consequently, when we believe that the Scriptures are the word of God, having no immediate revelation from God himself, our belief, faith, and trust is in the Church, whose word we take and acquiesce therein. And they that believe that which a prophet relates unto them in the name of God take the word of the prophet, do honor to him, and in him trust and believe touching the truth of what he relates, whether he be a true or a false prophet. And so it is also with all other history. For if I should not believe all that is written by historians of the glorious acts of Alexander or Caesar, I do not think the ghost of Alexander or Caesar had any just cause to be offended, or anybody else but the historian. If Livy say the gods made once a cow speak and we believe it not, we distrust not God therein but Livy.[1] So that it is evident that whatsoever we believe upon no other reason than what is drawn from authority of men only and their writings, whether they be sent from God or not, is faith in men only.

CHAPTER EIGHT

OF THE VIRTUES COMMONLY CALLED INTELLECTUAL AND THEIR CONTRARY DEFECTS

Intellectual virtue defined. Virtue generally, in all sorts of subjects, is somewhat that is valued for eminence, and consists in comparison. For if all things were equal in all men, nothing would be prized. And by *virtues intellectual* are always understood such abilities of the mind as men praise, value,

1 [The masterly history of Rome by Titus Livius (59 B.C.-A.D. 17) was constructed from traditional sources and is replete with the legends of early Rome.]

and desire should be in themselves and go commonly under the name of a *good wit,* though the same word *wit* be used also to distinguish one certain ability from the rest.

Wit, natural, or acquired. These *virtues* are of two sorts: *natural* and *acquired.* By natural, I mean not that which a man has from his birth for that is nothing else but sense, wherein men differ so little one from another and from brute beasts as it is not to be reckoned among virtues. But I mean that *wit* which is gotten by use only and experience, without method, culture, or instruction. This

Natural wit. NATURAL WIT consists principally in two things: *celerity of imagining*—that is, swift succession of one thought to another—*and steady direction* to some approved end. On the contrary, a slow imagination makes that defect or fault of the mind which is commonly called DULLNESS, *stupidity,* and sometimes by other names that signify slowness of motion or difficulty to be moved.

And this difference of quickness is caused by the difference of men's passions that love and dislike, some one thing, some another; and therefore some men's thoughts run one way, some another, and are held to and observe differently the things that pass through their imagination. And whereas in this succession of men's thoughts there is nothing to observe in the things they think on but either in what they be *like one another* or in what they be *unlike,* or *what they serve for* or *how they serve to such a purpose,* those that observe their similitudes, in case they be such as are but rarely observed by others, are said to have a

Good wit, or fancy. good wit, by which, in this occasion, is meant a good fancy. But they that observe their differences and dissimilitudes, which is called *distinguishing* and *discerning* and *judging* between thing and thing, in case such discerning be not easy are said to have a *good*

Good judgment. *judgment;* and particularly in matter of conversation and business wherein times, places, and persons are to be discerned, this virtue is called DISCRETION.

Discretion. The former—that is, fancy—without the help of judgment, is not commended as a virtue; but the latter, which is judgment and discretion, is commended for itself without the help of fancy. Besides the discretion of times, places, and persons necessary to a good fancy, there is required also an often application of his thoughts to their end—that is to say, to some use to be made of them. This done, he that has this virtue will be easily fitted with similitudes that will please, not only by illustrations of his discourse and adorning it with new and apt metaphors, but also by the rarity of their invention. But without steadiness and direction to some end, a great fancy is one kind of madness, such as they have that, entering into any discourse, are snatched from their purpose by everything that comes in their thought into so many and so long digressions and parentheses that they utterly lose themselves; which kind of folly I know no particular name for; but the cause of it is sometimes want of experience, whereby that seems to a man new and rare which does not so to others; sometimes pusillanimity, by which that seems great to him which other men think a trifle; and whatsoever is new or great, and therefore thought fit to be told, withdraws a man by degrees from the intended way of his discourse.

In a good poem, whether it be *epic* or *dramatic,* as also in *sonnets, epigrams,* and other pieces, both judgment and fancy are required; but the fancy must be more eminent, because they please for the extravagancy, but ought not to displease by indiscretion.

In a good history the judgment must be eminent, because the goodness consists in the method, in the truth, and in the choice of the actions that are most profitable to be known. Fancy has no place, but only in adorning the style.

In orations of praise and in invectives the fancy is predominant, because the design is not truth but to honor or dishonor, which is done by noble or by vile comparisons. The judgment does but suggest what circumstances make an action laudable or culpable.

In hortatives and pleadings, as truth or disguise serves best to the design in hand, so is the judgment or the fancy most required.

In demonstration, in counsel, and all rigorous search of truth, judgment does all, except sometimes the understanding have need to be opened by some apt similitude, and then there is so much use of fancy. But for metaphors, they are in this case utterly excluded. For seeing they openly profess deceit, to admit them into counsel or reasoning were manifest folly.

And in any discourse whatsoever, if the defect of discretion be apparent, how extravagant soever the fancy be, the whole discourse will be taken for a sign of want of wit; and so will it never when the discretion is manifest, though the fancy be never so ordinary.

The secret thoughts of a man run over all things—holy, profane, clean, obscene, grave, and light—without shame or blame, which verbal discourse cannot do farther than the judgment shall approve of the time, place, and persons. An anatomist or a physician may speak or write his judgment of unclean things because it is not to please but profit; but for another man to write his extravagant and pleasant fancies of the same is as if a man, from being tumbled into the dirt, should come and present himself before good company. And it is the want of discretion that makes the difference. Again, in professed remissness of mind and familiar company, a man may play with the sounds and equivocal significations of words, and that many times with encounters of extraordinary fancy; but in a sermon, or in public, or before persons unknown or whom we ought to reverence, there is no jingling of words that will not be accounted folly; and the difference is only in the want of discretion. So that where wit is wanting, it is not fancy that is wanting but discretion. Judgment therefore without fancy is wit, but fancy without judgment not.

When the thoughts of a man that has a design in hand, running over a multitude of things, observes how they conduce to that design, or what design they may conduce unto, if his observations be such as are not easy or usual this wit of his is called *Prudence.* PRUDENCE, and depends on much experience and memory of the like things and their consequences heretofore. In which there is not so much difference of men as there is in their fancies and judgment, because the experience of men equal in age is not much unequal as to the quantity but lies in different occasions, everyone having his private designs. To govern well a family and a kingdom are not different degrees of prudence but different sorts of business; no more than to draw a picture in little, or as great, or greater than the life are different degrees of art. A plain husbandman is more prudent in affairs of his own house than a privy councillor in the affairs of another man.

To prudence, if you add the use of unjust or dishonest means such as usually are prompted to men by fear or want, you have that crooked wisdom which is called CRAFT, which is a sign of pusillanimity. For magnanimity is contempt of unjust or dishonest helps. And that which the Latins call *versutia*—translated into English *shifting*—and is a putting off of a present danger or incommodity by engaging into a greater, as when a man robs one to pay another is but a shorter-sighted craft, called *versutia* from *versura*, which signifies taking money at usury for the present payment of interest.

Craft.

As for *acquired wit*—I mean acquired by method and instruction—there is none but reason, which is grounded on the right use of speech and produces the sciences. But of reason and science I have already spoken in the fifth and sixth chapters.

Acquired wit.

The causes of this difference of wits are in the passions, and the difference of passions proceeds partly from the different constitution of the body and partly from different education. For if the difference proceeded from the temper of the brain and the organs of sense, either exterior or interior, there would be no less difference of men in their sight, hearing, or other senses than in their fancies and discretions. It proceeds, therefore, from the passions, which are different not only from the difference of men's complexions, but also from their difference of customs and education.

The passions that most of all cause the difference of wit are principally the more or less desire of power, of riches, of knowledge, and of honor. All which may be reduced to the first—that is, desire of power. For riches, knowledge, and honor are but several sorts of power.

And therefore a man who has no great passion for any of these things but is, as men term it, indifferent, though he may be so far a good man as to be free from giving offense, yet he cannot possibly have either a great fancy or much judgment. For the thoughts are to the desires as scouts and spies, to range abroad and find the way to the things desired, all steadiness of the mind's motion, and all quickness of the same, proceeding from thence; for as to have no desire is to be dead, so to have weak passions is dullness; and to have passions indifferently for

Giddiness.　everything, GIDDINESS and *distraction;* and to have stronger and more vehement passions for anything than is ordinarily seen in others is that which men call MADNESS.

Madness.

Whereof there be almost as many kinds as of the passions themselves. Sometimes the extraordinary and extravagant passion proceeds from the evil constitution of the organs of the body or harm done them; and sometimes the hurt and indisposition of the organs is caused by the vehemence or long continuance of the passion. But in both cases the madness is of one and the same nature.

The passion whose violence or continuance makes madness is either great *vainglory,* which is commonly called *pride* and *self-conceit,* or great *dejection* of mind.

Pride subjects a man to anger, the excess whereof is the madness called RAGE and FURY. And thus it comes to pass that excessive desire of revenge, when it becomes habitual, hurts the organs and becomes rage; that excessive love, with jealousy, becomes also rage; excessive opinion of a man's own self, for divine inspiration, for wisdom, learning, form, and the like, becomes distraction and giddiness; the same, joined with envy, rage: vehement opinion of the truth of anything, contradicted by others, rage.

Melancholy.　Dejection subjects a man to causeless fears, which is a madness commonly called MELANCHOLY, apparent also in divers manners, as in haunting of solitudes and graves, in superstitious behavior, and in fearing some one, some another particular thing. In sum, all passions that produce strange and unusual behavior are called by the general name of madness. But of the several kinds of madness, he that would take the pains might enroll a legion. And if the excess be madness, there is no doubt but the passions themselves, when they tend to evil, are degrees of the same.

For example, though the effect of folly in them that are possessed of an opinion of being inspired be not visible always in one man by any very extravagant action that proceeds from such passion, yet when many of them conspire together the rage of the whole multitude is visible enough. For what argument of madness can there be greater than to clamor, strike, and throw stones at our best friends? Yet this is somewhat less than such a multitude will do. For they will clamor, fight against, and destroy those by whom all their lifetime before they have been protected and secured from injury. And if this be madness in the multitude, it is the same in every particular man. For as in the midst of the sea, though a man perceive no sound of that part of the water next him, yet he is well assured that part contributes as much to the roaring of the sea as any other part of the same quantity; so also, though we perceive no great unquietness in one or two men, yet we may be well assured that their singular passions are parts of the seditious roaring of a troubled nation. And if there were nothing else that betrayed their madness, yet that very arrogating such inspiration to themselves is argument enough. If some man in Bedlam [1] should entertain you with sober discourse and you desire, in taking leave, to know what he were, that you might another time requite his civility, and he should tell you he were God the Father, I think you need expect no extravagant action for argument of his madness.

This opinion of inspiration, called commonly private spirit, begins very often from some lucky finding of an error generally held by others; and not knowing, or not remembering, by what conduct of reason they came to so singular a truth (as they think it, though it be many times an untruth they light on), they presently admire themselves as being in the special grace of God Almighty, who has revealed the same to them supernaturally by his Spirit.

Again, that madness is nothing else but too much appearing passion may be gathered out of the effects of wine, which are the same with those of the evil disposition of the organs. For the variety of behavior in men that have drunk too much is the same with that of madmen: some of them raging, others loving, others laughing, all extravagantly but according to their several domineering passions; for the effect of the wine does but remove dissimulation and take from them the sight of the deformity of their passions. For I believe the most sober men, when they walk alone, without care and employment of the mind, would be unwilling the vanity and extravagance of their

1 [An insane asylum in London.]

thoughts at that time should be publicly seen, which is a confession that passions unguided are for the most part mere madness.

The opinions of the world, both in ancient and later ages, concerning the cause of madness have been two. Some deriving them from the passions, some from demons or spirits, either good or bad, which they thought might enter into a man, possess him, and move his organs in such strange and uncouth manner as madmen use to do. The former sort, therefore, called such men madmen; but the latter called them sometimes *demoniacs* —that is, possessed with spirits—sometimes *energumeni*—that is, agitated or moved with spirits—and now in Italy they are called not only *pazzi,* madmen, but also *spiritati,* men possessed.

There was once a great conflux of people in Abdera, a city of the Greeks, at the acting of the tragedy of *Andromeda* upon an extreme hot day; whereupon a great many of the spectators, falling into fevers, had this accident from the heat and from the tragedy together, that they did nothing but pronounce iambics with the names of Perseus and Andromeda; which, together with the fever, was cured by the coming on of winter; and this madness was thought to proceed from the passion imprinted by the tragedy.[2] Likewise there reigned a fit of madness in another Grecian city which seized only the young maidens and caused many of them to hang themselves. This was by most then thought an act of the devil. But one that suspected that contempt of life in them might proceed from some passion of the mind, and supposing that they did not contemn also their honor, gave counsel to the magistrates to strip such as so hanged themselves and let them hang out naked. This, the story says, cured that madness. But on the other side, the same Grecians did often ascribe madness to the operation of Eumenides or Furies, and sometimes of Ceres, Phoebus, and other gods—so much did men attribute to phantasms as to think them aerial living bodies and generally to call them spirits. And as the Romans in this held the same opinion with the Greeks, so also did the Jews; for they called madmen prophets or, according as they

[2] [A lost play of Euripides first performed at Athens in 412 B.C., the *Andromeda* treated the Greek myth in which Andromeda, tied to a rock as a sacrifice to a sea monster sent by Poseidon, is discovered and rescued by Perseus.]

thought the spirits good or bad, demoniacs; and some of them called both prophets and demoniacs madmen; and some called the same man both demoniac and madman. But for the gentiles it is no wonder, because diseases and health, vices and virtues, and many natural accidents were with them termed and worshiped as demons. So that a man was to understand by demon as well sometimes an ague as a devil. But for the Jews to have such opinion is somewhat strange. For neither Moses nor Abraham pretended to prophecy by possession of a spirit but from the voice of God or by a vision or dream; nor is there anything in his law, moral or ceremonial, by which they were taught there was any such enthusiasm or any possession. When God is said (Num. 11: 25) to take from the spirit that was in Moses and give to the seventy elders, the Spirit of God (taking it for the substance of God) is not divided. The Scriptures, by the Spirit of God in man, mean a man's spirit inclined to godliness. And where it is said (Exod. 28: 3) *whom I have filled with the spirit of wisdom to make garments for Aaron,* is not meant a spirit put into them that can make garments, but the wisdom of their own spirits in that kind of work. In the like sense, the spirit of man, when it produces unclean actions, is ordinarily called an unclean spirit, and so other spirits, though not always yet as often as the virtue or vice so styled is extraordinary and eminent. Neither did the other prophets of the Old Testament pretend enthusiasm or that God spoke in them; but to them, by voice, vision, or dream; and the *burthen of the Lord* [3] was not possession but command. How then could the Jews fall into this opinion of possession? I can imagine no reason but that which is common to all men, namely, the want of curiosity to search natural causes and their placing felicity in the acquisition of the gross pleasures of the senses and the things that most immediately conduce thereto. For they that see any strange and unusual ability or defect in a man's mind, unless they see withal from what cause it may probably proceed, can hardly think it natural; and if not natural, they must needs think it supernatural; and then what can it be but that either God or the devil is in him? And hence it came to pass, when our Saviour (Mark 3: 21) was compassed about with the multitude, those of the house doubted he was mad and went out to hold him; but the Scribes

3 [II Kings 9: 25.]

said he had Beelzebub, and that was it by which he cast out devils, as if the greater madman had awed the lesser; and that (John 10: 20) some said, *he hath a devil, and is mad,* whereas others holding him for a prophet said, *these are not the words of one that hath a devil.* So in the Old Testament he that came to anoint Jehu (II Kings 9: 11) was a prophet, but some of the company asked Jehu, *what came that madman for?* So that in sum, it is manifest that whosoever behaved himself in extraordinary manner was thought by the Jews to be possessed either with a good or evil spirit; except by the Sadducees,[4] who erred so far on the other hand as not to believe there were at all any spirits, which is very near to direct atheism, and thereby perhaps the more provoked others to term such men demoniacs rather than madmen.

But why then does our Saviour proceed in the curing of them as if they were possessed and not as if they were mad? To which I can give no other kind of answer but that which is given to those that urge the Scripture in like manner against the opinion of the motion of the earth. The Scripture was written to show unto men the kingdom of God and to prepare their minds to become his obedient subjects, leaving the world and the philosophy thereof to the disputation of men for the exercising of their natural reason. Whether the earth's or sun's motion make the day and night, or whether the exorbitant actions of men proceed from passion or from the devil, so we worship him not, it is all one as to our obedience and subjection to God Almighty, which is the thing for which the Scripture was written. As for that our Saviour speaks to the disease as to a person, it is the usual phrase of all that cure by words only, as Christ did and enchanters pretend to do, whether they speak to a devil or not. For is not Christ also said (Matt. 8: 26) to have rebuked the winds? Is not he said also (Luke 4: 39) to rebuke a fever? Yet this does not argue that a fever is a devil. And whereas many of the devils are said to confess Christ, it is not necessary to interpret those places otherwise than that those madmen confessed

4 [The Sadducees and Pharisees were the leading religious parties in the second Jewish commonwealth, which the Romans destroyed in A.D. 70. The more conservative party, the Sadducees denied the authority of the oral law and exegetical tradition and insisted upon the supremacy of the written law contained in the Pentateuch.]

him. And whereas our Saviour (Matt. 12: 43) speaks of an unclean spirit that, having gone out of a man, wanders through
dry places, seeking rest and finding none, and returning into the
same man with seven other spirits worse than himself, it is
manifestly a parable alluding to a man that, after a little endeavor to quit his lusts, is vanquished by the strength of them
and becomes seven times worse than he was. So that I see nothing at all in the Scripture that requires a belief that demoniacs
were any other thing but madmen.

Insignificant speech. There is yet another fault in the discourses of
some men which may also be numbered among
the sorts of madness—namely, that abuse of words whereof I
have spoken before in the fifth chapter by the name of absurdity. And that is when men speak such words as, put together,
have in them no signification at all, but are fallen upon by some
through misunderstanding of the words they have received and
repeat by rote, by others from intention to deceive by obscurity.
And this is incident to none but those that converse in questions of matters incomprehensible, as the Schoolmen, or in
questions of abstruse philosophy. The common sort of men
seldom speak insignificantly, and are therefore by those other
egregious persons counted idiots. But to be assured their words
are without anything correspondent to them in the mind, there
would need some examples, which if any man require, let him
take a Schoolman in his hands and see if he can translate any
one chapter concerning any difficult point, as the Trinity, the
Deity, the nature of Christ, transubstantiation, free will, etc.,
into any of the modern tongues so as to make the same intelligible, or into any tolerable Latin such as they were acquainted
withal that lived when the Latin tongue was vulgar. What is
the meaning of these words: *The first cause does not necessarily
inflow anything into the second, by force of the essential sub-
ordination of the second causes, by which it may help it to
work?* They are the translation of the title of the sixth chapter
of Suárez' first book, *Of the Concourse, Motion, and Help of
God.* When men write whole volumes of such stuff, are they not
mad or intend to make others so? And particularly in the question of transubstantiation where, after certain words spoken,
they that say the white*ness,* round*ness,* magni*tude,* quali*ty,* cor-

ruptibility—all which are incorporeal—etc., go out of the wafer into the body of our blessed Saviour, do they not make those *nesses, tudes,* and *ties* to be so many spirits possessing his body? For by spirits they mean always things that, being incorporeal, are nevertheless movable from one place to another. So that this kind of absurdity may rightly be numbered among the many sorts of madness, and all the time that, guided by clear thoughts of their worldly lust, they forbear disputing or writing thus, but lucid intervals. And thus much of the virtues and defects intellectual.

CHAPTER NINE

OF THE SEVERAL SUBJECTS OF KNOWLEDGE

There are of KNOWLEDGE two kinds, whereof one is *knowledge of fact,* the other *knowledge of the consequence of one affirmation to another.* The former is nothing else but sense and memory, and is *absolute knowledge,* as when we see a fact doing or remember it done; and this is the knowledge required in a witness. The latter is called *science,* and is *conditional,* as when we know that *if the figure shown be a circle, then any straight line through the center shall divide it into two equal parts.* And this is the knowledge required in a philosopher—that is to say, of him that pretends to reasoning.

The register of *knowledge of fact* is called *history.* Whereof there be two sorts: one called *natural history,* which is the history of such facts or effects of nature as have no dependence on man's *will,* such as are the histories of *metals, plants, animals, regions,* and the like. The other is *civil history,* which is the history of the voluntary actions of men in commonwealths.

The registers of science are such *books* as contain the *demonstrations* of consequences of one affirmation to another, and are commonly called *books of philosophy;* whereof the sorts are many, according to the diversity of the matter, and may be divided in such manner as I have divided them in the following table.

Consequences from the accidents
common to all bodies natural;
which are *quantity*, and *motion* . . . . . .

Consequences
from the
accidents of
bodies na-
tural; which
is called
NATURAL
PHILOSOPHY

Consequences from the qualities of bodies *transient*, such
as sometimes appear, sometimes vanish, *Meteorology*. .

PHYSICS or conse-
quences from
qualities.

Consequences
from the
qualities of
the *stars* . .

SCIENCE, that
is, knowledge of
consequences;
which is called
also PHILOSOPHY.

Consequences
from the
qualities of
bodies *per-
manent*.

Consequences
of the quali-
ties from
liquid bodies,
that fill the
space be-
tween the
stars; such as
are the *air*, or
substances
ethereal.

Consequences
from the
qualities of
*bodies terres-
trial*.

Consequences
from the
accidents of
politic bo-
dies; which
is called PO-
LITICS, and
CIVIL PHI-
LOSOPHY.

1. Of consequences from the *institution* of COMMON-
WEALTHS, to the *rights*, and *duties* of the *body
politic* or *sovereign*.
2. Of consequences from the same, to the *duty* and
right of the *subjects*.

Consequences from quantity, and motion *indeterminate*; which being the principles or first foundation of philosophy, is called *Philosophia Prima*. . . . . . . — PHILOSOPHIA PRIMA.

Consequences from motion and quantity *determined*.

  Consequences from quantity, and motion determined.
    By Figure . . ⎫
            ⎬ *Mathematics.* — GEOMETRY.
    By Number . ⎭   — ARITHMETIC.

  Consequences from the motion, and quantity of bodies in *special*.
    Consequences from the motion and quantity of the greater parts of the world, as the *earth* and *stars*. — *Cosmography.* ⎰ ASTRONOMY.
                                                       ⎱ GEOGRAPHY.

    Consequences from the motions of special kinds, and figures of body. ⎰ *Mechanics.* ⎧ *Science* of ENGINEERS.
                                                          ⎱ Doctrine of weight. ⎨ ARCHITECTURE
                                                                          ⎩ NAVIGATION.

. . . . METEOROLOGY

Consequences from the *light* of the stars. Out of this, and the motion of the sun, is made the science of . . . ⎱ SCIOGRAPHY.

Consequences from the *influences* of the stars. . — ASTROLOGY.

Consequences from the parts of the earth, that are *without sense*.
  Consequences from the qualities of *minerals*, as *stones, metals, &c.*

  Consequences from the qualities of *vegetables.*

Consequences from the qualities of *animals*.

  Consequences from the qualities of *animals* in general.
    Consequences from *vision* . . OPTICS.
    Consequences from *sounds* . . MUSIC.
    Consequences from the rest of the senses.

  Consequences from the qualities of *men* in *special*.
    Consequences from the *passions* of men . . . . . ⎬ ETHICS.

    Consequences from *speech*.
      In *magnifying, vilifying, &c.* ⎬ POETRY.
      In *persuading*, RHETORIC.
      In *reasoning*, LOGIC.
      In *contracting*, The *Science* of JUST and UNJUST.

CHAPTER TEN

OF POWER, WORTH, DIGNITY, HONOR, AND WORTHINESS

Power.   The POWER of a man, to take it universally, is his present means to obtain some future apparent good, and is either *original* or *instrumental*.

Natural power is the eminence of the faculties of body or mind, as extraordinary strength, form, prudence, arts, eloquence, liberality, nobility. *Instrumental* are those powers which, acquired by these or by fortune, are means and instruments to acquire more, as riches, reputation, friends, and the secret working of God, which men call good luck. For the nature of power is in this point like to fame, increasing as it proceeds; or like the motion of heavy bodies, which, the further they go, make still the more haste.

The greatest of human powers is that which is compounded of the powers of most men united by consent in one person, natural or civil, that has the use of all their powers depending on his will, such as is the power of a commonwealth; or depending on the wills of each particular, such as is the power of a faction or of divers factions leagued. Therefore to have servants is power; to have friends is power: for they are strengths united.

Also riches joined with liberality is power, because it procures friends and servants; without liberality, not so, because in this case they defend not, but expose men to envy, as a prey.

Reputation of power is power, because it draws with it the adherence of those that need protection.

So is reputation of love of a man's country, called popularity, for the same reason.

Also, what quality soever makes a man beloved or feared of many, or the reputation of such quality, is power, because it is a means to have the assistance and service of many.

Good success is power, because it makes reputation of wisdom or good fortune, which makes men either fear him or rely on him.

Affability of men already in power is increase of power, because it gains love.

Reputation of prudence in the conduct of peace or war is power, because to prudent men we commit the government of ourselves more willingly than to others.

Nobility is power, not in all places, but only in those commonwealths where it has privileges, for in such privileges consists their power.

Eloquence is power, because it is seeming prudence.

Form is power, because, being a promise of good, it recommends men to the favor of women and strangers.

The sciences are small power, because not eminent and therefore not acknowledged in any man; nor are at all but in a few, and in them but of a few things. For science is of that nature as none can understand it to be but such as in a good measure have attained it.

Arts of public use—as fortification, making of engines, and other instruments of war—because they confer to defense and victory, are power, and though the true mother of them be science—namely, the mathematics—yet, because they are brought into the light by the hand of the artificer, they be esteemed—the midwife passing with the vulgar for the mother—as his issue.

Worth. The *value* or WORTH of a man is, as of all other things, his price—that is to say, so much as would be given for the use of his power—and therefore is not absolute but a thing dependent on the need and judgment of another. An able conductor of soldiers is of great price in time of war present or imminent, but in peace not so. A learned and uncorrupt judge is much worth in time of peace, but not so much in war. And as in other things so in men, not the seller but the buyer determines the price. For let a man, as most men do, rate themselves at the highest value they can, yet their true value is no more than it is esteemed by others.

The manifestation of the value we set on one another is that which is commonly called honoring and dishonoring. To value a man at a high rate is to *honor* him, at a low rate is to *dishonor* him. But high and low, in this case, is to be understood by comparison to the rate that each man sets on himself.

The public worth of a man, which is the value set on him by

Dignity. the commonwealth, is that which men commonly call DIGNITY. And this value of him by the commonwealth is understood by offices of command, judicature, public employment, or by names and titles introduced for distinction of such value.

To pray to another for aid of any kind is *to* HONOR, because a sign we have an opinion he has power to help; and the more difficult the aid is, the more is the honor.

To honor and dishonor. To obey is to honor, because no man obeys them whom they think have no power to help or hurt them. And consequently to disobey is to *dishonor.*

To give great gifts to a man is to honor him, because it is buying of protection and acknowledging of power. To give little gifts is to dishonor, because it is but alms, and signifies an opinion of the need of small helps.

To be sedulous in promoting another's good, also to flatter, is to honor, as a sign we seek his protection or aid. To neglect is to dishonor.

To give way or place to another in any commodity is to honor, being a confession of greater power. To arrogate is to dishonor.

To show any sign of love or fear of another is to honor, for both to love and to fear is to value. To contemn, or less to love or fear than he expects, is to dishonor, for it is undervaluing.

To praise, magnify, or call happy is to honor, because nothing but goodness, power, and felicity is valued. To revile, mock, or pity is to dishonor.

To speak to another with consideration, to appear before him with decency and humility, is to honor him, as signs of fear to offend. To speak to him rashly, to do anything before him obscenely, slovenly, impudently, is to dishonor.

To believe, to trust, to rely on another is to honor him, sign of opinion of his virtue and power. To distrust or not believe is to dishonor.

To hearken to a man's counsel or discourse of what kind soever is to honor, as a sign we think him wise or eloquent or witty. To sleep or go forth or talk the while is to dishonor.

To do those things to another which he takes for signs of honor, or which the law or custom makes so, is to honor, because in approving the honor done by others he acknowledges the power which others acknowledge. To refuse to do them is to dishonor.

To agree with in opinion is to honor, as being a sign of approving his judgment and wisdom. To dissent is dishonor, and an upbraiding of error; and, if the dissent be in many things, of folly.

To imitate is to honor, for it is vehemently to approve. To imitate one's enemy is to dishonor.

To honor those another honors is to honor him, as a sign of approbation of his judgment. To honor his enemies is to dishonor him.

To employ in counsel or in actions of difficulty is to honor, as a sign of opinion of his wisdom or other power. To deny employment in the same cases to those that seek it is to dishonor.

All these ways of honoring are natural, and as well within as without commonwealths. But in commonwealths, where he or they that have the supreme authority can make whatsoever they please to stand for signs of honor, there be other honors.

A sovereign does honor a subject with whatsoever title or office or employment or action that he himself will have taken for a sign of his will to honor him.

The king of Persia honored Mordecai when he appointed he should be conducted through the streets in the king's garment, upon one of the king's horses, with a crown on his head, and a prince before him, proclaiming *thus shall it be done to him that the king will honor*.[1] And yet another king of Persia, or the same another time, to one that demanded for some great service to wear one of the king's robes, gave him leave so to do, but with this addition, that he should wear it as the king's fool, and then it was dishonor. So that of civil honor the fountain is in the person of the commonwealth and depends on the will of the sovereign, and is therefore temporary and called *civil honor:* such as magistracy, offices, titles, and in some places coats and scutcheons painted; and men honor such as have them as having so many signs of favor in the common-

Honorable.

wealth, which favor is power. *Honorable* is whatsoever possession, action, or quality is an argument and sign of power.

[1] [Esther 6:11.]

And therefore ~~to be honored, loved, or feared of many is~~
Dishonorable.   ~~honorable, as arguments of power.~~ To be honored of few or none, *dishonorable.*
~~Dominion and victory is honorable, because acquired by~~
~~power~~; and servitude, for need or fear, is dishonorable.

Good fortune, if lasting, honorable, as a sign of the favor of
God. Ill fortune and losses, dishonorable. Riches are honorable,
for they are power. Poverty, dishonorable. Magnanimity, liberality, hope, courage, confidence are honorable, for they proceed from the conscience of power. Pusillanimity, parsimony,
fear, diffidence are dishonorable.

Timely resolution, or determination of what a man is to do,
is honorable, as being the contempt of small difficulties and
dangers. And irresolution dishonorable, as a sign of too much
valuing of little impediments and little advantages; for when a
man has weighed things as long as the time permits and resolves
not, the difference of weight is but little; and therefore if he resolve not, he overvalues little things, which is pusillanimity.

All action and speeches that proceed, or seem to proceed,
from much experience, science, discretion, or wit are honorable,
for all these are powers. Actions or words that proceed from error, ignorance, or folly, dishonorable.

Gravity, as far forth as it seems to proceed from a mind employed on something else, is honorable, because employment is
a sign of power. But if it seem to proceed from a purpose to appear grave, it is dishonorable. For the gravity of the former is
like the steadiness of a ship laden with merchandise; but of the
latter, like the steadiness of a ship ballasted with sand and other
trash.

To be conspicuous—that is to say, to be known—for wealth,
office, great actions, or any eminent good is honorable, as a sign
of the power for which he is conspicuous. On the contrary, obscurity is dishonorable.

To be descended from conspicuous parents is honorable, because they the more easily attain the aids and friends of their
ancestors. On the contrary, to be descended from obscure par-
entage is dishonorable.

Actions proceeding from equity, joined with loss, are honorable, as signs of magnanimity; for magnanimity is a sign of

power. On the contrary, craft, shifting, neglect of equity is dishonorable.

Covetousness of great riches and ambition of great honors are honorable, as signs of power to obtain them. Covetousness and ambition of little gains or preferments is dishonorable.

Nor does it alter the case of honor whether an action, so it be great and difficult and consequently a sign of much power, be just or unjust, for honor consists only in the opinion of power. Therefore the ancient heathen did not think they dishonored but greatly honored the gods when they introduced them in their poems committing rapes, thefts, and other great but unjust or unclean acts; insomuch as nothing is so much celebrated in Jupiter as his adulteries, nor in Mercury as his frauds and thefts—of whose praises, in a hymn of Homer, the greatest is this: that, being born in the morning, he had invented music at noon and, before night, stolen away the cattle of Apollo from his herdsmen.

Also among men, till there were constituted great commonwealths, it was thought no dishonor to be a pirate or a highway thief but rather a lawful trade, not only among the Greeks but also among all other nations, as is manifest by the histories of ancient time. And at this day, in this part of the world, private duels are and always will be honorable, though unlawful, till such time as there shall be honor ordained for them that refuse and ignominy for them that make the challenge. For duels also are many times effects of courage, and the ground of courage is always strength or skill, which are power; though for the most part they be effects of rash speaking and of the fear of dishonor in one or both the combatants, who, engaged by rashness, are driven into the lists to avoid disgrace.

Coats of arms. Scutcheons and coats of arms hereditary, where they have any eminent privileges, are honorable, otherwise not; for their power consists either in such privileges or in riches or some such thing as is equally honored in other men. This kind of honor, commonly called gentry, has been derived from the ancient Germans. For there never was any such thing known where the German customs were unknown. Nor is it now anywhere in use where the Germans have not inhabited. The ancient Greek commanders, when they went to war, had their shields painted with such devices as they pleased, insomuch as an unpainted buckler was a sign of poverty and of a common soldier; but they transmitted not the inheritance of them. The Romans transmitted the marks of their families; but they were the images, not the devices, of their ancestors. Among the people of Asia, Africa, and America there is not, nor was ever, any such thing. The Germans only had that custom, from whom it has been derived into England, France, Spain, and Italy when in great numbers they either aided the Romans or made their own conquests in these western parts of the world.

For Germany being anciently, as all other countries in their beginnings, divided among an infinite number of little lords or masters of families that continually had wars one with another, those masters or lords, principally to the end they might, when they were covered with arms, be known by their followers, and partly for ornament, both painted their armor or their scutcheon or coat with the picture of some beast or other thing, and also put some eminent and visible mark upon the crest of their helmets. And this ornament, both of the arms and crest, descended by inheritance to their children, to the eldest pure and to the rest with some note of diversity, such as the old master— that is to say in Dutch, the *Here-alt*—thought fit. But when many such families, joined together, made a greater monarchy, this duty of the Herealt to distinguish scutcheons was made a private office apart. And the issue of these lords is the great and ancient gentry, which for the most part bear living creatures noted for courage and rapine, or castles, battlements, belts, weapons, bars, palisadoes, and other notes of war—nothing being then in honor but virtue military. Afterwards, not only kings but popular commonwealths gave divers manners of scutcheons to such as went forth to the war or returned from it for encouragement or recompense to their service. All which, by an observing reader, may be found in such ancient histories, Greek and Latin, as make mention of the German nation and manners in their times.

Titles of honor.   Titles of *honor,* such as are duke, count, marquis, and baron, are honorable, as signifying the value set upon them by the sovereign power of the commonwealth; which titles were in old times titles of office and command, derived some from the Romans, some from the Germans and French: dukes, in Latin *duces,* being generals in war; counts, *comites,* such as bear the general company out of friendship, and were left to govern and defend places conquered and pacified; marquises, *marchiones,* were counts that governed the marches or bounds of the empire. Which titles of duke, count, and marquis came into the empire, about the time of Constantine the Great, from the customs of the German *militia.* But baron seems to have been a title of the Gauls and signifies a great man, such as were the king's or prince's men whom they employed in war about their persons, and seems to be derived from *vir,* to *ber* and *bar,* that signified the same in the language of the Gauls that *vir* in Latin, and thence to *bero* and *baro;* so that such men were called *berones,* and after *barones,* and in Spanish *varones.* But he that would know more particularly the original of titles of honor may find it, as I have done this, in Mr. Selden's most excellent treatise of that subject.[2] In process of time these offices of honor, by occasion of trouble and for reasons of good and peaceable government, were turned into mere titles, serving for the most part to distinguish the precedence, place, and order of subjects in the commonwealth; and men were made dukes, counts, marquises, and barons of places wherein they had neither possession nor command; and other titles also were devised to the same end.

Worthiness. WORTHINESS is a thing different from the worth or value of a man, and also from his merit or desert, and consists in a particular power or ability for that whereof he is said to be worthy; which particular ability is usually named FITNESS or *aptitude.*

Fitness.

For he is worthiest to be a commander, to be a judge, or to have any other charge that is best fitted with the qualities required to the well discharging of it; and worthiest of riches that has the qualities most requisite for the well using of them—any of which qualities being absent, one may nevertheless be a worthy man, and valuable for something else. Again, a man may be worthy of riches, office, and employment that nevertheless can plead no right to have it before another and therefore

2 [John Selden, *Titles of Honour* (1614).]

cannot be said to merit or deserve it. For merit presupposes a right and that the thing deserved is due by promise, of which I shall say more hereafter when I shall speak of contracts.

CHAPTER ELEVEN

OF THE DIFFERENCE OF MANNERS

What is here meant   By MANNERS I mean not here decency of be-
by manners.   havior—as how one should salute another, or how a man should wash his mouth or pick his teeth before company, and such other points of the *small morals*—but those qualities of mankind that concern their living together in peace and unity. To which end we are to consider that the felicity of this life consists not in the repose of a mind satisfied. For there is no such *finis ultimus,* utmost aim, nor *summum bonum,* greatest good, as is spoken of in the books of the old moral philosophers. Nor can a man any more live whose desires are at an end than he whose senses and imaginations are at a stand. Felicity is a continual progress of the desire from one object to another, the attaining of the former being still but the way to the latter. The cause whereof is that the object of man's desire is not to enjoy once only and for one instant of time, but to assure forever the way of his future desire. And therefore the voluntary actions and inclinations of all men tend, not only to the procuring, but also to the assuring of a contented life; and differ only in the way, which arises partly from the diversity of passions in divers men, and partly from the difference of the knowledge or opinion each one has of the causes which produce the effect desired.

A restless desire of   So that, in the first place, I put for a general in-
power in all men.   clination of all mankind a perpetual and rest-
less desire of power after power that ceases only in death. And the cause of this is not always that a man hopes for a more intensive delight than he has already attained to, or that he cannot be content with a moderate power, but because he cannot assure the power and means to live well which he has present without the acquisition of more. And from hence

it is that kings, whose power is greatest, turn their endeavors to the assuring it at home by laws or abroad by wars; and when that is done, there succeeds a new desire—in some, of fame from new conquest; in others, of ease and sensual pleasure; in others, of admiration or being flattered for excellence in some art or other ability of the mind.

Love of contention from competition. Competition of riches, honor, command, or other power inclines to contention, enmity, and war, because the way of one competitor to the attaining of his desire is to kill, subdue, supplant, or repel the other. Particularly, competition of praise inclines to a reverence of antiquity. For men contend with the living, not with the dead—to these ascribing more than due, that they may obscure the glory of the other.

Civil obedience from love of ease. Desire of ease and sensual delight disposes men to obey a common power, because by such desires a man does abandon the protection that *From fear of death or wounds.* might be hoped for from his own industry and labor. Fear of death and wounds disposes to the same, and for the same reason. On the contrary, needy men and hardy, not contented with their present condition, as also all men that are ambitious of military command, are inclined to continue the causes of war, and to stir up trouble and sedition; for there is no honor military but by war, nor any such hope to mend an ill game as by causing a new shuffle.

And from love of arts. Desire of knowledge and arts of peace inclines men to obey a common power, for such desire contains a desire of leisure, and consequently protection from some other power than their own.

Love of virtue from love of praise. Desire of praise disposes to laudable actions, such as please them whose judgment they value; for of those men whom we contemn, we contemn also the praises. Desire of fame after death does the same. And though after death there be no sense of the praise given us on earth, as being joys that are either swallowed up in the unspeakable joys of heaven or extinguished in the extreme torments of hell, yet is not such fame vain; because men have a present delight therein from the foresight of it and of the benefit that may redound thereby to their posterity, which, though they now see not, yet they imagine; and anything that is pleasure to the sense, the same also is pleasure in the imagination.

To have received from one to whom we think *Hate, from difficulty of requiting great benefits.* ourselves equal greater benefits than there is hope to requite disposes to counterfeit love, but really secret hatred; and puts a man into the estate of a desperate debtor that, in declining the sight of his creditor, tacitly wishes him there where he might never see him more. For benefits oblige, and obligation is thralldom, and unrequitable obligation perpetual thralldom—which is to one's equal hateful. But to have received benefits from one whom we acknowledge for superior inclines to love, because the obligation is no new depression, and cheerful acceptation, which men call *gratitude,* is such an honor done to the obliger as is taken generally for retribution. Also to receive benefits, though from an equal or inferior, as long as there is hope of requital, disposes to love; for in the intention of the receiver, the obligation is of aid and service mutual; from whence proceeds an emulation of who shall exceed in benefiting—the most noble and profitable contention possible, wherein the victor is pleased with his victory and the other revenged by confessing it.

And from conscience of deserving to be hated. To have done more hurt to a man than he can or is willing to expiate inclines the doer to hate the sufferer. For he must expect revenge or forgiveness, both which are hateful.

Promptness to hurt, from fear. Fear of oppression disposes a man to anticipate or to seek aid by society, for there is no other way by which a man can secure his life and liberty. *And from distrust of their own wit.* Men that distrust their own subtlety are, in tumult and sedition, better disposed for victory than they that suppose themselves wise or crafty. For these love to consult, the other, fearing to be circumvented, to strike first. And in sedition, men being always in the precincts of battle, to hold together and use all advantages of force is a better stratagem than any that can proceed from subtlety of wit.

Vain undertaking from vainglory. Vainglorious men such as, without being conscious to themselves of great sufficiency, delight in supposing themselves gallant men are inclined only to ostentation but not to attempt, because when danger or difficulty appears they look for nothing but to have their insufficiency discovered.

Vainglorious men such as estimate their sufficiency by the flattery of other men or the fortune of some precedent action, without assured ground of hope from the true knowledge of themselves, are inclined to rash engaging; and in the approach of danger or difficulty to retire if they can, because, not seeing the way of safety, they will rather hazard their honor, which may be salved with an excuse, than their lives, for which no salve is sufficient. Men that have a strong opinion of their own wisdom in matter of government are disposed to ambition. Because without public employment in council or magistracy the honor of their wisdom is lost. And therefore eloquent speakers are inclined to ambition, for eloquence seems wisdom, both to themselves and others.

Ambition, from opinion of sufficiency.

Pusillanimity disposes men to irresolution, and consequently to lose the occasions and fittest opportunities of action. For after men have been in deliberation till the time of action approach, if it be not then manifest what is best to be done, it is a sign the difference of motives, the one way and the other, are not great; therefore not to resolve them is to lose the occasion by weighing of trifles, which is pusillanimity.

Irresolution, from too great valuing of small matters.

Frugality, though in poor men a virtue, makes a man unapt to achieve such actions as require the strength of many men at once; for it weakens their endeavor, which is to be nourished and kept in vigor by reward.

Eloquence, with flattery, disposes men to confide in them that have it; because the former is seeming wisdom, the latter seeming kindness.

Confidence in others, from ignorance of the marks of wisdom and kindness.

Add to them military reputation, and it disposes men to adhere and subject themselves to those men that have them. The two former having given them caution against danger from him, the latter gives them caution against danger from others.

Want of science—that is, ignorance of causes—disposes, or rather constrains, a man to rely on the advice and authority of others. For all men whom the truth concerns, if they rely not on their own, must

And from ignorance of natural causes.

rely on the opinion of some other whom they think wiser than
themselves, and see not why he should deceive them.

And from want of understanding. Ignorance of the signification of words, which
is want of understanding, disposes men to take
on trust, not only the truth they know not, but
also the errors and, which is more, the nonsense of them they
trust; for neither error nor nonsense can, without a perfect understanding of words, be detected.

From the same it proceeds that men give different names to
one and the same thing from the difference of their own passions: as they that approve a private opinion call it opinion,
but they that mislike it, heresy; and yet heresy signifies no more
than private opinion, but has only a greater tincture of choler.

From the same also it proceeds that men cannot distinguish,
without study and great understanding, between one action of
many men and many actions of one multitude: as for example
between one action of all the senators of Rome in killing Cataline, and the many actions of a number of senators in killing
Caesar; [1] and therefore are disposed to take for the action of the
people that which is a multitude of actions done by a multitude
of men, led perhaps by the persuasion of one.

Adherence to cus-tom, from ignorance of the nature of right and wrong. Ignorance of the causes and original constitution of right, equity, law, and justice disposes a
man to make custom and example the rule of
his actions; in such manner as to think that un-
just which it has been the custom to punish, and that just of the
impunity and approbation whereof they can produce an example or, as the lawyers which only use this false measure of
justice barbarously call it, a precedent; like little children that
have no other rule of good and evil manners but the correction
they receive from their parents and masters, save that children
are constant to their rule, whereas men are not so; because,
grown old and stubborn, they appeal from custom to reason
and from reason to custom as it serves their turn, receding from
custom when their interest requires it and setting themselves
against reason as oft as reason is against them; which is the

1 [The Roman senator Cataline was indicted for conspiracy by Cicero in
one of his most famous orations (63 B.C.); he withdrew from Rome and was
shortly defeated and killed. For the assassination of Caesar, see ch. 2, n. 2.]

cause that the doctrine of right and wrong is perpetually disputed, both by the pen and the sword, whereas the doctrine of lines and figures is not so; because men care not, in that subject, what be truth, as a thing that crosses no man's ambition, profit, or lust. For I doubt not but if it had been a thing contrary to any man's right of dominion, or to the interest of men that have dominion, *that the three angles of a triangle should be equal to two angles of a square,* that doctrine should have been, if not disputed, yet, by the burning of all books of geometry, suppressed, as far as he whom it concerned was able.

Adherence to private men, from ignorance of the causes of peace. Ignorance of remote causes disposes men to attribute all events to the causes immediate and instrumental, for these are all the causes they perceive. And hence it comes to pass that in all places men that are grieved with payments to the public discharge their anger upon the publicans—that is to say, farmers, collectors, and other officers of the public revenue—and adhere to such as find fault with the public government, and thereby, when they have engaged themselves beyond hope of justification, fall also upon the supreme authority for fear of punishment or shame of receiving pardon.

Credulity, from ignorance of nature. Ignorance of natural causes disposes a man to credulity, so as to believe many times impossibilities; for such know nothing to the contrary but that they may be true, being unable to detect the impossibility. And credulity, because men like to be hearkened unto in company, disposes them to lying, so that ignorance itself without malice is able to make a man both to believe lies and tell them—and sometimes also to invent them.

Curiosity to know, from care of future time. Anxiety for the future time disposes men to inquire into the causes of things, because the knowledge of them makes men the better able to order the present to their best advantage.

Natural religion from the same. Curiosity, or love of the knowledge of causes, draws a man from the consideration of the effect to seek the cause; and again, the cause of that cause; till of necessity he must come to this thought at last: that there is some cause whereof there is no former cause but is eternal—which is it men call God. So that it is impossible to make any profound inquiry into natural causes without being inclined thereby to believe there is one God eternal, though they cannot have any idea of him in their mind answerable to his nature. For as a man that is born blind, hearing men talk of warming themselves by the fire and being brought to warm himself by the same, may easily conceive and assure himself there is somewhat there which men call *fire* and is the cause of the heat he feels, but cannot imagine what it is like nor have an idea of it in his mind such as they have that see it; so also by the visible things in this world, and their admirable order, a man may conceive there is a cause of them, which men call God, and yet not have an idea or image of him in his mind.

And they that make little or no inquiry into the natural causes of things, yet from the fear that proceeds from the ignorance itself of what it is that has the power to do them much good or harm, are inclined to suppose, and feign unto themselves, several kinds of powers invisible; and to stand in awe of their own imaginations; and in time of distress to invoke them; as also in the time of an expected good success to give them thanks; making the creatures of their own fancy their gods. By which means it has come to pass that, from the innumerable variety of fancy, men have created in the world innumerable sorts of gods. And this fear of things invisible is the natural seed of that which everyone in himself calls religion, and in them that worship, or fear that power otherwise than they do, superstition.

And this seed of religion having been observed by many, some of those that have observed it have been inclined thereby to nourish, dress, and form it into laws; and to add to it of their own invention any opinion of the causes of future events by which they thought they should be best able to govern others and make unto themselves the greatest use of their powers.

CHAPTER TWELVE

OF RELIGION

Religion in man only. Seeing there are no signs nor fruit of *religion* but in man only, there is no cause to doubt but that the seed of *religion* is also only in man, and consists in some peculiar quality, or at least in some eminent degree thereof, not to be found in any other living creatures.

First, from his desire of knowing causes. And first, it is peculiar to the nature of man to be inquisitive into the causes of the events they see— some more, some less, but all men so much as to be curious in the search of the causes of their own good and evil fortune.

From the consideration of the beginning of things. Secondly, upon the sight of anything that has a beginning, to think also it had a cause which determined the same to begin then when it did rather than sooner or later.

From his observation of the sequel of things. Thirdly, whereas there is no other felicity of beasts but the enjoying of their quotidian food, ease, and lusts—as having little or no foresight of the time to come for want of observation and memory of the order, consequence, and dependence of the things they see—man observes how one event has been produced by another, and remembers in them antecedence and consequence; and when he cannot assure himself of the true causes of things (for the causes of good and evil fortune for the most part are invisible), he supposes causes of them, either such as his own fancy suggests, or trusts the authority of other men such as he thinks to be his friends and wiser than himself.

The natural cause of religion, the anxiety of the time to come. The two first make anxiety. For being assured that there be causes of all things that have arrived hitherto or shall arrive hereafter, it is impossible for a man who continually endeavors to secure himself against the evil he fears and procure the good he desires not to be in a perpetual solicitude of the time to come, so that every man, especially those that are over provident, are in a state like to that of Prometheus. For as Prometheus—which interpreted is *the prudent man*—was bound to the hill Caucasus, a place of large prospect, where an eagle feeding on his liver devoured in the day as much as was repaired in the night, so that man which looks too far before him in the care of future time has his heart all the day long gnawed on by fear of death, poverty, or other calamity, and has no repose nor pause of his anxiety but in sleep.

Which makes them fear the power of invisible things. This perpetual fear, always accompanying mankind in the ignorance of causes, as it were in the dark, must needs have for object something. And therefore when there is nothing to be seen there is nothing to accuse, either of their good or evil fortune, but some *power* or agent *invisible;* in which sense perhaps it was that some of the old poets said that the gods were at first created by human fear; which, spoken of the gods—that is to say, of the many gods of the Gentiles—is very true. But the acknowledging of one God, eternal, infinite, and omnipotent, may more easily be derived from the desire men have to know the causes of natural bodies and their several virtues and operations than from the fear of what was to befall them in time to come. For he that from any effect he sees come to pass should reason to the next and immediate cause thereof, and from thence to the cause of that cause, and plunge himself profoundly in the pursuit of causes, shall at last come to this: that there must be, as even the heathen philosophers confessed, one first mover—that is, a first and an eternal cause of all things— which is that which men mean by the name of God; and all this without thought of their fortune, the solicitude whereof both inclines to fear and hinders them from the search of the causes of other things, and thereby gives occasion of feigning of as many gods as there be men that feign them.

And suppose them incorporeal. And for the matter or substance of the invisible agents, so fancied, they could not by natural cogitation fall upon any other conceit but that it was the same with that of the soul of man; and that the soul of man was of the same substance with that which appears in a dream to one that sleeps, or in a looking glass to one that is awake; which men, not knowing that such apparitions are nothing else but creatures of the fancy, think to be real and external substances, and therefore call them ghosts; as the Latins called them *imagines* and *umbrae,* and thought them spirits—that is, thin aerial bodies—and those invisible agents, which they feared, to be like them, save that they appear and vanish when they please. But the opinion that such spirits were incorporeal or immaterial could never enter into the mind of any man by nature because, though men may put together words of contradictory signification, as *spirit* and *incorporeal,* yet they can never have the imagination of anything answering to them; and therefore men that by their own meditation arrive to the acknowledgment of one infinite, omnipotent, and eternal God choose rather to confess he is incomprehensible and above their understanding than to define his nature by *spirit incorporeal* and then confess their definition to be unintelligible; or if they give him such a title, it is not *dogmatically,* with intention to make the divine nature understood, but *piously,* to honor him with attributes of significations as remote as they can from the grossness of bodies visible.

But know not the way how they effect any thing. Then, for the way by which they think these invisible agents wrought their effects—that is to say, what immediate causes they used in bringing things to pass—men that know not what it is that we call *causing*—that is, almost all men—have no other rule to guess by but by observing and remembering what they have seen to precede the like effect at some other time or times before, without seeing between the antecedent and subsequent event any dependence or connection at all; and therefore from the like things past they expect the like things to come, and hope for good or evil luck, superstitiously, from things that have no part at all in the causing of it: as the Athenians did for their war at Lepanto demand another Phormio; the Pompeian faction for their war in Africa, another Scipio; [1] and others have done in divers other occasions since. In like manner they attribute their fortune to a stander by, to a lucky or unlucky place, to words spoken, especially if the name of God be among

1 [Phormio (5th cent. B.C.), an Athenian admiral, won a series of brilliant naval victories over Peloponnesian fleets in the war with Sparta. Publius Cornelius Scipio (236-184 B.C.) received the title Africanus for his successful African campaign in the Second Punic War, climaxed by his victory over Hannibal at Zama (202 B.C.).]

them—as charming and conjuring (the liturgy of witches)—insomuch as to believe they have power to turn a stone into bread, bread into a man, or anything into anything.

But honor them as they honor men.

Thirdly, for the worship which naturally men exhibit to powers invisible, it can be no other but such expressions of their reverence as they would use toward men: gifts, petitions, thanks, submission of body, considerate addresses, sober behavior, premeditated words, swearing—that is, assuring one another of their promises —by invoking them. Beyond that reason suggests nothing, but leaves them either to rest there or, for further ceremonies, to rely on those they believe to be wiser than themselves.

Lastly, concerning how these invisible powers declare to men the things which shall hereafter come to pass, especially concerning their good or evil fortune in general, or good or ill success in any particular undertaking, men are

And attribute to them all extraordinary events.

naturally at a stand; save that using to conjecture of the time to come by the time past, they are very apt, not only to take casual things, after one or two encounters, for prognostics of the like encounter ever after, but also to believe the like prognostics from other men of whom they have once conceived a good opinion.

Four things, natural seeds of religion.

And in these four things—opinion of ghosts, ignorance of second causes, devotion toward what men fear, and taking of things casual for prognostics—consists the natural seed of *religion,* which, by reason of the different fancies, judgments, and passions of several men, has grown up into ceremonies so different that those which are used by one man are for the most part ridiculous to another.

Made difficult by culture.

For these seeds have received culture from two sorts of men. One sort have been they that have nourished and ordered them according to their own invention. The other have done it by God's commandment and direction. But both sorts have done it with a purpose to make those men that relied on them the more apt to obedience, laws, peace, charity, and civil society. So that the religion of the former sort is a part of human politics, and teaches part of the duty which earthly kings require of their subjects. And the religion of the latter sort is divine politics, and contains precepts to those that have yielded themselves subjects in the kingdom of God. Of the former sort were all the founders of commonwealths and the lawgivers of the gentiles; of the latter sort were Abraham, Moses, and our blessed Saviour, by whom have been derived unto us the laws of the kingdom of God.

The absurd opinion of gentilism. And for that part of religion which consists in opinions concerning the nature of powers invisible, there is almost nothing that has a name that has not been esteemed among the gentiles, in one place or another, a god or devil, or by their poets feigned to be inanimated, inhabited, or possessed by some spirit or other.

The unformed matter of the world was a god by the name of Chaos.

The heaven, the ocean, the planets, the fire, the earth, the winds were so many gods.

Men, women, a bird, a crocodile, a calf, a dog, a snake, an onion, a leek, were deified. Besides that, they filled almost all places with spirits called *demons:* the plains with Pan and Panises or satyrs; the woods with fauns and nymphs; the sea with Tritons and other nymphs; every river and fountain with a ghost of his name and with nymphs; every house with its *lares* or familiars; every man with his *genius;* hell with ghosts and spiritual officers, as Charon, Cerberus, and the Furies; and in the nighttime, all places with *larvae, lemures,* ghosts of men deceased, and a whole kingdom of fairies and bugbears. They have also ascribed divinity and built temples to mere accidents and qualities, such as are time, night, day, peace, concord, love, contention, virtue, honor, health, rust, fever, and the like; which, when they prayed for or against, they prayed to, as if there were ghosts of those names hanging over their heads and letting fall or withholding that good or evil for or against which they prayed. They invoked also their own wit, by the name of Muses; their own ignorance, by the name of Fortune; their own lusts, by the name of Cupid; their own rage, by the name of Furies; their own privy members, by the name of Priapus; and attributed their pollutions to incubi and succubi: insomuch as there was nothing which a poet could introduce as a person in his poem which they did not make either a *god* or a *devil.*

The same authors of the religion of the gentiles, observing the second ground for religion—which is men's ignorance of causes—and thereby their aptness to attribute their fortune to causes on which there was no dependence at all apparent, took occasion to obtrude on their ignorance, instead of second causes, a kind of second and ministerial gods, ascribing the cause of fecundity to Venus, the cause of arts to Apollo, of subtlety and craft to Mercury, of tempests and storms to Aeolus, and of other effects to other gods: insomuch as there was among the heathen almost as great variety of gods as of business.

And to the worship which naturally men conceived fit to be used toward their gods—namely, oblations, prayers, thanks, and the rest formerly named—the same legislators of the gentiles have added their images, both in picture and sculpture, that the more ignorant sort—that is to say, the most part or generality of the people—thinking the gods for whose representation they were made were really included and, as it were, housed within them, might so much the more stand in fear of them; and endowed them with lands and houses and officers and revenues set apart from all other human uses—that is, consecrated and made holy to those their idols—as caverns, groves, woods, mountains, and whole islands; and have attributed to them, not only the shapes, some of men, some of beasts, some of monsters, but also the faculties and passions of men and beasts, as sense, speech, sex, lust, generation, and this not only by mixing one with another to propagate the kind of gods, but also by mixing with men and women to beget mongrel gods, and but inmates of heaven, as Bacchus, Hercules, and others; besides anger, revenge, and other passions of living creatures, and the actions proceeding from them, as fraud, theft, adultery, sodomy, and any vice that may be taken for an effect of power or a cause of pleasure; and all such vices as among men are taken to be against law rather than against honor.

Lastly, to the prognostics of time to come—which are naturally but conjectures upon experience of time past, and supernaturally divine revelation—the same authors of the religion of the gentiles, partly upon pretended experience, partly upon pretended revelation, have added innumerable other superstitious ways of divination, and made men believe they should find their fortunes, sometimes in the ambiguous or senseless

answers of the priests at Delphi, Delos, Ammon, and other famous oracles—which answers were made ambiguous by design
to own the event both ways, or absurd by the intoxicating vapor
of the place, which is very frequent in sulphurous caverns;
sometimes in the leaves of the Sybils, of whose prophecies, like
those perhaps of Nostradamus [2] (for the fragments now extant
seem to be the invention of later times), there were some books
in reputation in the time of the Roman republic; sometimes in
the insignificant speeches of madmen, supposed to be possessed
with a divine spirit, which possession they called enthusiasm,
and these kinds of foretelling events were accounted theomancy
or prophecy; sometimes in the aspect of the stars at their na-
tivity, which was called horoscopy and esteemed a part of judi-
ciary astrology; sometimes in their own hopes and fears, called
thumomancy or presage; sometimes in the prediction of witches
that pretended conference with the dead, which is called necro-
mancy, conjuring, and witchcraft, and is but juggling and con-
federate knavery; sometimes in the casual flight or feeding of
birds, called augury; sometimes in the entrails of a sacrificed
beast, which was *aruspicina;* sometimes in dreams; sometimes
in croaking of ravens or chattering of birds; sometimes in the
lineaments of the face, which was called metoposcopy, or by
palmistry in the lines of the hand, in casual words called *omina;*
sometimes in monsters or unusual accidents, as eclipses, comets,
rare meteors, earthquakes, inundations, uncouth births, and
the like, which they called *portenta* and *ostenta* because they
thought them to portend or foreshow some great calamity to
come; sometimes in mere lottery, as cross and pile, counting
holes in a sieve, dipping of verses in Homer and Virgil, and innumerable other such vain conceits. So easy are men to be
drawn to believe anything from such men as have gotten credit
with them and can with gentleness and dexterity take hold of
their fear and ignorance.

The designs of the authors of the religion of the heathen. And therefore the first founders and legislators
of commonwealths among the gentiles, whose
ends were only to keep the people in obedience
and peace, have in all places taken care, first,
to imprint in their minds a belief that those precepts which

2 [Reference is here to Nostradamus' well-known work, *Centuries* (1555),
a collection of prophecies made on the basis of astrological speculations.]

they gave concerning religion might not be thought to proceed from their own device but from the dictates of some god or other spirit, or else that they themselves were of a higher nature than mere mortals, that their laws might the more easily be received: so Numa Pompilius pretended to receive the ceremonies he instituted among the Romans from the nymph Egeria; and the first king and founder of the kingdom of Peru pretended himself and his wife to be the children of the Sun; and Mohammed, to set up his new religion, pretended to have conferences with the Holy Ghost in form of a dove. Secondly, they have had a care to make it believed that the same things were displeasing to the gods which were forbidden by the laws. Thirdly, to prescribe ceremonies, supplications, sacrifices, and festivals, by which they were to believe the anger of the gods might be appeased; and that ill success in war, great contagions of sickness, earthquakes, and each man's private misery came from the anger of the gods, and their anger from the neglect of their worship, or the forgetting or mistaking some point of the ceremonies required. And though among the ancient Romans men were not forbidden to deny that which in the poets is written of the pains and pleasures after this life, which divers of great authority and gravity in that state have in their harangues openly derided, yet that belief was always more cherished than the contrary.

And by these and such other institutions they obtained in order to their end, which was the peace of the commonwealth, that the common people in their misfortunes, laying the fault on neglect or error in their ceremonies, or on their own disobedience to the laws, were the less apt to mutiny against their governors; and being entertained with the pomp and pastime of festivals and public games made in honor of the gods, needed nothing else but bread to keep them from discontent, murmuring, and commotion against the state. And therefore the Romans, that had conquered the greatest part of the then known world, made no scruple of tolerating any religion whatsoever in the city of Rome itself, unless it had something in it that could not consist with their civil government; nor do we read that any religion was there forbidden but that of the Jews, who, being the peculiar kingdom of God, thought it unlawful to acknowledge subjection to any mortal king or state whatsoever. And thus you see how the religion of the gentiles was a part of their policy.

The true religion and the laws of God's kingdom the same. But where God himself, by supernatural revelation, planted religion, there he also made to himself a peculiar kingdom, and gave laws, not only of behavior toward himself, but also toward one another; and thereby in the kingdom of God the policy and laws civil are a part of religion, and therefore the distinction of temporal and spiritual domination has there no place. It is true that God is king of all the earth; yet may he be king of a peculiar and chosen nation. For there is no more incongruity therein than that he that has the general command of the whole army should have withal a peculiar regiment or company of his own. God is king of all the earth by his power, but of his chosen people he is king by covenant. But to speak more largely of the kingdom of God, both by nature and covenant, I have in the following discourse assigned another place (chapter xxxv).[3]

The causes of change in religion. From the propagation of religion it is not hard to understand the causes of the resolution of the same into its first seeds or principles—which are only an opinion of a deity and powers invisible and supernatural—that can never be so abolished out of human nature but that new religions may again be made to spring out of them by the culture of such men as for such purpose are in reputation.

For seeing all formed religion is founded at first upon the faith which a multitude has in some one person, whom they believe not only to be a wise man and to labor to procure their happiness, but also to be a holy man to whom God himself vouchsafes to declare his will supernaturally, it follows necessarily when they that have the government of religion shall come to have either the wisdom of those men, their sincerity, or their love suspected, or when they shall be unable to show any probable token of divine revelation, that the religion which they desire to uphold must be suspected likewise, and, without the fear of the civil sword, contradicted and rejected.

[3] [In Part III, "Of a Christian Commonwealth," not included in the present edition.]

Enjoining belief of impossibilities. That which takes away the reputation of wisdom in him that forms a religion or adds to it when it is already formed is the enjoining of a belief of contradictories; for both parts of a contradiction cannot possibly be true, and therefore to enjoin the belief of them is an argument of ignorance, which detects the author in that and discredits him in all things else he shall propound as from revelation supernatural; which revelation a man may indeed have of many things above, but of nothing against natural reason.

Doing contrary to the religion they establish. That which takes away the reputation of sincerity is the doing or saying of such things as appear to be signs that what they require other men to believe is not believed by themselves; all which doings or sayings are therefore called scandalous, because they be stumbling blocks that make men to fall in the way of religion—as injustice, cruelty, profaneness, avarice, and luxury. For who can believe that he that does ordinarily such actions as proceed from any of these roots believes there is any such invisible power to be feared as he affrights other men withal for lesser faults?

That which takes away the reputation of love is the being detected of private ends, as when the belief they require of others conduces or seems to conduce to the acquiring of dominion, riches, dignity, or secure pleasure to themselves only or specially. For that which men reap benefit by to themselves they are thought to do for their own sakes, and not for love of others.

Want of the testimony of miracles. Lastly, the testimony that men can render of divine calling can be no other than the operation of miracles, or true prophecy, which also is a miracle, or extraordinary felicity. And therefore, to those points of religion which have been received from them that did such miracles, those that are added by such as approve not their calling by some miracle obtain no greater belief than what the custom and laws of the places in which they be educated have wrought into them. For as in natural things men of judgment require natural signs and arguments, so in supernatural things they require signs supernatural, which are miracles, before they consent inwardly and from their hearts.

All which causes of the weakening of men's faith do manifestly appear in the examples following. First, we have the example of the children of Israel, who, when Moses, that had approved his calling to them by miracles and by the happy conduct of them out of Egypt, was absent but forty days, revolted
from the worship of the true God recommended to them by
him, and, setting up (Exod. 32: 1-2) a golden calf for their god,
relapsed into the idolatry of the Egyptians, from whom they
had been so lately delivered. And again, after Moses, Aaron,
Joshua, and that generation which had seen the great works of
God in Israel (Judges 2: 11) were dead, another generation arose
and served Baal. So that miracles failing, faith also failed.

Again, when the sons of Samuel (I Sam. 8: 3), being constituted by their father judges in Bersabee, received bribes and
judged unjustly, the people of Israel refused any more to have
God to be their king in other manner than he was king of other
people, and therefore cried out to Samuel to choose them a king
after the manner of the nations. So that justice failing, faith
also failed, insomuch as they deposed their God from reigning
over them.

And whereas in the planting of Christian religion, the oracles
ceased in all parts of the Roman empire and the number of
Christians increased wonderfully every day and in every place
by the preaching of the Apostles and Evangelists, a great part of
that success may reasonably be attributed to the contempt into
which the priests of the gentiles of that time had brought themselves by their uncleanness, avarice, and juggling between
princes. Also the religion of the Church of Rome was, partly for
the same cause, abolished in England and many other parts of
Christendom, insomuch as the failing of virtue in the pastors
makes faith fail in the people; and partly from bringing of the
philosophy and doctrine of Aristotle into religion by the
Schoolmen, from whence there arose so many contradictions
and absurdities as brought the clergy into a reputation both of
ignorance and of fraudulent intention, and inclined people to
revolt from them, either against the will of their own princes as
in France and Holland, or with their will as in England.

Lastly, among the points by the Church of Rome declared
necessary for salvation, there be so many manifestly to the ad-

vantage of the pope and of his spiritual subjects residing in the territories of other Christian princes that, were it not for the mutual emulation of those princes, they might without war or trouble exclude all foreign authority as easily as it has been excluded in England. For who is there that does not see to whose benefit it conduces to have it believed that a king has not his authority from Christ unless a bishop crown him? That a king, if he be a priest, cannot marry? That whether a prince be born in lawful marriage or not must be judged by authority from Rome? That subjects may be freed from their allegiance if by the court of Rome the king be judged an heretic? That a king, as Childeric of France, may be deposed by a pope, as Pope Zachary, for no cause, and his kingdom given to one of his subjects? [4] That the clergy and regulars, in what country soever, shall be exempt from the jurisdiction of their king in cases criminal? Or who does not see to whose profit redound the fees of private masses and vales of purgatory—with other signs of private interest, enough to mortify the most lively faith if, as I said, the civil magistrate and custom did not more sustain it than any opinion they have of the sanctity, wisdom, or probity of their teachers? So that I may attribute all the changes of religion in the world to one and the same cause, and that is, unpleasing priests; and those not only among Catholics, but even in that church that has presumed most of reformation.[5]

CHAPTER THIRTEEN

OF THE NATURAL CONDITION OF MANKIND AS CONCERNING THEIR FELICITY AND MISERY

Men by nature equal.   Nature has made men so equal in the faculties of the body and mind as that, though there be found one man sometimes manifestly stronger in body or of quicker mind than another, yet, when all is reckoned together,

---

[4] [Childeric III (d. *c.* 751), last of the Merovingian kings of the Franks; St. Zacharias, pope from 741 to 752.]

[5] [Hobbes refers to Calvinism and especially to Puritanism.]

the difference between man and man is not so considerable as that one man can thereupon claim to himself any benefit to which another may not pretend as well as he. For as to the strength of body, the weakest has strength enough to kill the strongest, either by secret machination or by confederacy with others that are in the same danger with himself.

And as to the faculties of the mind, setting aside the arts grounded upon words, and especially that skill of proceeding upon general and infallible rules called science—which very few have and but in few things, as being not a native faculty born with us, nor attained, as prudence, while we look after somewhat else—I find yet a greater equality among men than that of strength. For prudence is but experience, which equal time equally bestows on all men in those things they equally apply themselves unto. That which may perhaps make such equality incredible is but a vain conceit of one's own wisdom, which almost all men think they have in a greater degree than the vulgar—that is, than all men but themselves and a few others whom, by fame or for concurring with themselves, they approve. For such is the nature of men that howsoever they may acknowledge many others to be more witty or more eloquent or more learned, yet they will hardly believe there be many so wise as themselves; for they see their own wit at hand and other men's at a distance. But this proves rather that men are in that point equal than unequal. For there is not ordinarily a greater sign of the equal distribution of anything than that every man is contented with his share.

From equality proceeds diffidence. From this equality of ability arises equality of hope in the attaining of our ends. And therefore if any two men desire the same thing, which nevertheless they cannot both enjoy, they become enemies; and in the way to their end, which is principally their own conservation, and sometimes their delectation only, endeavor to destroy or subdue one another. And from hence it comes to pass that where an invader has no more to fear than another man's single power, if one plant, sow, build, or possess a convenient seat, others may probably be expected to come prepared with forces united to dispossess and deprive him, not only of the fruit of his labor, but also of his life or liberty. And the invader again is in the like danger of another.

From diffidence war. And from this diffidence of one another there is no way for any man to secure himself so reasonable as anticipation—that is, by force or wiles to master the persons of all men he can, so long till he see no other power great enough to endanger him; and this is no more than his own conservation requires, and is generally allowed. Also, because there be some that take pleasure in contemplating their own power in the acts of conquest, which they pursue farther than their security requires, if others that otherwise would be glad to be at ease within modest bounds should not by invasion increase their power, they would not be able, long time, by standing only on their defense, to subsist. And by consequence, such augmentation of dominion over men being necessary to a man's conservation, it ought to be allowed him.

Again, men have no pleasure, but on the contrary a great deal of grief, in keeping company where there is no power able to overawe them all. For every man looks that his companion should value him at the same rate he sets upon himself; and upon all signs of contempt or undervaluing naturally endeavors, as far as he dares (which among them that have no common power to keep them in quiet is far enough to make them destroy each other), to extort a greater value from his contemners by damage and from others by the example.

So that in the nature of man we find three principal causes of quarrel: first, competition; secondly, diffidence; thirdly, glory.

The first makes men invade for gain, the second for safety, and the third for reputation. The first use violence to make themselves masters of other men's persons, wives, children, and cattle; the second, to defend them; the third, for trifles, as a word, a smile, a different opinion, and any other sign of undervalue, either direct in their persons or by reflection in their kindred, their friends, their nation, their profession, or their name.

Out of civil states, there is always war of every one against every one. Hereby it is manifest that, during the time men live without a common power to keep them all in awe, they are in that condition which is called war, and such a war as is of every man against every man. For WAR consists not in battle only, or the act of fighting, but in a tract of time wherein the

will to contend by battle is sufficiently known; and therefore
the notion of *time* is to be considered in the nature of war as it
is in the nature of weather. For as the nature of foul weather
lies not in a shower or two of rain but in an inclination thereto
of many days together, so the nature of war consists not in actual fighting but in the known disposition thereto during all
the time there is no assurance to the contrary. All other time is
PEACE.

The incommodities of such a war. Whatsoever, therefore, is consequent to a time
of war where every man is enemy to every man,
the same is consequent to the time wherein
men live without other security than what their own strength
and their own invention shall furnish them withal. In such condition there is no place for industry, because the fruit thereof is
uncertain: and consequently no culture of the earth; no navigation nor use of the commodities that may be imported by sea;
no commodious building; no instruments of moving and removing such things as require much force; no knowledge of the
face of the earth; no account of time; no arts; no letters; no society; and, which is worst of all, continual fear and danger of
violent death; and the life of man solitary, poor, nasty, brutish,
and short.

It may seem strange to some man that has not well weighed
these things that nature should thus dissociate and render men
apt to invade and destroy one another; and he may therefore,
not trusting to this inference made from the passions, desire
perhaps to have the same confirmed by experience. Let him
therefore consider with himself—when taking a journey he arms
himself and seeks to go well accompanied, when going to sleep
he locks his doors, when even in his house he locks his chests,
and this when he knows there be laws and public officers,
armed, to revenge all injuries shall be done him—what opinion
he has of his fellow subjects when he rides armed, of his fellow
citizens when he locks his doors, and of his children and servants when he locks his chests. Does he not there as much accuse
mankind by his actions as I do by my words? But neither of us
accuse man's nature in it. The desires and other passions of
man are in themselves no sin. No more are the actions that proceed from those passions till they know a law that forbids them,

which, till laws be made, they cannot know, nor can any law be made till they have agreed upon the person that shall make it.

It may peradventure be thought there was never such a time nor condition of war as this, and I believe it was never generally so over all the world; but there are many places where they live so now. For the savage people in many places of America, except the government of small families, the concord whereof depends on natural lust, have no government at all and live at this day in that brutish manner as I said before. Howsoever, it may be perceived what manner of life there would be where there were no common power to fear by the manner of life which men that have formerly lived under a peaceful government use to degenerate into in a civil war.

But though there had never been any time wherein particular men were in a condition of war one against another, yet in all times kings and persons of sovereign authority, because of their independency, are in continual jealousies and in the state and posture of gladiators, having their weapons pointing and their eyes fixed on one another—that is, their forts, garrisons, and guns upon the frontiers of their kingdoms, and continual spies upon their neighbors—which is a posture of war. But because they uphold thereby the industry of their subjects, there does not follow from it that misery which accompanies the liberty of particular men.

In such a war nothing is unjust. To this war of every man against every man, this also is consequent: that nothing can be unjust. The notions of right and wrong, justice and injustice, have there no place. Where there is no common power, there is no law; where no law, no injustice. Force and fraud are in war the two cardinal virtues. Justice and injustice are none of the faculties neither of the body nor mind. If they were, they might be in a man that were alone in the world, as well as his senses and passions. They are qualities that relate to men in society, not in solitude. It is consequent also to the same condition that there be no propriety, no dominion, no *mine* and *thine* distinct; but only that to be every man's that he can get, and for so long as he can keep it. And thus much for the ill condition which man by mere nature is actually placed in, though with a possibility to come out of it consisting partly in the passions, partly in his reason.

The passions that incline men to peace.

The passions that incline men to peace are fear of death, desire of such things as are necessary to commodious living, and a hope by their industry to obtain them. And reason suggests convenient articles of peace, upon which men may be drawn to agreement. These articles are they which otherwise are called the Laws of Nature, whereof I shall speak more particularly in the two following chapters.

CHAPTER FOURTEEN

OF THE FIRST AND SECOND NATURAL LAWS, AND OF CONTRACTS

Right of nature what.

The RIGHT OF NATURE, which writers commonly call *jus naturale,* is the liberty each man has to use his own power, as he will himself, for the preservation of his own nature—that is to say, of his own life—and consequently of doing anything which, in his own judgment and reason, he shall conceive to be the aptest means thereunto.

Liberty what.

By LIBERTY is understood, according to the proper signification of the word, the absence of external impediments; which impediments may oft take away part of a man's power to do what he would, but cannot hinder him from using the power left him according as his judgment and reason shall dictate to him.

A law of nature what.

A LAW OF NATURE, *lex naturalis,* is a precept or general rule, found out by reason, by which a man is forbidden to do that which is destructive of his life or takes away the means of preserving the same and to omit that by which he thinks it may be best preserved. For though they that speak of this subject use to confound *jus* and *lex,* *right* and *law,* yet they ought to be distinguished; be-

Difference of right and law.

cause RIGHT consists in liberty to do or to forbear, whereas LAW determines and binds to one of them; so that law and right differ as much as obligation and liberty, which in one and the same matter are inconsistent.

And because the condition of man, as has been

Naturally every man has right to every thing. declared in the precedent chapter, is a condition of war of every one against every one—in which case everyone is governed by his own reason and there is nothing he can make use of that may not be a help unto him in preserving his life against his enemies—it follows that in such a condition every man has a right to everything, even to one another's body. And therefore, as long as this natural right of every man to everything endures, there can be no security to any man, how strong or wise soever he be, of living out the time which nature ordinarily allows men to live. And consequently it is a precept or general rule of reason *that*

The fundamental law of nature. *every man ought to endeavor peace, as far as he has hope of obtaining it; and when he cannot obtain it, that he may seek and use all helps and advantages of war.* The first branch of which rule contains the first and fundamental law of nature, which is *to seek peace and follow it.* The second, the sum of the right of nature, which is, *by all means we can to defend ourselves.*

From this fundamental law of nature, by which men are commanded to endeavor peace, is derived this second law: *that a*

The second law of nature. *man be willing, when others are so too, as far forth as for peace and defense of himself he shall think it necessary, to lay down this right to all things, and be contented with so much liberty against other men as he would allow other men against himself.* For as long as every man holds this right of doing anything he likes, so long are all men in the condition of war. But if other men will not lay down their right as well as he, then there is no reason for anyone to divest himself of his, for that were to expose himself to prey, which no man is bound to, rather than to dispose himself to peace. This is that law of the gospel: *whatsoever you require that others should do to you, that do ye to them.* And that law of all men, *quod tibi fieri non vis, alteri ne feceris.*[1]

1 [Matt. 7:12; Luke 6:31. The Latin expresses the same rule negatively: "What you would not have done to you, do not do to others."]

To *lay down* a man's *right* to anything is to divest himself of the *liberty* of hindering another of the benefit of his own right to the

What it is to lay down a right.

same. For he that renounces or passes away his right gives not to any other man a right which he had not before—because there is nothing to which every man had not right by nature—but only stands out of his way, that he may enjoy his own original right without hindrance from him, not without hindrance from another. So that the effect which redounds to one man by another man's defect of right is but so much diminution of impediments to the use of his own right original. Right is laid aside either by simply renouncing it or by transferring it to another. By *simply* RENOUNCING, when he cares not to whom the benefit thereof redounds. By TRANSFERRING, when he intends the benefit thereof to some certain person or persons. And when a man has in either

Renouncing a right, what it is.

Transferring right what. Obligation.

manner abandoned or granted away his right, then he is said to be OBLIGED or BOUND not to hinder those to whom such right is granted or abandoned from the benefit of it; and that he *ought,* and it is his DUTY, not to make void that voluntary act of his own; and that such hindrance is INJUSTICE and INJURY as

Duty.

Injustice.

being *sine jure,*[2] the right being before renounced or transferred. So that *injury* or *injustice* in the controversies of the world is somewhat like to that which in the disputations of scholars is called *absurdity.* For as it is there called an absurdity to contradict what one maintained in the beginning, so in the world it is called injustice and injury voluntarily to undo that which from the beginning he had voluntarily done. The way by which a man either simply renounces or transfers his right is a declaration or signification by some voluntary and sufficient sign or signs that he does so renounce or transfer, or has so renounced or transferred, the same to him that accepts it. And these signs are either words only or actions only; or as it happens most often, both words and actions. And the same are the BONDS by which men are bound and obliged—bonds that have their strength, not from their own nature, for nothing is more

2 [Without legal basis.]

easily broken than a man's word, but from fear of some evil consequence upon the rupture.

Whensoever a man transfers his right or renounces it, it is either in consideration of some right reciprocally transferred to himself or for some other good he hopes for thereby. For it is a voluntary act; and of the voluntary acts of every man, the object is some *good to himself*.

Not all rights are alienable.

And therefore there be some rights which no man can be understood by any words or other signs to have abandoned or transferred. As, first, a man cannot lay down the right of resisting them that assault him by force to take away his life, because he cannot be understood to aim thereby at any good to himself. The same may be said of wounds and chains and imprisonment, both because there is no benefit consequent to such patience as there is to the patience of suffering another to be wounded or imprisoned, as also because a man cannot tell, when he sees men proceed against him by violence, whether they intend his death or not. And, lastly, the motive and end for which this renouncing and transferring of right is introduced is nothing else but the security of a man's person in his life and in the means of so preserving life as not to be weary of it. And therefore if a man by words or other signs seem to despoil himself of the end for which those signs were intended, he is not to be understood as if he meant it or that it was his will, but that he was ignorant of how such words and actions were to be interpreted.

Contract what.

The mutual transferring of right is that which men call CONTRACT.

There is difference between transferring of right to the thing and transferring, or tradition—that is, delivery—of the thing itself. For the thing may be delivered together with the translation of the right, as in buying and selling with ready money or exchange of goods or lands, and it may be delivered some time after.

Again, one of the contractors may deliver the thing contracted for on his part and leave the other to perform his part at some determinate time after and in the meantime be trusted, and then the contract on his part is called PACT or COVENANT; or both parts may contract now to perform hereafter, in which cases he that is to perform in

Covenant what.

time to come, being trusted, his performance is called *keeping of promise* or faith, and the failing of performance, if it be voluntary, *violation of faith.*

When the transferring of right is not mutual, but one of the parties transfers in hope to gain thereby friendship or service from another or from his friends, or in hope to gain the reputation of charity or magnanimity, or to deliver his mind from the
Free gift.   pain of compassion, or in hope of reward in
          heaven—this is not contract but GIFT, FREE
GIFT, GRACE, which words signify one and the same thing.

          Signs of contract are either *express* or *by in-*
Signs of contract   *ference.* Express are words spoken with under-
express.
          standing of what they signify, and such words
are either of the time *present* or *past*—as *I give, I grant, I have given, I have granted, I will that this be yours*—or of the future —as *I will give, I will grant*—which words of the future are called PROMISE.

          Signs by inference are sometimes the conse-
Signs of contract   quence of words, sometimes the consequence
by inference.
          of silence, sometimes the consequence of actions, sometimes the consequence of forbearing an action; and generally a sign by inference of any contract is whatsoever sufficiently argues the will of the contractor.

Words alone, if they be of the time to come and contain a bare
          promise, are an insufficient sign of a free gift
Free gift passes by and therefore not obligatory. For if they be of
words of the pres-
ent or past.   the time to come, as *tomorrow I will give,* they
are a sign I have not given yet and consequently that my right is not transferred but remains till I transfer it by some other act. But if the words be of the time present or past, as *I have given* or *do give to be delivered tomorrow,* then is my tomorrow's right given away today, and that by the virtue of the words though there were no other argument of my will. And there is a great difference in the signification of these words: *volo hoc tuum esse cras* and *cras dabo*—that is, between *I will that this be yours tomorrow* and *I will give it you tomorrow*—for the word *I will,* in the former manner of speech, signifies an act of the will present, but in the latter it signifies a promise of an act of the will to come; and therefore the former words, being of the present, transfer a future right; the latter,

that be of the future, transfer nothing. But if there be other signs of the will to transfer a right besides words, then, though the gift be free, yet may the right be understood to pass by words of the future: as if a man propound a prize to him that comes first to the end of a race, the gift is free; and though the words be of the future, yet the right passes; for if he would not have his words so be understood, he should not have let them run.

Signs of contract are words both of the past, present, and future. In contracts, the right passes not only where the words are of the time present or past but also where they are of the future, because all contract is mutual translation or change of right, and therefore he that promises only because he has already received the benefit for which he promises is to be understood as if he intended the right should pass; for unless he had been content to have his words so understood, the other would not have performed his part first. And for that cause, in buying and selling and other acts of contract a promise is equivalent to a covenant and therefore obligatory.

Merit what. He that performs first in the case of a contract is said to MERIT that which he is to receive by the performance of the other; and he has it as *due.* Also when a prize is propounded to many which is to be given to him only that wins, or money is thrown among many to be enjoyed by them that catch it, though this be a free gift, yet so to win or so to catch is to *merit* and to have it as DUE. For the right is transferred in the propounding of the prize and in throwing down the money, though it be not determined to whom but by the event of the contention. But there is between these two sorts of merit this difference: that in contract I merit by virtue of my own power and the contractor's need, but in this case of free gift I am enabled to merit only by the benignity of the giver; in contract I merit at the contractor's hand that he should depart with his right, in this case of gift I merit not that the giver should part with his right but that when he has parted with it, it should be mine rather than another's. And this I think to be the meaning of that distinction of the Schools between *meritum congrui* and *meritum condigni.*[3] For God Almighty having

[3] [Merit based on conformity and merit based on worthiness.]

promised Paradise to those men, hoodwinked with carnal desires, that can walk through this world according to the precepts and limits prescribed by him, they say he that shall so
walk shall merit Paradise *ex congruo*. But because no man can
demand a right to it, by his own righteousness or any other
power in himself, but by the free grace of God only, they say no
man can merit Paradise *ex condigno*. This, I say, I think is the
meaning of that distinction; but because disputers do not agree
upon the signification of their own terms of art longer than it
serves their turn, I will not affirm anything of their meaning;
only this I say: when a gift is given indefinitely, as a prize to be
contended for, he that wins merits and may claim the prize
as due.

Covenants of mutual trust, when invalid. If a covenant be made wherein neither of the
parties perform presently but trust one an-
other, in the condition of mere nature, which
is a condition of war of every man against
every man, upon any reasonable suspicion, it is void; but if
there be a common power set over them both, with right and
force sufficient to compel performance, it is not void. For he
that performs first has no assurance the other will perform
after, because the bonds of words are too weak to bridle men's
ambition, avarice, anger, and other passions without the fear of
some coercive power which in the condition of mere nature,
where all men are equal and judges of the justness of their own
fears, cannot possibly be supposed. And therefore he which performs first does but betray himself to his enemy, contrary to the
right he can never abandon of defending his life and means of
living.

But in a civil estate, where there is a power set up to constrain
those that would otherwise violate their faith, that fear is no
more reasonable; and for that cause, he which by the covenant
is to perform first is obliged so to do.

The cause of fear which makes such a covenant invalid must
be always something arising after the covenant made, as some
new fact or other sign of the will not to perform; else it cannot
make the covenant void. For that which could not hinder a man
from promising ought not to be admitted as a hindrance of
performing.

Right to the end contains right to the means. He that transfers any right transfers the means of enjoying it, as far as lies in his power. As he that sells land is understood to transfer the herbage and whatsoever grows upon it; nor can he that sells a mill turn away the stream that drives it. And they that give to a man the right of government in sovereignty are understood to give him the right of levying money to maintain soldiers and of appointing magistrates for the administration of justice.

No covenant with beasts. To make covenants with brute beasts is impossible because, not understanding our speech, they understand not nor accept of any translation of right, nor can translate any right to another; and without mutual acceptation there is no covenant.

Nor with God without special revelation. To make covenant with God is impossible but by mediation of such as God speaks to, either by revelation supernatural or by his lieutenants that govern under him and in his name; for otherwise we know not whether our covenants be accepted or not. And therefore they that vow anything contrary to any law of nature vow in vain, as being a thing unjust to pay such vow. And if it be a thing commanded by the law of nature, it is not the vow but the law that binds them.

No covenant but of possible and future. The matter or subject of a covenant is always something that falls under deliberation, for to covenant is an act of the will—that is to say, an act, and the last act, of deliberation—and is therefore always understood to be something to come, and which is judged possible for him that covenants to perform.

And therefore to promise that which is known to be impossible is no covenant. But if that prove impossible afterwards which before was thought possible, the covenant is valid, and binds, though not to the thing itself, yet to the value, or, if that also be impossible, to the unfeigned endeavor of performing as much as is possible, for to more no man can be obliged.

Covenants how made void. Men are freed of their covenants two ways: by performing or by being forgiven. For performance is the natural end of obligation, and forgiveness the restitution of liberty, as being a retransferring of that right in which the obligation consisted.

Covenants entered into by fear, in the condi-
Covenants extorted by fear are valid. tion of mere nature, are obligatory. For example, if I covenant to pay a ransom or service for
my life to an enemy, I am bound by it; for it is a contract,
wherein one receives the benefit of life, the other is to receive
money or service for it; and consequently, where no other law,
as in the condition of mere nature, forbids the performance, the
covenant is valid. Therefore prisoners of war, if trusted with
the payment of their ransom, are obliged to pay it; and if a
weaker prince make a disadvantageous peace with a stronger,
for fear, he is bound to keep it; unless, as has been said before,
there arises some new and just cause of fear to renew the war.
And even in commonwealths, if I be forced to redeem myself
from a thief by promising him money, I am bound to pay it
till the civil law discharge me. For whatsoever I may lawfully do
without obligation, the same I may lawfully covenant to do
through fear; and what I lawfully covenant, I cannot lawfully
The former covenant break. A former covenant makes void a later.
to one makes void For a man that has passed away his right to one
the later to another. man today has it not to pass tomorrow to another; and therefore the later promise passes no right, but is null.

A man's covenant A covenant not to defend myself from force by
not to defend him- force is always void. For, as I have showed be-
self is void. fore, no man can transfer or lay down his right
to save himself from death, wounds, and imprisonment, the
avoiding whereof is the only end of laying down any right; and
therefore the promise of not resisting force in no covenant transfers any right, nor is obliging. For though a man may covenant
thus: *unless I do so or so, kill me,* he cannot covenant thus:
*unless I do so or so, I will not resist you when you come to kill
me.* For man by nature chooses the lesser evil, which is danger
of death in resisting, rather than the greater, which is certain
and present death in not resisting. And this is granted to be true
by all men, in that they lead criminals to execution and prison
with armed men, notwithstanding that such criminals have
consented to the law by which they are condemned.

No man obliged to A covenant to accuse oneself, without assurance
accuse himself. of pardon, is likewise invalid. For in the condition of nature, where every man is judge,
there is no place for accusation; and in the civil state, the accu-

sation is followed with punishment, which, being force, a man is not obliged not to resist. The same is also true of the accusation of those by whose condemnation a man falls into misery, as of a father, wife, or benefactor. For the testimony of such an accuser, if it be not willingly given, is presumed to be corrupted by nature, and therefore not to be received; and where a man's testimony is not to be credited, he is not bound to give it. Also accusations upon torture are not to be reputed as testimonies. For torture is to be used but as means of conjecture and light in the further examination and search of truth; and what is in that case confessed tends to the ease of him that is tortured, not to the informing of the torturers, and therefore ought not to have the credit of a sufficient testimony; for whether he deliver himself by true or false accusation, he does it by the right of preserving his own life.

The end of an oath. The force of words being, as I have formerly noted, too weak to hold men to the performance of their covenants, there are in man's nature but two imaginable helps to strengthen it. And those are either a fear of the consequence of breaking their word, or a glory or pride in appearing not to need to break it. This latter is a generosity too rarely found to be presumed on, especially in the pursuers of wealth, command, or sensual pleasure—which are the greatest part of mankind. The passion to be reckoned upon is fear, whereof there be two very general objects: one, the power of spirits invisible; the other, the power of those men they shall therein offend. Of these two, though the former be the greater power, yet the fear of the latter is commonly the greater fear. The fear of the former is in every man his own religion, which has place in the nature of man before civil society. The latter has not so, at least not place enough to keep men to their promises, because in the condition of mere nature the inequality of power is not discerned but by the event of battle. So that before the time of civil society, or in the interruption thereof by war, there is nothing can strengthen a covenant of peace agreed on against the temptations of avarice, ambition, lust, or other strong desire but the fear of that invisible power, which they everyone worship as God and fear as a revenger of their perfidy. All therefore that can be done between two men not subject to civil power is to put one another to swear by the God he fears,

The form of an oath. which *swearing* or OATH is a *form of speech,* *added to a promise, by which he that promises* *signifies that, unless he perform, he renounces the mercy of his* *God, or calls to him for vengeance on himself.* Such was the heathen form, *Let Jupiter kill me else, as I kill this beast.* So is our form, *I shall do thus and thus, so help me God.* And this, with the rites and ceremonies which everyone uses in his own religion, that the fear of breaking faith might be the greater.

By this it appears that an oath taken according to any other form or rite than his that swears is in vain and no oath, and that *No oath but by God.* there is no swearing by anything which the swearer thinks not God. For though men have sometimes used to swear by their kings, for fear or flattery, yet they would have it thereby understood they attributed to them divine honor. And that swearing unnecessarily by God is but profaning of his name; and swearing by other things, as men do in common discourse, is not swearing but an impious custom gotten by too much vehemence of talking.

An oath adds nothing to the obligation. It appears also that the oath adds nothing to the obligation. For a covenant, if lawful, binds in the sight of God without the oath as much as with it; if unlawful, binds not at all, though it be confirmed with an oath.

CHAPTER FIFTEEN

OF OTHER LAWS OF NATURE

The third law of nature, justice. From that law of nature by which we are obliged to transfer to another such rights as, being retained, hinder the peace of mankind, there follows a third, which is this: *that men perform their covenants made;* without which covenants are in vain and but empty words, and, the right of all men to all things remaining, we are still in the condition of war.

Justice and injustice what. And in this law of nature consists the fountain and original of JUSTICE. For where no covenant has preceded there has no right been transferred, and every man has right to every thing; and consequently no action can be unjust. But when a covenant is made, then to break it is *unjust;* and the definition of INJUSTICE is no other than *the not performance of covenant.* And whatsoever is not unjust is *just.*

Justice and propri-ety begin with the constitution of commonwealth.

But because covenants of mutual trust, where there is a fear of not performance on either part, as has been said in the former chapter, are invalid, though the original of justice be the making of covenants, yet injustice actually there can be none till the cause of such fear be taken away, which, while men are in the natural condition of war, cannot be done. Therefore, before the names of just and unjust can have place, there must be some coercive power to compel men equally to the perform-ance of their covenants by the terror of some punishment greater than the benefit they expect by the breach of their cove-nant, and to make good that propriety which by mutual con-tract men acquire in recompense of the universal right they abandon; and such power there is none before the erection of a commonwealth. And this is also to be gathered out of the ordi-nary definition of justice in the Schools, for they say that *justice is the constant will of giving to every man his own.* And there-fore where there is no *own*—that is, no propriety—there is no in-justice; and where there is no coercive power erected—that is, where there is no commonwealth—there is no propriety, all men having right to all things; therefore, where there is no common-wealth, there nothing is unjust. So that the nature of justice consists in keeping of valid covenants; but the validity of cove-nants begins not but with the constitution of a civil power suf-ficient to compel men to keep them; and then it is also that pro-priety begins.

Justice not contrary to reason.

The fool hath said in his heart, there is no such thing as justice; [1] and sometimes also with his tongue, seriously alleging that, every man's conservation and contentment being committed to his own care, there could be no reason why every man might not do what he thought conduced thereunto; and therefore also to make or not make, keep or not keep covenants was not against reason when it conduced to one's benefit. He does not therein deny that

1 [Pss. 14, 53.]

there be covenants and that they are sometimes broken, some-times kept, and that such breach of them may be called injus-tice and the observance of them justice; but he questions whether injustice, taking away the fear of God—for the same fool hath said in his heart there is no God—may not sometimes stand with that reason which dictates to every man his own good, and particularly then when it conduces to such a benefit as shall put a man in a condition to neglect not only the dis-praise and revilings, but also the power of other men. The king-dom of God is gotten by violence; but what if it could be gotten by unjust violence? Were it against reason so to get it, when it is impossible to receive hurt by it? And if it be not against rea-son, it is not against justice, or else justice is not to be approved for good. From such reasoning as this, successful wickedness has obtained the name of virtue; and some that in all other things have disallowed the violation of faith yet have allowed it when it is for the getting of a kingdom. And the heathen that believed that Saturn was deposed by his son Jupiter believed nevertheless the same Jupiter to be the avenger of injustice—somewhat like to a piece of law in Coke's *Commentaries on Littleton* [2] where he says: if the right heir of the crown be attainted of treason, yet the crown shall descend to him and *eo instante* the attainder be void; from which instances a man will be very prone to infer that when the heir apparent of a kingdom shall kill him that is in possession, though his father, you may call it injustice or by what other name you will, yet it can never be against reason, seeing all the voluntary actions of men tend to the benefit of themselves, and those actions are most reasonable that conduce most to their ends. This specious reasoning is nevertheless false.

For the question is not of promises mutual where there is no security of performance on either side—as when there is no civil power erected over the parties promising—for such promises are no covenants; but either where one of the parties has performed already or where there is a power to make him perform, there is the question whether it be against reason—that is, against the

---

[2] [Sir Edward Coke (1552-1634), English jurist, the first Lord Chief Justice of England. The first volume of his *Institutes* was a translation of, and com-mentary on, the *Treatise on Tenures* of Sir Thomas de Littleton (*c.* 1407-1481). It is commonly called *Coke on Littleton.*]

benefit of the other—to perform or not. And I say it is not against reason. For the manifestation whereof we are to consider, first, that when a man does a thing which, notwithstanding anything can be foreseen and reckoned on, tends to his own destruction, howsoever some accident which he could not expect, arriving, may turn it to his benefit, yet such events do not make it reasonably or wisely done. Secondly, that in a condition of war, wherein every man to every man, for want of a common power to keep them all in awe, is an enemy, there is no man who can hope by his own strength or wit to defend himself from destruction without the help of confederates, where everyone expects the same defense by the confederation that anyone else does; and therefore he which declares he thinks it reason to deceive those that help him can in reason expect no other means of safety than what can be had from his own single power. He, therefore, that breaks his covenant, and consequently declares that he thinks he may with reason do so, cannot be received into any society that unite themselves for peace and defense, but by the error of them that receive him; nor, when he is received, be retained in it without seeing the danger of their error, which errors a man cannot reasonably reckon upon as the means of his security; and therefore if he be left or cast out of society he perishes, and if he live in society, it is by the errors of other men, which he could not foresee nor reckon upon, and consequently against the reason of his preservation; and so, as all men that contribute not to his destruction, forbear him only out of ignorance of what is good for themselves.

As for the instance of gaining the secure and perpetual felicity of heaven by any way, it is frivolous, there being but one way imaginable, and that is not breaking but keeping of covenant.

And for the other instance of attaining sovereignty by rebellion, it is manifest that, though the event follow, yet because it cannot reasonably be expected, but rather the contrary, and because by gaining it so others are taught to gain the same in like manner, the attempt thereof is against reason. Justice, therefore—that is to say, keeping of covenant—is a rule of reason by which we are forbidden to do anything destructive to our life, and consequently a law of nature.

There be some that proceed further and will not have the law

of nature to be those rules which conduce to the preservation of
man's life on earth but to the attaining of an eternal felicity
after death, to which they think the breach of covenant may
conduce and consequently be just and reasonable; such are they
that think it a work of merit to kill or depose or rebel against
the sovereign power constituted over them by their own consent.
But because there is no natural knowledge of man's estate after
death—much less of the reward that is then to be given to breach
of faith—but only a belief grounded upon other men's saying
that they know it supernaturally, or that they know those that
knew them that knew others that knew it supernaturally, breach
of faith cannot be called a precept of reason or nature.

Covenants not dis-
charged by the vice
of the person to
whom they are
made.
Others that allow for a law of nature the keeping of faith do nevertheless make exception of
certain persons, as heretics and such as use not
to perform their covenant to others; and this
also is against reason. For if any fault of a man
be sufficient to discharge our covenant made, the same ought in
reason to have been sufficient to have hindered the making of it.

Justice of men and
justice of actions
what.
The names of just and unjust, when they are
attributed to men, signify one thing, and when
they are attributed to actions, another. When
they are attributed to men, they signify conformity or inconformity of manners to reason. But when they
are attributed to actions, they signify the conformity or inconformity to reason, not of manners or manner of life, but of particular actions. A just man, therefore, is he that takes all the care
he can that his actions may be all just; and an unjust man is he
that neglects it. And such men are more often in our language
styled by the names of righteous and unrighteous than just and
unjust, though the meaning be the same. Therefore a righteous
man does not lose that title by one or a few unjust actions that
proceed from sudden passion or mistake of things or persons;
nor does an unrighteous man lose his character for such actions
as he does or forbears to do for fear, because his will is not
framed by the justice but by the apparent benefit of what he is
to do. That which gives to human actions the relish of justice is
a certain nobleness or gallantness of courage, rarely found, by
which a man scorns to be beholden for the contentment of his

life to fraud or breach of promise. This justice of the manners is that which is meant where justice is called a virtue and injustice a vice.

But the justice of actions denominates men, not just, but *guiltless;* and the injustice of the same, which is also called injury, gives them but the name of *guilty.*

Justice of manners, and justice of actions. Again, the injustice of manners is the disposition or aptitude to do injury, and is injustice before it proceed to act and without supposing any individual person injured. But the injustice of an action—that is.to say, injury—supposes an individual person injured—namely, him to whom the covenant was made—and therefore many times the injury is received by one man when the damage redounds to another. As when the master commands his servant to give money to a stranger: if it be not done, the injury is done to the master, whom he had before covenanted to obey; but the damage redounds to the stranger, to whom he had no obligation and therefore could not injure him. And so also in commonwealths private men may remit to one another their debts but not robberies or other violences whereby they are endamaged; because the detaining of debt is an injury to themselves, but robbery and violence are injuries to the person of the commonwealth.

Nothing done to a man by his own consent can be injury. Whatsoever is done to a man, conformable to his own will signified to the doer, is no injury to him. For if he that does it has not passed away his original right to do what he please by some antecedent covenant, there is no breach of covenant and therefore no injury done him. And if he have, then his will to have it done, being signified, is a release of that covenant, and so again there is no injury done him.

Justice commutative and distributive. Justice of actions is by writers divided into *commutative* and *distributive;* and the former they say consists in proportion arithmetical, the latter in proportion geometrical. Commutative, therefore, they place in the equality of value of the things contracted for, and distributive in the distribution of equal benefit to men of equal merit. As if it were injustice to sell dearer than we buy, or to give more to a man than he merits. The value of all things contracted for is measured by the appetite of the contractors, and therefore the just value is that which they be contented to give. And merit (besides that which is by covenant, where the performance on one part merits the performance of the other part, and falls under justice commutative, not distributive) is not due by justice, but is rewarded of grace only. And therefore this distinction, in the sense wherein it uses to be expounded, is not right. To speak properly, commutative justice is the justice of a contractor—that is, a performance of covenant in buying and selling, hiring and letting to hire, lending and borrowing, exchanging, bartering, and other acts of contract.

And distributive justice, the justice of an arbitrator—that is to say, the act of defining what is just. Wherein, being trusted by them that make him arbitrator, if he perform his trust, he is said to distribute to every man his own; and this is indeed just distribution, and may be called, though improperly, distributive justice, but more properly equity, which also is a law of nature, as shall be shown in due place. [P. 128.]

The fourth law of nature, gratitude. As justice depends on antecedent covenant, so does GRATITUDE depend on antecedent grace—that is to say, antecedent free gift—and is the fourth law of nature, which may be conceived in this form: *that a man which receives benefit from another of mere grace endeavor that he which gives it have no reasonable cause to repent him of his good will.* For no man gives but with intention of good to himself, because gift is voluntary, and of all voluntary acts the object is to every man his own good; of which if men see they shall be frustrated, there will be no beginning of benevolence or trust nor consequently of mutual help nor of reconciliation of one man to another; and therefore they are to remain still in the condition of *war,* which is contrary to the first and fundamental law of nature, which commands men to *seek peace.* The breach of this law is called *ingratitude,* and has the same relation to grace that injustice has to obligation by covenant.

The fifth mutual accommodation, or complaisance. A fifth law of nature is COMPLAISANCE—that is to say, *that every man strive to accommodate himself to the rest.* For the understanding whereof we may consider that there is in men's aptness to society a diversity of nature rising from their diversity of affections not unlike to that we see in stones brought together for building of an edifice. For as that stone which by the asperity and irregularity of figure takes more room from others than itself fills, and for the hardness cannot be easily made plain and thereby hinders the building, is by the builders cast away as unprofitable and troublesome, so also a man that by asperity of nature will strive to retain those things which to himself are superfluous and to others necessary, and for the stubbornness of his passions cannot be corrected, is to be left or cast out of society as cumbersome thereunto. For seeing every man, not only by right but also by necessity of nature, is supposed to endeavor all he can to obtain that which is necessary for his conservation, he that shall oppose himself against it for things superfluous is guilty of the war that thereupon is to follow, and therefore does that which is contrary to the fundamental law of nature, which commands *to seek peace*. The observers of this law may be called SOCIABLE (the Latins call them *commodi*), the contrary *stubborn, insociable, froward, intractable*.

The sixth, facility to pardon. A sixth law of nature is this: *that upon caution of the future time, a man ought to pardon the offenses past of them that, repenting, desire it.* For PARDON is nothing but granting of peace, which, though granted to them that persevere in their hostility, be not peace but fear, yet, not granted to them that give caution of the future time, is sign of an aversion to peace, and therefore contrary to the law of nature.

The seventh, that in revenges men respect only the future good. A seventh is *that in revenges*—that is, retribution of evil for evil—*men look not at the greatness of the evil past, but the greatness of the good to follow*. Whereby we are forbidden to inflict punishment with any other design than for correction of the offender or direction of others. For this law is consequent to the next before it that commands pardon upon security of the future time. Besides, revenge without respect to the example and profit to come is a triumph or glorying in the hurt of another, tending to no end; for the end is always somewhat to come, and glorying to no end is vainglory and contrary to reason; and to hurt without reason tends to the introduction of war, which is against the law of nature and is commonly styled by the name of *cruelty*.

The eighth, against contumely. And because all signs of hatred or contempt provoke to fight, insomuch as most men choose rather to hazard their life than not to be revenged, we may in the eighth place for a law of nature set down this precept: *that no man by deed, word, countenance, or gesture declare hatred or contempt of another.* The breach of which law is commonly called *contumely.*

The ninth, against pride. The question who is the better man has no place in the condition of mere nature, where, as has been shown before, all men are equal. The inequality that now is has been introduced by the laws civil. I know that Aristotle in the first book of his *Politics,* for a foundation of his doctrine, makes men by nature some more worthy to command, meaning the wiser sort such as he thought himself to be for his philosophy, others to serve, meaning those that had strong bodies but were not philosophers as he; as if master and servant were not introduced by consent of men but by difference of wit, which is not only against reason but also against experience. For there are very few so foolish that had not rather govern themselves than be governed by others; nor when the wise in their own conceit contend by force with them who distrust their own wisdom, do they always, or often, or almost at any time, get the victory. If nature therefore have made men equal, that equality is to be acknowledged; or if nature have made men unequal, yet because men that think themselves equal will not enter into conditions of peace but upon equal terms, such equality must be admitted. And therefore for the ninth law of nature, I put this: *that every man acknowledge another for his equal by nature.* The breach of this precept is *pride.*

The tenth, against arrogance. On this law depends another: *that at the entrance into conditions of peace, no man require to reserve to himself any right which he is not content should be reserved to every one of the rest.* As it is necessary for all men that seek peace to lay down certain rights of nature—that is to say, not to have liberty to do all they list—so is it necessary for man's life to retain some, as right to govern their own bodies, enjoy air, water, motion, ways to go from place to place, and all things else without which a man cannot live or not live well. If in this case, at the making of peace, men require for themselves that which they would not have to be granted to others, they do contrary to the precedent law that commands the acknowledgment of natural equality and therefore also against the law of nature. The observers of this law are those we call *modest,* and the breakers *arrogant* men. The Greeks call the violation of this law πλεονεξία—that is, a desire of more than their share.

The eleventh, equity.

Also if *a man be trusted to judge between man and man,* it is a precept of the law of nature *that he deal equally between them.* For without that, the controversies of men cannot be determined but by war. He, therefore, that is partial in judgment does what in him lies to deter men from the use of judges and arbitrators, and consequently, against the fundamental law of nature, is the cause of war.

The observance of this law, from the equal distribution to each man of that which in reason belongs to him, is called EQUITY and, as I have said before, distributive justice; the violation, *acception of persons, προσωποληψία.*

The twelfth, equal use of things common.

And from this follows another law: *that such things as cannot be divided be enjoyed in common, if it can be; and if the quantity of the thing permit, without stint; otherwise proportionably to the number of them that have right.* For otherwise the distribution is unequal and contrary to equity.

The thirteenth, of lot.

But some things there be that can neither be divided nor enjoyed in common. Then the law of nature, which prescribes equity, requires *that the entire right, or else—making the use alternate—the first possession, be determined by lot.* For equal distribution is of the law of nature; and other means of equal distribution cannot be imagined.

The fourteenth, of primogeniture and first seizing.

Of *lots* there be two sorts: *arbitrary* and *natural.* Arbitrary is that which is agreed on by the competitors; natural is either *primogeniture* (which the Greek calls κληρονομία, which signifies *given by lot*) or *first seizure.*

And therefore those things which cannot be enjoyed in common, nor divided, ought to be adjudged to the first possessor; and in some cases to the first-born, as acquired by lot.

The fifteenth, of mediators. It is also a law of nature *that all men that mediate peace be allowed safe conduct.* For the law that commands peace, as the *end,* commands intercession, as the *means;* and to intercession the means is safe conduct.

The sixteenth, of submission to arbitrement. And because, though men be never so willing to observe these laws, there may nevertheless arise questions concerning a man's action— first, whether it were done or not done; secondly, if done, whether against the law or not against the law; the former whereof is called a question *of fact,* the latter a question *of right*—therefore, unless the parties to the question covenant mutually to stand to the sentence of another, they are as far from peace as ever. This other to whose sentence they submit is called an ARBITRATOR. And therefore it is of the law of nature *that they that are at controversy submit their right to the judgment of an arbitrator.*

The seventeenth, no man is his own judge. And seeing every man is presumed to do all things in order to his own benefit, no man is a fit arbitrator in his own cause; and if he were never so fit, yet, equity allowing to each party equal benefit, if one be admitted to be judge the other is to be admitted also; and so the controversy—that is, the cause of war— remains against the law of nature.

The eighteenth, no man to be judge that has in him a natural cause of partiality. For the same reason no man in any cause ought to be received for arbitrator to whom greater profit or honor or pleasure apparently arises out of the victory of one party than of the other; for he has taken, though an unavoidable bribe, yet a bribe, and no man can be obliged to trust him. And thus also the controversy and the condition of war remains, contrary to the law of nature.

The nineteenth, of witnesses. And in a controversy of *fact,* the judge being to give no more credit to one than to the other, if there be no other arguments, must give credit to a third, or to a third and fourth, no more; for else the question is undecided and left to force, contrary to the law of nature.

These are the laws of nature dictating peace for a means of the conservation of men in multitudes, and which only concern the doctrine of civil society. There be other things tending to the destruction of particular men—as drunkenness and all other parts of intemperance—which may therefore also be reckoned among those things which the law of nature has forbidden, but are not necessary to be mentioned nor are pertinent enough to this place.

A rule by which the laws of nature may easily be examined. And though this may seem too subtle a deduction of the laws of nature to be taken notice of by all men—whereof the most part are too busy in getting food and the rest too negligent to understand—yet to leave all men inexcusable they have been contracted into one easy sum, intelligible even to the meanest capacity, and that is *Do not that to another which you would not have done to yourself;* which shows him that he has no more to do in learning the laws of nature but, when weighing the actions of other men with his own they seem too heavy, to put them into the other part of the balance and his own into their place, that his own passions and self-love may add nothing to the weight, and then there is none of these laws of nature that will not appear unto him very reasonable.

The laws of nature oblige in conscience always, but in effect then only when there is security. The laws of nature oblige *in foro interno*[3]— that is to say, they bind to a desire they should take place—but *in foro externo*[4]—that is, to the putting them in act—not always. For he that should be modest and tractable and perform all he promises in such time and place where no man else should do so should but make himself a prey to others and procure his own certain ruin, contrary to the ground of all laws of nature, which tend to nature's preservation. And again, he that, having sufficient security that others shall observe the same laws toward him, observes them not himself, seeks not peace but war and consequently the destruction of his nature by violence.

And whatsoever laws bind *in foro interno* may be broken, not only by a fact contrary to the law, but also by a fact according to it, in case a man think it contrary. For though his action in this

3 [In conscience.]   4 [In civil law.]

case be according to the law, yet his purpose was against the law, which, where the obligation is *in foro interno*, is a breach.

The laws of nature are eternal. The laws of nature are immutable and eternal, for injustice, ingratitude, arrogance, pride, iniquity, acception of persons, and the rest can never be made lawful. For it can never be that war shall preserve life and peace destroy it.

And yet easy. The same laws, because they oblige only to a desire and endeavor—I mean an unfeigned and constant endeavor—are easy to be observed. For in that they require nothing but endeavor, he that endeavors their performance fulfills them; and he that fulfills the law is just.

The science of these laws is the true moral philosophy. And the science of them is the true and only moral philosophy. For moral philosophy is nothing else but the science of what is *good* and *evil* in the conversation and society of mankind. *Good* and *evil* are names that signify our appetites and aversions, which in different tempers, customs, and doctrines of men are different; and divers men differ not only in their judgment on the senses of what is pleasant and unpleasant to the taste, smell, hearing, touch, and sight but also of what is conformable or disagreeable to reason in the actions of common life. Nay, the same man in divers times differs from himself, and one time praises—that is, calls good—what another time he dispraises and calls evil; from whence arise disputes, controversies, and at last war. And therefore so long as a man is in the condition of mere nature, which is a condition of war, private appetite is the measure of good and evil; and consequently all men agree on this: that peace is good, and therefore also the way or means of peace, which, as I have showed before, are *justice, gratitude, modesty, equity, mercy,* and the rest of the laws of nature, are good—that is to say, *moral virtues*—and their contrary *vices* evil. Now the science of virtue and vice is moral philosophy; and therefore the true doctrine of the laws of nature is the true moral philosophy. But the writers of moral philosophy, though they acknowledge the same virtues and vices, yet, not seeing wherein consisted their goodness nor that they come to be praised as the means of peaceable, sociable, and comfortable living, place them in a mediocrity of passions; as if not the cause but the degree of daring made fortitude, or not the cause but the quantity of a gift made liberality.

These dictates of reason men used to call by the name of laws, but improperly, for they are but conclusions or theorems concerning what conduces to the conservation and defense of themselves, whereas law, properly, is the word of him that by right has command over others. But yet if we consider the same theorems as delivered in the word of God, that by right commands all things, then are they properly called laws.

CHAPTER SIXTEEN

OF PERSONS, AUTHORS, AND THINGS PERSONATED

A person what.   A person is he *whose words or actions are considered either as his own or as representing the words or actions of another man or of any other thing to whom they are attributed, whether truly or by fiction.*

Person natural, and artificial.   When they are considered as his own, then is he called a *natural person;* and when they are considered as representing the words and actions of another, then is he a *feigned* or *artificial person.*

The word person, whence.   The word *person* is Latin, instead whereof the Greeks have πρόσωπον, which signifies the *face,* as *persona* in Latin signifies the *disguise* or *outward appearance* of a man, counterfeited on the stage, and sometimes more particularly that part of it which disguises the face, as a mask or vizard; and from the stage has been translated to any representer of speech and action, as well in tribunals as theaters. So that a *person* is the same that an *actor* is, both on the stage and in common conversation; and to *personate* is to *act* or *represent* himself or another; and he that acts another is said to bear his person or act in his name—in which sense Cicero uses it where he says, *Unus sustineo tres personas: mei, adversarii, et judicis;* I bear three persons: my own, my adversary's, and the judge's—and is called in divers occasions diversely, as a *representer* or *representative*, a *lieutenant*, a *vicar*, an *attorney*, a *deputy*, a *procurator*, an *actor*, and the like.

Of persons artificial, some have their words and actions
Actor. owned by those whom they represent. And then
the person is the *actor*, and he that owns his
Author. words and actions is the AUTHOR; in which case
the actor acts by authority. For that which in
speaking of goods and possessions is called an *owner*—and in
Latin *dominus,* in Greek κύριος—speaking of actions is called
author. And as the right of possession is called dominion, so the
Authority. right of doing any action is called AUTHORITY.
So that by *authority* is always understood a
right of doing any act; and *done by authority,* done by commission or license from him whose right it is.

From hence it follows that when the actor
Covenants by makes a covenant by authority, he binds
authority bind thereby the author no less than if he had made
the author. it himself, and no less subjects him to all the
consequences of the same. And therefore all that has been said
formerly (chap. xiv) of the nature of covenants between man
and man in their natural capacity is true also when they are
made by their actors, representers, or procurators that have authority from them, so far forth as is in their commission, but no
further.

And therefore he that makes a covenant with the actor or representer, not knowing the authority he has, does it at his own
peril. For no man is obliged by a covenant whereof he is not
author, nor consequently by a covenant made against or beside
But not the actor. the authority he gave. When the actor does anything against the law of nature by command of
the author, if he be obliged by former covenant to obey him,
not he but the author breaks the law of nature, for though the
action be against the law of nature, yet it is not his; but contrarily, to refuse to do it is against the law of nature that forbids
breach of covenant.

And he that makes a covenant with the author by mediation
The authority is to of the actor, not knowing what authority he
be shown. has, but only takes his word, in case such authority be not made manifest unto him upon
demand, is no longer obliged; for the covenant made with the

author is not valid without his counterassurance. But if he that so covenants knew beforehand he was to expect no other assurance than the actor's word, then is the covenant valid, because the actor in this case makes himself the author. And therefore, as when the authority is evident the covenant obliges the author, not the actor, so when the authority is feigned it obliges the actor only, there being no author but himself.

Things personated, inanimate. There are few things that are incapable of being represented by fiction. Inanimate things, as a church, a hospital, a bridge, may be personated by a rector, master, or overseer. But things inanimate cannot be authors, nor therefore give authority to their actors; yet the actors may have authority to procure their maintenance, given them by those that are owners or governors of those things. And therefore such things cannot be personated before there be some state of civil government. Like-

Irrational. wise children, fools, and madmen that have no use of reason may be personated by guardians or curators; but can be no authors, during that time, of any action done by them longer than, when they shall recover the use of reason, they shall judge the same reasonable. Yet during the folly, he that has right of governing them may give authority to the guardian. But this again has no place but in a state civil, because before such estate there is no dominion of persons.

False gods. An idol or mere figment of the brain may be personated, as were the gods of the heathen, which by such officers as the state appointed were personated and held possessions and other goods and rights which men from time to time dedicated and consecrated unto them. But idols cannot be authors, for an idol is nothing. The authority proceeded from the state, and therefore, before introduction of civil government, the gods of the heathen could not be personated.

The true God. The true God may be personated. As he was, first, by Moses, who governed the Israelites, that were not his but God's people, not in his own name, with *hoc dicit Moses,* but in God's name, with *hoc dicit Dominus.*[1] Secondly, by the Son of man, his own Son, our blessed Saviour Jesus Christ, that

1 [Thus saith Moses; thus saith the Lord.]

came to reduce the Jews and induce all nations into the kingdom of his father, not as of himself, but as sent from his father.
And thirdly, by the Holy Ghost, or Comforter, speaking and
working in the Apostles, which Holy Ghost was a Comforter
that came not of himself, but was sent and proceeded from them
both.

A multitude of men, how one person. A multitude of men are made *one* person when
they are by one man or one person represented,
so that it be done with the consent of every one
of that multitude in particular. For it is the *unity* of the representer, not the *unity* of the represented, that makes the person
one. And it is the representer that bears the person, and but one
person; and *unity* cannot otherwise be understood in multitude.

Everyone is author. And because the multitude naturally is not *one*
but *many,* they cannot be understood for one
but many authors of everything their representative says or does
in their name, every man giving their common representer authority from himself in particular and owning all the actions
the representer does, in case they give him authority without
stint; otherwise, when they limit him in what and how far he
shall represent them, none of them owns more than they gave
him commission to act.

An actor may be many men made one by plurality of voices. And if the representative consist of many men,
the voice of the greater number must be con-
sidered as the voice of them all. For if the lesser
number pronounce, for example, in the affirm-
ative, and the greater in the negative, there will be negatives
more than enough to destroy the affirmatives; and thereby the
excess of negatives, standing uncontradicted, are the only voice
the representative has.

Representatives, when the number is even, unprofitable. And a representative of even number, especially when the number is not great, whereby
the contradictory voices are oftentimes equal,
is therefore oftentimes mute and incapable of
action. Yet in some cases contradictory voices equal in number
may determine a question, as in condemning or absolving equality of votes, even in that they condemn not, do absolve, but not
on the contrary condemn in that they absolve not. For when a

cause is heard, not to condemn is to absolve; but on the contrary, to say that not absolving is condemning is not true. The like it is in a deliberation of executing presently or deferring till another time, for when the voices are equal, the not decreeing execution is a decree of dilation.

Negative voice. Or if the number be odd, as three or more men or assemblies, whereof everyone has by a negative voice authority to take away the effect of all the affirmative voices of the rest, this number is no representative; because by the diversity of opinions and interests of men it becomes oftentimes, and in cases of the greatest consequence, a mute person and unapt, as for many things else, so for the government of a multitude, especially in time of war.

Of authors there be two sorts. The first simply so called, which I have before defined to be him that owns the action of another simply. The second is he that owns an action or covenant of another conditionally—that is to say, he undertakes to do it if the other does it not at or before a certain time. And these authors conditional are generally called SURETIES—in Latin *fidejussores* and *sponsores,* and particularly for debt, *prædes,* and for appearance before a judge or magistrate, *vades.*

OF COMMONWEALTH

PART TWO: OF COMMONWEALTH

CHAPTER SEVENTEEN

OF THE CAUSES, GENERATION, AND DEFINITION OF A COMMONWEALTH

The end of commonwealth, particular security. The final cause, end, or design of men, who naturally love liberty and dominion over others, in the introduction of that restraint upon themselves in which we see them live in commonwealths is the foresight of their own preservation, and of a more contented life thereby—that is to say, of getting themselves out from that miserable condition of war which is necessarily consequent, as has been shown (chapter XIII), to the natural passions of men when there is no visible power to keep them in awe and tie them by fear of punishment to the performance of their covenants and observation of those laws of nature set down in the fourteenth and fifteenth chapters.

Which is not to be had from the law of nature. For the laws of nature—as *justice, equity, modesty, mercy,* and, in sum, *doing to others as we would be done to*—of themselves, without the terror of some power to cause them to be observed, are contrary to our natural passions, that carry us to partiality, pride, revenge, and the like. And covenants without the sword are but words, and of no strength to secure a man at all. Therefore, notwithstanding the laws of nature (which everyone has then kept when he has the will to keep them, when he can do it safely), if there be no power erected, or not great enough for our security, every man will—and may lawfully—rely on his own strength and art for caution against all other men. And in all places where men have lived by small families, to rob and spoil one another has been a trade, and so far from being reputed against the law of nature that the greater spoils they gained, the greater was their honor; and men observed no other laws therein but the laws of honor—that is, to abstain from cruelty, leaving to men their lives and instruments of husbandry. And as small families did then, so now do cities and kingdoms, which are but greater families, for their own security enlarge their dominions upon all pretenses of danger and fear of invasion or assistance that may be given to invaders, and endeavor as much as they can to subdue or weaken their neighbors by open force and secret arts, for want of other caution, justly; and are remembered for it in after ages with honor.

Nor from the conjunction of a few men or families. Nor is it the joining together of a small number of men that gives them this security, because in small numbers small additions on the one side or the other make the advantage of strength so great as is sufficient to carry the victory, and therefore gives encouragement to an invasion. The multitude sufficient to confide in for our security is not determined by any certain number but by comparison with the enemy we fear, and is then sufficient when the odds of the enemy is not of so visible and conspicuous moment to determine the event of war as to move him to attempt.

Nor from a great multitude, unless directed by one judgment. And be there never so great a multitude, yet if their actions be directed according to their particular judgments and particular appetites, they can expect thereby no defense nor protection, neither against a common enemy nor against the injuries of one another. For being distracted in opinions concerning the best use and application of their strength, they do not help but hinder one another, and reduce their strength by mutual opposition to nothing; whereby they are easily not only subdued by a very few that agree together, but also, when there is no common enemy, they make war upon each other for their particular interest. For if we could suppose a great multitude of men to consent in the observation of justice and other laws of nature without a common power to keep them all in awe, we might as well suppose all mankind to do the same; and then there neither would be, nor need to be, any civil government or commonwealth at all, because there would be peace without subjection.

Nor is it enough for the security which men de-
And that con-
tinually.
sire should last all the time of their life that
they be governed and directed by one judg-
ment for a limited time, as in one battle or one war. For though
they obtain a victory by their unanimous endeavor against a
foreign enemy, yet afterwards, when either they have no common enemy or he that by one part is held for an enemy is by another part held for a friend, they must needs, by the difference
of their interests, dissolve and fall again into a war among
themselves.

It is true that certain living creatures, as bees
Why certain crea-
tures without reason
or speech do never-
theless live in soci-
ety, without any
coercive power.
and ants, live sociably one with another—
which are therefore by Aristotle numbered
among political creatures—and yet have no
other direction than their particular judgments and appetites, nor speech whereby one
of them can signify to another what he thinks expedient for the
common benefit; and therefore some man may perhaps desire
to know why mankind cannot do the same. To which I answer:

First, that men are continually in competition for honor and
dignity, which these creatures are not; and consequently among
men there arises on that ground envy and hatred and finally
war, but among these not so.

Secondly, that among these creatures the common good differs
not from the private; and being by nature inclined to their private, they procure thereby the common benefit. But man, whose
joy consists in comparing himself with other men, can relish
nothing but what is eminent.

Thirdly, that these creatures—having not, as man, the use of
reason—do not see nor think they see any fault in the administration of their common business; whereas among men there
are very many that think themselves wiser and abler to govern
the public better than the rest, and these strive to reform and
innovate, one this way, another that way, and thereby bring it
into distraction and civil war.

Fourthly, that these creatures, though they have some use of
voice in making known to one another their desires and other
affections, yet they want that art of words by which some men
can represent to others that which is good in the likeness of evil,

and evil in the likeness of good, and augment or diminish the apparent greatness of good and evil, discontenting men and troubling their peace at their pleasure.

Fifthly, irrational creatures cannot distinguish between *injury* and *damage,* and therefore, as long as they be at ease, they are not offended with their fellows; whereas man is then most troublesome when he is most at ease, for then it is that he loves to show his wisdom and control the actions of them that govern the commonwealth.

Lastly, the agreement of these creatures is natural, that of men is by covenant only, which is artificial; and therefore it is no wonder if there be somewhat else required besides covenant to make their agreement constant and lasting, which is a common power to keep them in awe and to direct their actions to the common benefit.

The only way to erect such a common power as *The generation of a* may be able to defend them from the invasion *commonwealth.* of foreigners and the injuries of one another, and thereby to secure them in such sort as that by their own industry and by the fruits of the earth they may nourish themselves and live contentedly, is to confer all their power and strength upon one man, or upon one assembly of men that may reduce all their wills, by plurality of voices, unto one will; which is as much as to say, to appoint one man or assembly of men to bear their person, and everyone to own and acknowledge himself to be author of whatsoever he that so bears their person shall act or cause to be acted in those things which concern the common peace and safety, and therein to submit their wills every one to his will, and their judgments to his judgment. This is more than consent or concord; it is a real unity of them all in one and the same person, made by covenant of every man with every man, in such manner as if every man should say to every man, *I authorize and give up my right of governing myself to this man, or to this assembly of men, on this condition, that you give up your right to him and authorize all his actions in like manner.* This done, the multitude so united in one person is called a COMMONWEALTH, in Latin CIVITAS. This is the generation of that great LEVIATHAN (or rather, to speak more reverently, of that *mortal god*) to which we owe, under the *im-*

mortal God, our peace and defense. For by this authority, given him by every particular man in the commonwealth, he has the use of so much power and strength conferred on him that, by terror thereof, he is enabled to form the wills of them all to peace at home and mutual aid against their enemies abroad. And in him consists the essence of the commonwealth, which,

The definition of a commonwealth.
to define it, is *one person, of whose acts a great multitude, by mutual covenants one with another, have made themselves every one the author, to the end he may use the strength and means of them all as he shall think expedient for their peace and common defense.*

Sovereign and subject, what.
And he that carries this person is called SOVEREIGN and said to have *sovereign power;* and everyone besides, his SUBJECT.

The attaining to this sovereign power is by two ways. One, by natural force, as when a man makes his children to submit themselves and their children to his government, as being able to destroy them if they refuse, or by war subdues his enemies to his will, giving them their lives on that condition. The other is when men agree among themselves to submit to some man or assembly of men voluntarily, on confidence to be protected by him against all others. This latter may be called a political commonwealth, or commonwealth by *institution,* and the former a commonwealth by *acquisition.* And first I shall speak of a commonwealth by institution.

CHAPTER EIGHTEEN

OF THE RIGHTS OF SOVEREIGNS BY INSTITUTION

The act of instituting a commonwealth, what.
A *commonwealth* is said to be *instituted* when a *multitude* of men do agree and *covenant, every one with every one,* that to whatsoever *man* or *assembly of men* shall be given by the major part the *right* to *present* the person of them all—that is to say, to be their

representative—every one, as well he that *voted for it* as he that *voted against it,* shall *authorize* all the actions and judgments of that man or assembly of men in the same manner as if they were his own, to the end to live peaceably among themselves and be protected against other men.

The consequences to such institutions, are: From this institution of a commonwealth are derived all the *rights* and *faculties* of him or them on whom the sovereign power is conferred by the consent of the people assembled.

1. *The subjects cannot change the form of government.* First, because they covenant, it is to be understood they are not obliged by former covenant to anything repugnant hereunto. And consequently they that have already instituted a commonwealth, being thereby bound by covenant to own the actions and judgments of one, cannot lawfully make a new covenant among themselves to be obedient to any other, in anything whatsoever, without his permission. And therefore, they that are subjects to a monarch cannot without his leave cast off monarchy and return to the confusion of a disunited multitude, nor transfer their person from him that bears it to another man or other assembly of men; for they are bound, every man to every man, to own and be reputed author of all that he that already is their sovereign shall do and judge fit to be done; so that any one man dissenting, all the rest should break their covenant made to that man, which is injustice; and they have also every man given the sovereignty to him that bears their person, and therefore if they depose him they take from him that which is his own, and so again it is injustice. Besides, if he that attempts to depose his sovereign be killed or punished by him for such attempt, he is author of his own punishment, as being by the institution author of all his sovereign shall do; and because it is injustice for a man to do anything for which he may be punished by his own authority, he is also upon that title unjust. And whereas some men have pretended for their disobedience to their sovereign a new covenant, made not with men but with God, this also is unjust; for there is no covenant with God but by mediation of somebody that represents God's person, which none does but God's lieutenant, who has the sovereignty under God. But this

pretense of covenant with God is so evident a lie, even in the pretenders' own consciences, that it is not only an act of an unjust but also of a vile and unmanly disposition.

Secondly, because the right of bearing the person of them all is given to him they make sovereign by covenant only of one to another and not of him to any of them, there can happen no breach of covenant on the part of the sovereign; and consequently none of his subjects, by any pretense of forfeiture, can be freed from his subjection. That he which is made sovereign makes no covenant with his subjects beforehand is manifest, because either he must make it with the whole multitude, as one party to the covenant, or he must make a several covenant with every man. With the whole, as one party, it is impossible because as yet they are not one person; and if he make so many several covenants as there be men, those covenants after he has the sovereignty are void because what act soever can be pretended by any one of them for breach thereof is the act both of himself and of all the rest, because done in the person and by the right of every one of them in particular. Besides, if any one or more of them pretend a breach of the covenant made by the sovereign at his institution, and others, or one other of his subjects, or himself alone, pretend there was no such breach, there is in this case no judge to decide the controversy; it returns therefore to the sword again, and every man recovers the right of protecting himself by his own strength, contrary to the design they had in the institution. It is therefore in vain to grant sovereignty by way of precedent covenant. The opinion that any monarch receives his power by covenant—that is to say, on condition—proceeds from want of understanding this easy truth: that covenants, being but words and breath, have no force to oblige, contain, constrain, or protect any man but what it has from the public sword—that is, from the untied hands of that man or assembly of men that has the sovereignty, and whose actions are avouched by them all and performed by the strength of them all in him united. But when an assembly of men is made sovereign, then no man imagines any such covenant to have passed in the institution; for no man is so dull as to say, for example, the peo-

2. Sovereign power cannot be forfeited.

ple of Rome made a covenant with the Romans to hold the sovereignty on such or such conditions, which not performed, the Romans might lawfully depose the Roman people. That men see not the reason to be alike in a monarchy and in a popular government proceeds from the ambition of some that are kinder to the government of an assembly, whereof they may hope to participate, than of monarchy, which they despair to enjoy.

3. No man can without injustice protest against the institution of the sovereign declared by the major part. Thirdly, because the major part has by consenting voices declared a sovereign, he that dissented must now consent with the rest—that is, be contented to avow all the actions he shall do —or else justly be destroyed by the rest. For if he voluntarily entered into the congregation of them that were assembled, he sufficiently declared thereby his will, and therefore tacitly covenanted, to stand to what the major part should ordain; and therefore, if he refuse to stand thereto or make protestation against any of their decrees, he does contrary to his covenant, and therefore unjustly. And whether he be of the congregation or not, and whether his consent be asked or not, he must either submit to their decrees or be left in the condition of war he was in before, wherein he might without injustice be destroyed by any man whatsoever.

4. The sovereign's actions cannot be justly accused by the subject. Fourthly, because every subject is by this institution author of all the actions and judgments of the sovereign instituted, it follows that whatsoever he does, it can be no injury to any of his subjects; nor ought he to be by any of them accused of injustice. For he that does anything by authority from another does therein no injury to him by whose authority he acts; but by this institution of a commonwealth, every particular man is author of all the sovereign does; and consequently he that complains of injury from his sovereign complains of that whereof he himself is author, and therefore ought not to accuse any man but himself—no, nor himself of injury, because to do injury to one's self is impossible. It is true that they that have sovereign power may commit iniquity, but not injustice or injury in the proper signification.

5. *Whatsoever the sovereign does is unpunishable by the subject.*

Fifthly, and consequently to that which was said last, no man that has sovereign power can justly be put to death or otherwise in any manner by his subjects punished. For seeing every subject is author of the actions of his sovereign, he punishes another for the actions committed by himself.

6. *The sovereign is judge of what is necessary for the peace and defense of his subjects.*

And because the end of this institution is the peace and defense of them all, and whosoever has right to the end has right to the means, it belongs of right to whatsoever man or assembly that has the sovereignty to be judge both of the means of peace and defense and also of the hindrances and disturbances of the same, and to do whatsoever he shall think necessary to be done, both beforehand, for the preserving of peace and security by prevention of discord at home and hostility from abroad, and, when peace and security are lost, for the recovery of the same. And therefore,

And judge of what doctrines are fit to be taught them.

Sixthly, it is annexed to the sovereignty to be judge of what opinions and doctrines are averse and what conducing to peace, and consequently on what occasions, how far, and what men are to be trusted withal in speaking to multitudes of people, and who shall examine the doctrines of all books before they be published. For the actions of men proceed from their opinions, and in the well-governing of opinions consists the well-governing of men's actions, in order to their peace and concord. And though in matter of doctrine nothing ought to be regarded but the truth, yet this is not repugnant to regulating the same by peace. For doctrine repugnant to peace can no more be true than peace and concord can be against the law of nature. It is true that in a commonwealth, where by the negligence or unskillfulness of governors and teachers false doctrines are by time generally received, the contrary truths may be generally offensive. Yet the most sudden and rough bustling in of a new truth that can be does never break the peace but only sometimes awake the war. For those men that are so remissly governed that they dare take up arms to defend or introduce an opinion are still in war, and their condition not peace but only a cessation of arms for fear of one another, and they live, as it were, in the precincts of battle continually. It belongs therefore to him that has the sovereign power to be judge or constitute all judges of opinions and doctrines as a thing necessary to peace, thereby to prevent discord and civil war.

7. The right of making rules; whereby the subjects may every man know what is so his own, as no other subject can without injustice take it from him. Seventhly is annexed to the sovereignty the whole power of prescribing the rules whereby every man may know what goods he may enjoy and what actions he may do without being molested by any of his fellow subjects; and this is it men call *propriety*. For before constitution of sovereign power, as has already been shown, all men had right to all things, which necessarily causes war; and therefore this propriety, being necessary to peace and depending on sovereign power, is the act of that power in order to the public peace. These rules of propriety, or *meum* and *tuum*,[1] and of *good, evil, lawful,* and *unlawful* in the actions of subjects, are the civil laws—that is to say, the laws of each commonwealth in particular—though the name of civil law be now restrained to the ancient civil laws of the city of Rome, which being the head of a great part of the world, her laws at that time were in these parts the civil law.

8. To him also belongs the right of all judicature and decision of controversy. Eighthly is annexed to the sovereignty the right of judicature—that is to say, of hearing and deciding all controversies which may arise concerning law, either civil or natural, or concerning fact. For without the decision of controversies, there is no protection of one subject against the injuries of another; the laws concerning *meum* and *tuum* are in vain; and to every man remains, from the natural and necessary appetite of his own conservation, the right of protecting himself by his private strength, which is the condition of war and contrary to the end for which every commonwealth is instituted.

9. And of making war and peace as he shall think best. Ninthly is annexed to the sovereignty the right of making war and peace with other nations and commonwealths—that is to say, of judging when it is for the public good, and how great forces are to be assembled, armed, and paid for that end, and to

1 [Mine and thine.]

levy money upon the subjects to defray the expenses thereof. For the power by which the people are to be defended consists in their armies, and the strength of an army in the union of their strength under one command, which command the sovereign instituted therefore has; because the command of the *militia,* without other institution, makes him that has it sovereign. And therefore whosoever is made general of an army, he that has the sovereign power is always generalissimo.

10. *And of choosing all counselors and ministers, both of peace and war.*   Tenthly is annexed to the sovereignty the choosing of all counselors, ministers, magistrates, and officers, both in peace and war. For seeing the sovereign is charged with the end, which is the common peace and defense, he is understood to have power to use such means as he shall think most fit for his discharge.

11. *And of rewarding and punishing, and that (where no former law has determined the measure of it) arbitrarily.*   Eleventhly, to the sovereign is committed the power of rewarding with riches or honor, and of punishing with corporal or pecuniary punishment or with ignominy, every subject according to the law he has formerly made; or if there be no law made, according as he shall judge most to conduce to the encouraging of men to serve the commonwealth or deterring of them from doing disservice to the same.

12. *And of honor and order.*   Lastly, considering what value men are naturally apt to set upon themselves, what respect they look for from others, and how little they value other men—from whence continually arise among them emulation, quarrels, factions, and at last war, to the destroying of one another and diminution of their strength against a common enemy—it is necessary that there be laws of honor and a public rate of the worth of such men as have deserved or are able to deserve well of the commonwealth, and that there be force in the hands of some or other to put those laws in execution. But it has already been shown that not only the whole *militia* or forces of the commonwealth, but also the judicature of all controversies is annexed to the sovereignty. To the sovereign therefore it belongs also to give titles of honor, and to appoint what order of place and dignity each man shall hold, and

what signs of respect, in public or private meetings, they shall give to one another.

These rights are indivisible. These are the rights which make the essence of sovereignty, and which are the marks whereby a man may discern in what man or assembly of men the sovereign power is placed and resides. For these are incommunicable and inseparable. The power to coin money, to dispose of the estate and persons of infant heirs, to have preemption in markets, and all other statute prerogatives may be transferred by the sovereign, and yet the power to protect his subjects be retained. But if he transfer the *militia,* he retains the judicature in vain for want of execution of the laws; or if he grant away the power of raising money, the *militia* is in vain; or if he give away the government of doctrines, men will be frighted into rebellion with the fear of spirits. And so if we consider any one of the said rights, we shall presently see that the holding of all the rest will produce no effect in the conservation of peace and justice, the end for which all commonwealths are instituted. And this division is it whereof it is said *a kingdom divided in itself cannot stand;* [2] for unless this division precede, division into opposite armies can never happen. If there had not first been an opinion received of the greatest part of England that these powers were divided between the King and the Lords and the House of Commons, the people had never been divided and fallen into this civil war—first between those that disagreed in politics and after between the dissenters about the liberty of religion—which has so instructed men in this point of sovereign right that there be few now in England that do not see that these rights are inseparable and will be so generally acknowledged at the next return of peace; [3] and so continue till their miseries are forgotten, and no longer, except the vulgar be better taught than they have hitherto been.

2 [Matt. 12: 25; Mark 3: 24; Luke 11: 17.]

3 [Hobbes wrote in the midst of the Great Rebellion, the English civil wars (1641-46, 1648-52) which grew out of the conflict between King and Parliament over those powers which Hobbes declares to be indivisibly the possession of the sovereign. The civil wars and later constitutional developments firmly established the supremacy of Parliament.]

And can by no grant pass away without direct renouncing of the sovereign power. And because they are essential and inseparable rights, it follows necessarily that in whatsoever words any of them seem to be granted away, yet if the sovereign power itself be not in direct terms renounced and the name of sovereign no more given by the grantees to him that grants them, the grant is void; for when he has granted all he can, if we grant back the sovereignty all is restored as inseparably annexed thereunto.

The power and honor of subjects vanishes in the presence of the power sovereign. This great authority being indivisible and inseparably annexed to the sovereignty, there is little ground for the opinion of them that say of sovereign kings, though they be *singulis majores,* of greater power than every one of their subjects, yet they be *universis minores,* or less power than them all together. For if by *all together* they mean not the collective body as one person, then *all together* and *every one* signify the same, and the speech is absurd. But if by *all together* they understand them as one person, which person the sovereign bears, then the power of all together is the same with the sovereign's power, and so again the speech is absurd; which absurdity they see well enough when the sovereignty is in an assembly of the people, but in a monarch they see it not; and yet the power of sovereignty is the same in whomsoever it be placed.

And as the power, so also the honor of the sovereign ought to be greater than that of any or all the subjects. For in the sovereignty is the fountain of honor. The dignities of lord, earl, duke, and prince are his creatures. As in the presence of the master the servants are equal, and without any honor at all, so are the subjects in the presence of the sovereign. And though they shine some more, some less, when they are out of his sight, yet in his presence they shine no more than the stars in the presence of the sun.

Sovereign power not so hurtful as the want of it, and the hurt proceeds for the greatest part from not submitting readily to a less. But a man may here object that the condition of subjects is very miserable, as being obnoxious to the lusts and other irregular passions of him or them that have so unlimited a power in their hands. And commonly they that live under a monarch think it the fault of monarchy, and they that live under the government of democracy or other sovereign assembly attribute all the inconvenience to that form of commonwealth, whereas the power in all forms, if they be perfect enough to protect them, is the same—not considering that the state of man can never be without some incommodity or other, and that the greatest that in any form of government can possibly happen to the people in general is scarce sensible in respect of the miseries and horrible calamities that accompany a civil war or that dissolute condition of masterless men, without subjection to laws and a coercive power to tie their hands from rapine and revenge; nor considering that the greatest pressure of sovereign governors proceeds not from any delight or profit they can expect in the damage or weakening of their subjects, in whose vigor consists their own strength and glory, but in the restiveness of themselves that, unwillingly contributing to their own defense, make it necessary for their governors to draw from them what they can in time of peace that they may have means on any emergent occasion or sudden need to resist or take advantage on their enemies. For all men are by nature provided of notable multiplying glasses—that is, their passions and self-love—through which every little payment appears a great grievance, but are destitute of those prospective glasses—namely, moral and civil science—to see afar off the miseries that hang over them and cannot without such payments be avoided.

CHAPTER NINETEEN

OF THE SEVERAL KINDS OF COMMONWEALTH BY INSTITUTION, AND OF SUCCESSION OF THE SOVEREIGN POWER

The different forms of commonwealths but three. The difference of commonwealths consists in the difference of the sovereign, or the person representative of all and every one of the multitude. And because the sovereignty is either in one man or in an assembly of more than one, and into that assembly either every man has right to enter, or not every one but certain men distinguished from the rest, it is manifest there can be but three kinds of commonwealth. For the representative must needs be one man or more, and if more then it is the assembly of all or but of a part. When the representative is one man, then is the commonwealth a MONARCHY; when an assembly of all that will come together, then it is a DEMOCRACY or popular commonwealth; when an assembly of a part only, then it is called an ARISTOCRACY. Other kind of commonwealth there can be none, for either one or more or all must have the sovereign power, which I have shown to be indivisible, entire.

Tyranny and oligarchy but different names of monarchy and aristocracy. There be other names of government in the histories and books of policy, as *tyranny* and *oligarchy;* but they are not the names of other forms of government, but of the same forms misliked. For they that are discontented under *monarchy* call it *tyranny,* and they that are displeased with *aristocracy* call it *oligarchy;* so also, they which find themselves grieved under a *democracy* call it *anarchy,* which signifies want of government, and yet I think no man believes that want of government is any new kind of government; nor by the same reason ought they to believe that the government is of one kind when they like it and another when they mislike it or are oppressed by the governors.

Subordinate representatives dangerous. It is manifest that men who are in absolute liberty may, if they please, give authority to one man to represent them every one as well as give such authority to any assembly of men whatsoever, and consequently may subject themselves, if they think good, to a monarch as absolutely as to any other representative. Therefore, where there is already erected a sovereign power, there can be no other representative of the same people, but only to certain particular ends, by the sovereign limited. For that were to erect two sovereigns, and every man to have his person represented by two actors that, by opposing one another, must needs divide that power which, if men will live in peace, is indivisible, and thereby reduce the multitude into the condition of war, contrary to the end for which all sovereignty is instituted. And therefore as it is absurd to think that a sovereign assembly, inviting the people of their dominion to send up their deputies with power to make known their advice or desires, should therefore hold such deputies rather than themselves for the absolute representatives of the people, so it is absurd also to think the same in a monarchy. And I know not how this so manifest a truth should of late be so little observed that in a monarchy he that had the sovereignty from a descent of six hundred years, was alone called sovereign, had the title of Majesty from every one of his subjects, and was unquestionably taken by them for their king, was notwithstanding never considered as their representative, the name without contradiction passing for the title of those men which at his command were sent up by the people to carry their petitions and give him, if he permitted it, their advice.[1] Which may serve as an admonition for those that are the true and absolute representative of a people to instruct men in the nature of that office, and to take heed how they admit of any other general representation upon any occasion whatsoever, if they mean to discharge the trust committed to them.

Comparison of monarchy with sovereign assemblies. The difference between these three kinds of commonwealth consists not in the difference of power but in the difference of convenience or aptitude to produce the peace and security of the people, for which end they were instituted. And to compare monarchy with the other two, we may observe, first, that whosoever bears the person of the people, or is one of that assembly that bears it, bears also his own natural person. And though he be careful in his politic person to procure the common interest, yet he is more or no less careful to procure the private good of himself, his family, kindred, and friends; and for the most part, if the public interest chance to cross the private, he prefers the private; for the passions of men are commonly more potent than their reason. From whence it follows that where the public and private interest are most closely united, there is the public most advanced. Now in monarchy the private interest is the same with the public. The riches, power, and honor of a monarch arise only from the riches, strength, and reputation of his subjects. For no king can be rich nor glorious nor secure whose

1 [Hobbes is speaking of Charles I, in whose reign, which began in 1625, the contest between King and Parliament culminated in civil war. Charles was beheaded in 1649.]

subjects are either poor or contemptible or too weak through want or dissension to maintain a war against their enemies; whereas in a democracy or aristocracy, the public prosperity confers not so much to the private fortune of one that is corrupt or ambitious as does many times a perfidious advice, a treacherous action, or a civil war.

Secondly, that a monarch receives counsel of whom, when, and where he pleases, and consequently may hear the opinion of men versed in the matter about which he deliberates of what rank or quality soever, and as long before the time of action and with as much secrecy as he will. But when a sovereign assembly has need of counsel, none are admitted but such as have a right thereto from the beginning, which for the most part are of those who have been versed more in the acquisition of wealth than of knowledge, and are to give their advice in long discourses which may and do commonly excite men to action but not govern them in it. For the *understanding* is by the flame of the passions never enlightened but dazzled. Nor is there any place or time wherein an assembly can receive counsel with secrecy because of their own multitude.

Thirdly, that the resolutions of a monarch are subject to no other inconstancy than that of human nature; but in assemblies, besides that of nature, there arises an inconstancy from the number. For the absence of a few that would have the resolution, once taken, continue firm—which may happen by security, negligence, or private impediments—or the diligent appearance of a few of the contrary opinion undoes today all that was concluded yesterday.

Fourthly, that a monarch cannot disagree with himself out of envy or interest, but an assembly may, and that to such a height as may produce a civil war.

Fifthly, that in monarchy there is this inconvenience: that any subject, by the power of one man, for the enriching of a favorite or flatterer, may be deprived of all he possesses, which I confess is a great and inevitable inconvenience. But the same may as well happen where the sovereign power is in an assembly; for their power is the same, and they are as subject to evil counsel and to be seduced by orators as a monarch by flatterers, and, becoming one another's flatterers, serve one another's covetousness and ambition by turns. And whereas the favorites of monarchs are few, and they have none else to advance but their own kindred, the favorites of an assembly are many, and the kindred much more numerous than of any monarch. Besides, there is no favorite of a monarch which cannot as well succor his friends as hurt his enemies; but orators—that is to say, favorites of sovereign assemblies—though they have great power to hurt, have little to save. For to accuse requires less eloquence— such is man's nature—than to excuse; and condemnation than absolution more resembles justice.

Sixthly, that it is an inconvenience in monarchy that the sovereignty may descend upon an infant or one that cannot discern between good and evil, and consists in this: that the use of his power must be in the hand of another man or of some assembly of men which are to govern by his right and in his name as curators and protectors of his person and authority. But to say there is inconvenience in putting the use of the sovereign power into the hand of a man or an assembly of men is to say that all government is more inconvenient than confusion and civil war. And therefore all the danger that can be pretended must arise from the contention of those that for an office of so great honor and profit may become competitors. To make it appear that this inconvenience proceeds not from that form of government we call monarchy, we are to consider that the precedent monarch has appointed who shall have the tuition of his infant successor, either expressly by testament or tacitly by not controlling the custom in that case received; and then such inconvenience, if it happen, is to be attributed not to the monarchy but to the ambition and injustice of the subjects, which in all kinds of government where the people are not well instructed in their duty and the rights of sovereignty is the same. Or else the precedent monarch has not at all taken order for such tuition; and then the law of nature has provided this sufficient rule: that the tuition shall be in him that has by nature most interest in the preservation of the authority of the infant, and to whom least benefit can accrue by his death or diminution. For seeing every man by nature seeks his own benefit and promotion, to put an infant into the power of those that can promote themselves by his destruction or damage is not tuition but treachery. So that

sufficient provision being taken against all just quarrel about
the government under a child, if any contention arise to the disturbance of the public peace, it is not to be attributed to the
form of monarchy but to the ambition of subjects and ignorance of their duty. On the other side, there is no great commonwealth the sovereignty whereof is in a great assembly which
is not, as to consultations of peace and war and making of laws,
in the same condition as if the government were in a child. For
as a child wants the judgment to dissent from counsel given
him, and is thereby necessitated to take the advice of them or
him to whom he is committed, so an assembly wants the liberty
to dissent from the counsel of the major part, be it good or bad.
And as a child has need of a tutor or protector to preserve his
person and authority; so also in great commonwealths the sovereign assembly, in all great dangers and troubles, have need of
custodes libertatis [2]—that is, of dictators or protectors of their
authority—which are as much as temporary monarchs to whom
for a time they may commit the entire exercise of their power,
and have at the end of that time been oftener deprived thereof
than infant kings by their protectors, regents, or any other
tutors.

Though the kinds of sovereignty be, as I have now shown,
but three—that is to say, monarchy, where one man has it; or
democracy, where the general assembly of subjects has it; or
aristocracy, where it is in an assembly of certain persons nomi-
nated or otherwise distinguished from the rest—yet he that shall
consider the particular commonwealths that have been and are
in the world will not perhaps easily reduce them to three, and
may thereby be inclined to think there be other forms arising
from these mingled together. As, for example, elective kingdoms where kings have the sovereign power put into their
hands for a time, or kingdoms wherein the king has a power
limited, which governments are nevertheless by most writers
called monarchy. Likewise if a popular or aristocratical commonwealth subdue an enemy's country, and govern the same by
a president, procurator, or other magistrate, this may seem perhaps at first sight to be a democratical or aristocratical govern-

2 [Guardians of liberty.]

ment. But it is not so. For elective kings are not sovereigns but ministers of the sovereign, nor limited kings sovereigns but ministers of them that have the sovereign power; nor are those provinces which are in subjection to a democracy or aristocracy of another commonwealth democratically or aristocratically governed, but monarchically.

And first, concerning an elective king, whose power is limited to his life, as it is in many places of Christendom at this day, or to certain years or months, as the dictator's power among the Romans: if he have right to appoint his successor, he is no more elective but hereditary. But if he have no power to elect his successor, then there is some other man or assembly known which after his decease may elect anew, or else the commonwealth dies and dissolves with him and returns to the condition of war. If it be known who have the power to give the sovereignty after his death, it is known also that the sovereignty was in them before; for none have right to give that which they have not right to possess and keep to themselves if they think good. But if there be none that can give the sovereignty after the decease of him that was first elected, then has he power—nay, he is obliged by the law of nature—to provide, by establishing his successor, to keep those that had trusted him with the government from relapsing into the miserable condition of civil war. And consequently he was, when elected, a sovereign absolute.

Secondly, that king whose power is limited is not superior to him or them that have the power to limit it; and he that is not superior is not supreme—that is to say, not sovereign. The sovereignty, therefore, was always in that assembly which had the right to limit him; and by consequence the government not monarchy, but either democracy or aristocracy—as of old time in Sparta, where the kings had a privilege to lead their armies, but the sovereignty was in the Ephori.[3]

Thirdly, whereas heretofore the Roman people governed the land of Judea, for example, by a president, yet was not Judea therefore a democracy, because they were not governed by any

[3] [From the 5th century B.C. through the 2nd century A.D., the Spartan state was dominated by the five annually elected Ephors. As the interpreters of the laws, they arrogated to themselves executive and judicial authority greater even than the kings', whom they entirely controlled.]

assembly into the which any of them had right to enter; nor an aristocracy, because they were not governed by any assembly into which any man could enter by their election; but they were governed by one person, which, though as to the people of Rome was an assembly of the people, or democracy, yet as to the people of Judea, which had no right at all of participating in the government, was a monarch. For though where the people are governed by an assembly, chosen by themselves out of their own number, the government is called a democracy or aristocracy, yet when they are governed by an assembly not of their own choosing, it is a monarchy, not of *one* man over another man, but of one people over another people.

Of all these forms of government, the matter *Of the right of* being mortal, so that not only monarchs but *succession.* also whole assemblies die, it is necessary for the conservation of the peace of men that as there was order taken for an artificial man, so there be order also taken for an artificial eternity of life; without which men that are governed by an assembly should return into the condition of war in every age, and they that are governed by one man as soon as their governor dies. This artificial eternity is that which men call the right of *succession*.

There is no perfect form of government where the disposing of the succession is not in the present sovereign. For if it be in any other particular man or private assembly, it is in a person subject and may be assumed by the sovereign at his pleasure; and consequently the right is in himself. And if it be in no particular man but left to a new choice, then is the commonwealth dissolved and the right is in him that can get it, contrary to the intention of them that did institute the commonwealth for their perpetual, and not temporary, security.

In a democracy, the whole assembly cannot fail unless the multitude that are to be governed fail. And therefore questions of the right of succession have in that form of government no place at all.

In an aristocracy, when any of the assembly dies, the election of another into his room belongs to the assembly, as the sovereign to whom belongs the choosing of all counselors and officers. For that which the representative does as actor, every one of the subjects does as author. And though the sovereign assembly may give power to others to elect new men for supply of their court, yet it is still by their authority that the election is made; and by the same it may, when the public shall require it, be recalled.

The present monarch has right to dispose of the succession. The greatest difficulty about the right of succession is in monarchy; and the difficulty arises from this, that at first sight it is not manifest who is to appoint the successor, nor many times who it is whom he has appointed. For in both these cases there is required a more exact ratiocination than every man is accustomed to use. As to the question who shall appoint the successor of a monarch that has the sovereign authority—that is to say, who shall determine of the right of inheritance (for elective kings and princes have not the sovereign power in propriety, but in use only)—we are to consider that either he that is in possession has right to dispose of the succession, or else that right is again in the dissolved multitude. For the death of him that has the sovereign power in propriety leaves the multitude without any sovereign at all—that is, without any representative in whom they should be united and be capable of doing any one action at all—and therefore they are incapable of election of any new monarch, every man having equal right to submit himself to such as he thinks best able to protect him or, if he can, protect himself by his own sword, which is a return to confusion and to the condition of a war of every man against every man, contrary to the end for which monarchy had its first institution. Therefore it is manifest that by the institution of monarchy the disposing of the successor is always left to the judgment and will of the present possessor.

And for the question, which may arise sometimes, who it is that the monarch in possession has designed to the succession and inheritance of his power, it is determined by his express words and testament, or by other tacit signs sufficient.

Succession passes by express words; By express words or testament, when it is declared by him in his lifetime, *viva voce* or by writing, as the first emperors of Rome declared who should be their heirs. For the word heir does not of itself imply the children or nearest kindred of a man, but whomsoever a man shall any way declare he would have to succeed him in his estate. If therefore a monarch declare expressly that such a man shall be his heir, either by word or writing, then is that man, immediately after the decease of his predecessor, invested in the right of being monarch.

Or by not controlling a custom; But where testament and express words are wanting, other natural signs of the will are to be followed, whereof the one is custom. And therefore where the custom is that the next of kindred absolutely succeeds, there also the next of kindred has right to the succession; for that, if the will of him that was in possession had been otherwise, he might easily have declared the same in his lifetime. And likewise where the custom is that the next of the male kindred succeeds, there also the right of succession is in the next of the kindred male, for the same reason. And so it is if the custom were to advance the female. For whatsoever custom a man may by a word control, and does not, it is a natural sign he would have that custom stand.

Or by presumption of natural affection. But where neither custom nor testament has preceded, there it is to be understood, first, that a monarch's will is that the government remain monarchical, because he has approved that government in himself. Secondly, that a child of his own, male or female, be preferred before any other, because men are presumed to be more inclined by nature to advance their own children than the children of other men; and of their own rather a male than a female, because men are naturally fitter than women for actions of labor and danger. Thirdly, where his own issue fails, rather a brother than a stranger; and so still the nearer in blood rather than the more remote, because it is always presumed that the nearer of kin is the nearer in affection, and it is evident that a man receives always, by reflection, the most honor from the greatness of his nearest kindred.

To dispose of the succession, though to a king of another nation, not unlawful. But if it be lawful for a monarch to dispose of the succession by words of contract or testament, men may perhaps object a great inconvenience; for he may sell or give his right of governing to a stranger, which, because strangers—that is, men not used to live under the same government nor speaking the same language—do commonly undervalue one another, may turn to the oppression of his subjects; which is indeed a great inconvenience, but it proceeds not necessarily from the subjection to a stranger's government but from the unskillfulness of the governors, ignorant of the true rules of politics. And therefore the Romans, when they had subdued many nations, to make their government digestible were wont to take away that grievance as much as they thought necessary by giving sometimes to whole nations, and sometimes to principal men of every nation they conquered, not only the privileges but also the name of Romans, and took many of them into the senate and offices of charge, even in the Roman city. And this was it our most wise king, King James, aimed at in endeavoring the union of his two realms of England and Scotland.[4] Which if he could have obtained, had in all likelihood prevented the civil wars which make both those kingdoms, at this present, miserable. It is not, therefore, any injury to the people for a monarch to dispose of the succession by will, though by the fault of many princes it has been sometimes found inconvenient. Of the lawfulness of it, this also is an argument: that whatsoever inconveniences can arrive by giving a kingdom to a stranger may arrive also by so marrying with strangers, as the right of succession may descend upon them; yet this by all men is accounted lawful.

CHAPTER TWENTY

OF DOMINION PATERNAL AND DESPOTICAL

A commonwealth by acquisition. A *commonwealth by acquisition* is that where the sovereign power is acquired by force; and it is acquired by force when men singly, or many together by plurality of voices, for fear of death or bonds do authorize all the actions of that man or assembly that has their lives and liberty in his power.

4 [James VI of Scotland succeeded to the throne of England in 1603 as James I. He reigned in both countries until his death in 1625. England and Scotland became the single kingdom of Great Britain by the Act of Union of 1707.]

Wherein different from a commonwealth by institution. And this kind of dominion or sovereignty differs from sovereignty by institution only in this, that men who choose their sovereign do it for fear of one another and not of him whom they institute, but in this case they subject themselves to him they are afraid of. In both cases they do it for fear—which is to be noted by them that hold all such covenants as proceed from fear of death or violence void, which if it were true, no man, in any kind of commonwealth, could be obliged to obedience. It is true that in a commonwealth once instituted or acquired promises proceeding from fear of death or violence are no covenants nor obliging when the thing promised is contrary to the laws; but the reason is not because it was made upon fear but because he that promises has no right in the thing promised. Also, when he may lawfully perform and does not, it is not the invalidity of the covenant that absolves him but the sentence of the sovereign. Otherwise, whensoever a man lawfully promises, he unlawfully breaks; but when the sovereign, who is the actor, acquits him, then he is acquitted by him that extorted the promise, as by the author of such absolution.

The right of sovereignty the same in both. But the rights and consequences of sovereignty are the same in both. His power cannot, without his consent, be transferred to another; he cannot forfeit it; he cannot be accused by any of his subjects of injury; he cannot be punished by them; he is judge of what is necessary for peace and judge of doctrines; he is sole legislator, and supreme judge of controversies and of the times and occasions of war and peace; to him it belongs to choose magistrates, counselors, commanders, and all other officers and ministers, and to determine of rewards and punishments, honor and order. The reasons whereof are the same which are alleged in the precedent chapter for the same rights and consequences of sovereignty by institution.

Dominion paternal how attained. Dominion is acquired two ways: by generation and by conquest. The right of dominion by generation is that which the parent has over his children, and is called PATERNAL. And is *Not by generation, but by contract;* not so derived from the generation, as if therefore the parent had dominion over his child because he begat him, but from the child's consent, either express or by other sufficient arguments declared. For as to the generation, God has ordained to man a helper, and there be always two that are equally parents; the dominion therefore over the child should belong equally to both and he be equally subject to both, which is impossible, for no man can obey two masters.[1] And whereas some have attributed the dominion to the man only as being of the more excellent sex, they misreckon in it. For there is not always that difference of strength or prudence between the man and the woman as that the right can be determined without war. In commonwealths, this controversy is decided by the civil law; and for the most part, but not always, the sentence is in favor of the father because for the most part commonwealths have been erected by the fathers, not by the mothers of families. But the question lies now in the state of mere nature where there are supposed no laws of matrimony, no laws for the education of children, but the law of nature and the natural inclination of the sexes, one to another and to their children. In this condition of mere nature, either the parents between themselves dispose of the dominion over the child by contract or do not dispose thereof at all. If they dispose thereof, the right passes according to the contract. We find in history that the Amazons [2] contracted with the men of the neighboring countries, to whom they had recourse for issue, that the issue male should be sent back, but the female remain with themselves; so that the dominion of the females was in the mother.

Or education;   If there be no contract, the dominion is in the mother. For in the condition of mere nature, where there are no matrimonial laws, it cannot be known who is the father unless it be declared by the mother; and therefore the right of dominion over the child depends on her will, and is consequently hers. Again, seeing the infant is first in the power of the mother so as she may either nourish or expose it, if she nourish it, it owe its life to the mother and is therefore obliged to obey her rather than any other, and by consequence the dominion over it is hers. But if she expose it, and another find and nourish it, the dominion is in him that nourishes it. For it ought to obey him by whom it is preserved, because preserva-

1 [Cf. Luke 16:13.]
2 [A mythological nation of female hunters and warriors.]

tion of life being the end for which one man becomes subject to another, every man is supposed to promise obedience to him in whose power it is to save or destroy him.

Or precedent sub-jection of one of the parents to the other.

If the mother be the father's subject, the child is in the father's power; and if the father be the mother's subject, as when a sovereign queen marries one of her subjects, the child is subject to the mother because the father also is her subject.

If a man and woman, monarchs of two several kingdoms, have a child, and contract concerning who shall have the dominion of him, the right of the dominion passes by the contract. If they contract not, the dominion follows the dominion of the place of his residence. For the sovereign of each country has dominion over all that reside therein.

He that has the dominion over the child has dominion also over the children of the child and over their children's children. For he that has dominion over the person of a man has dominion over all that is his, without which dominion were but a title without the effect. The right of succession to paternal domin-

The right of succes-sion follows the rules of the right of possession.

ion proceeds in the same manner as does the right of succession of monarchy, of which I have already sufficiently spoken in the preced-ent chapter.

Despotical dominion how attained.

Dominion acquired by conquest or victory in war is that which some writers call DESPOTICAL

—from Δεσπότης, which signifies a *lord* or *mas-ter*—and is the dominion of the master over his servant. And this dominion is then acquired to the victor when the van-quished, to avoid the present stroke of death, covenants either in express words or by other sufficient signs of the will that, so long as his life and the liberty of his body is allowed him, the victor shall have the use thereof at his pleasure. And after such covenant made, the vanquished is a SERVANT, and not before; for by the word *servant*—whether it be derived from *servire*, to serve, or from *servare*, to save, which I leave to grammarians to dispute—is not meant a captive which is kept in prison or bonds till the owner of him that took him or bought him of one that did shall consider what to do with him; for such men, com-monly called slaves, have no obligation at all, but may break their bonds or the prison, and kill or carry away captive their master, justly; but one that, being taken, has corporal liberty allowed him, and upon promise not to run away nor to do violence to his master is trusted by him. It is not,

Not by the victory, therefore, the victory that gives the right of do-
but by the consent minion over the vanquished but his own cove-
of the vanquished. nant. Nor is he obliged because he is con-
quered—that is to say, beaten and taken, or put to flight—but because he comes in and submits to the victor; nor is the victor obliged by an enemy's rendering himself, without promise of life, to spare him for this his yielding to discretion, which obliges not the victor longer than in his own discretion he shall think fit.

And that which men do when they demand, as it is now called, *quarter*—which the Greeks called Ζωγρία, *taking alive*—is to evade the present fury of the victor by submission, and to compound for their life with ransom or service; and therefore he that has quarter has not his life given but deferred till further deliberation, for it is not a yielding on condition of life but to discretion. And then only is his life in security and his service due when the victor has trusted him with his corporal liberty. For slaves that work in prisons or fetters do it not of duty but to avoid the cruelty of their taskmasters.

The master of the servant is master also of all he has and may exact the use thereof—that is to say, of his goods, of his labor, of his servants, and of his children, as often as he shall think fit. For he holds his life of his master by the covenant of obedience —that is, of owning and authorizing whatsoever the master shall do. And in case the master, if he refuse, kill him or cast him into bonds or otherwise punish him for his disobedience, he is himself the author of the same and cannot accuse him of injury.

In sum, the rights and consequences of both *paternal* and *despotical* dominion are the very same with those of a sovereign by institution, and for the same reasons—which reasons are set down in the precedent chapter. So that for a man that is monarch of divers nations, whereof he has in one the sovereignty by institution of the people assembled and in another by conquest —that is, by the submission of each particular to avoid death or bonds—to demand of one nation more than of the other from the title of conquest, as being a conquered nation, is an act of ignorance of the rights of sovereignty; for the sovereign is absolute over both alike, or else there is no sovereignty at all and so every man may lawfully protect himself, if he can, with his own sword, which is the condition of war.

Difference between a family and a kingdom. By this it appears that a great family, if it be not part of some commonwealth, is of itself, as to the rights of sovereignty, a little monarchy— whether that family consist of a man and his children, or of a man and his servants, or of a man and his children and servants together—wherein the father or master is the sovereign. But yet a family is not properly a commonwealth unless it be of that power by its own number or by other opportunities as not to be subdued without the hazard of war. For where a number of men are manifestly too weak to defend themselves united, every one may use his own reason in time of danger to save his own life, either by flight or by submission to the enemy as he shall think best, in the same manner as a very small company of soldiers, surprised by an army, may cast down their arms and demand quarter or run away rather than be put to the sword. And thus much shall suffice concerning what I find by speculation and deduction of sovereign rights from the nature, need, and designs of men in erecting of commonwealths and putting themselves under monarchs or assemblies entrusted with power enough for their protection.

The rights of monarchy from Scripture. Let us now consider what the Scripture teaches in the same point. To Moses, the children of Israel say thus: *Speak thou to us, and we will hear thee; but let not God speak to us, lest we die* (Exod. 20: 19). This is absolute obedience to Moses. Concerning the right of kings, God himself, by the mouth of Samuel, says (I Sam. 8: 11-17): *This shall be the right of the king you will have to reign over you. He shall take your sons, and set them to drive his chariots, and to be his horsemen, and to run before his chariots; and gather in his harvest; and to make his engines of war, and instruments of his chariots; and shall take your daughters to make perfumes, to be his cooks and bakers. He shall take your fields, your vineyards, and your olive yards, and give them to his servants. He shall take the tithe of your*

*corn and wine and give it to the men of his chamber and to his
other servants. He shall take your manservants and your maid-
servants and the choice of your youth, and employ them in his
business. He shall take the tithe of your flocks; and you shall be
his servants.* This is absolute power, and summed up in the last
words, *you shall be his servants.* Again, when the people heard
what power their king was to have, yet they consented thereto,
and say thus (verse 19): *We will be as all other nations, and our
king shall judge our causes, and go before us to conduct our
wars.* Here is confirmed the right that sovereigns have, both to
the *militia* and to all *judicature,* in which is contained as absolute power as one man can possibly transfer to another. Again,
the prayer of King Solomon to God was this (I Kings 3: 9): *Give
to thy servant understanding, to judge thy people, and to discern between good and evil.* It belongs therefore to the sovereign to be *judge,* and to prescribe the rules of *discerning good
and evil;* which rules are laws, and therefore in him is the legislative power. Saul sought the life of David, yet when it was in
his power to slay Saul, and his servants would have done it,
David forbade them, saying (I Sam. 24: 6): *God forbid I should
do such an act against my Lord, the anointed of God.* For obedience of servants St. Paul says (Col. 3: 22): *Servants obey your
masters in all things;* and (Col. 3: 20): *Children obey your parents in all things.* There is simple obedience in those that are
subject to paternal or despotical dominion. Again (Matt. 23: 2-
3): *The Scribes and Pharisees sit in Moses' chair, and therefore
all that they shall bid you observe, that observe and do.* There
again is simple obedience. And St. Paul (Titus 3: 2): *Warn them
that they subject themselves to princes, and to those that are in
authority, and obey them.* This obedience is also simple. Lastly,
our Saviour himself acknowledges that men ought to pay such
taxes as are by kings imposed where he says, *give to Caesar that
which is Caesar's,*[3] and paid such taxes himself. And that the
king's word is sufficient to take anything from any subject when
there is need, and that the king is judge of that need; for he
himself, as king of the Jews, commanded his disciples to take
the ass and ass's colt to carry him into Jerusalem, saying (Matt.
21: 2-3): *Go into the village over against you, and you shall find*

---

[3] [Matt. 22: 21.]

a she ass tied, and her colt with her, untie them, and bring them to me. And if any man ask you what you mean by it, say the Lord hath need of them: and they will let them go. They will not ask whether his necessity be a sufficient title, nor whether he be judge of that necessity, but acquiesce in the will of the Lord.

To these places may be added also that of Genesis (3: 5): *Ye shall be as gods, knowing good and evil.* And (verse 11): *Who told thee that thou wast naked? hast thou eaten of the tree, of which I commanded thee thou shouldst not eat?* For the cognizance or judicature of *good* and *evil* being forbidden by the name of the fruit of the tree of knowledge as a trial of Adam's obedience, the devil, to inflame the ambition of the woman, to whom that fruit already seemed beautiful, told her that by tasting it they should be as gods, knowing *good* and *evil.* Whereupon having both eaten, they did indeed take upon them God's office, which is judicature of good and evil, but acquired no new ability to distinguish between them aright. And whereas it is said that, having eaten, they saw they were naked, no man has so interpreted that place as if they had been formerly blind and saw not their own skins; the meaning is plain, that it was then they first judged their nakedness, wherein it was God's will to create them, to be uncomely, and, by being ashamed, did tacitly censure God himself. And thereupon God said: *Hast thou eaten,* etc., as if he should say, dost thou that owest me obedience take upon thee to judge of my commandments? Whereby it is clearly, though allegorically, signified that the commands of them that have the right to command are not by their subjects to be censured nor disputed.

Sovereign power ought in all commonwealths to be absolute.
So that it appears plainly, to my understanding, both from reason and Scripture, that the sovereign power, whether placed in one man as in monarchy, or in one assembly of men as in popular and aristocratical commonwealths, is as great as possibly men can be imagined to make it. And though of so unlimited a power men may fancy many evil consequences, yet the consequences of the want of it, which is perpetual war of every man against his neighbor, are much worse. The condition of man in this life shall never be without inconveniences; but there happens in no commonwealth any great inconvenience

but what proceeds from the subject's disobedience and breach of those covenants from which the commonwealth has its being. And whosoever, thinking sovereign power too great, will seek to make it less must subject himself to the power that can limit it—that is to say, to a greater.

The greatest objection is that of the practice, when men ask where and when such power has by subjects been acknowledged. But one may ask them again when or where has there been a kingdom long free from sedition and civil war. In those nations whose commonwealths have been long-lived and not been destroyed but by foreign war, the subjects never did dispute of the sovereign power. But howsoever, an argument from the practice of men that have not sifted to the bottom, and with exact reason weighed the causes and nature of commonwealths, and suffer daily those miseries that proceed from the ignorance thereof, is invalid. For though in all places of the world men should lay the foundation of their houses on the sand, it could not thence be inferred that so it ought to be. The skill of making and maintaining commonwealths consists in certain rules, as do arithmetic and geometry, not, as tennis-play, on practice only; which rules neither poor men have the leisure, nor men that have had the leisure have hitherto had the curiosity or the method to find out.

CHAPTER TWENTY-ONE

OF THE LIBERTY OF SUBJECTS

Liberty, what.   LIBERTY, or FREEDOM, signifies properly the absence of opposition—by opposition I mean external impediments of motion—and may be applied no less to irrational and inanimate creatures than to rational. For whatsoever is so tied or environed as it cannot move but within a certain space, which space is determined by the opposition of some external body, we say it has not liberty to go farther. And so of all living creatures while they are imprisoned or restrained with walls or chains, and of the water while it is kept in by banks or vessels

that otherwise would spread itself into a larger space, we use to
say they are not at liberty to move in such manner as without
those external impediments they would. But when the impediment of motion is in the constitution of the thing itself, we use
not to say it wants the liberty but the power to move—as when a
stone lies still or a man is fastened to his bed by sickness.

What it is to be free. And according to this proper and generally received meaning of the word, a FREEMAN *is he
that in those things which by his strength and wit he is able to
do is not hindered to do what he has a will to.* But when the
words *free* and *liberty* are applied to anything but *bodies,* they
are abused, for that which is not subject to motion is not subject
to impediment; and therefore, when it is said, for example, the
way is free, no liberty of the way is signified but of those that
walk in it without stop. And when we say a gift is free, there is
not meant any liberty of the gift but of the giver, that was not
bound by any law or covenant to give it. So when we *speak
freely,* it is not the liberty of voice or pronunciation but of the
man, whom no law has obliged to speak otherwise than he did.
Lastly, from the use of the word *free will,* no liberty can be inferred of the will, desire, or inclination but the liberty of the
man, which consists in this: that he finds no stop in doing what
he has the will, desire, or inclination to do.

Fear and liberty consistent. Fear and liberty are consistent, as when a man
throws his goods into the sea for *fear* the ship
should sink, he does it nevertheless very will-
ingly, and may refuse to do it if he will: it is therefore the action
of one that was *free;* so a man sometimes pays his debt only for
fear of imprisonment, which, because nobody hindered him
from detaining, was the action of a man at *liberty.* And generally all actions which men do in commonwealths for *fear* of
the law are actions which the doers had *liberty* to omit.

Liberty and neces-sity consistent. *Liberty* and *necessity* are consistent, as in the
water that has not only *liberty* but a *necessity*
of descending by the channel; so likewise in
the actions which men voluntarily do, which, because they proceed from their will, proceed from *liberty,* and yet—because
every act of man's will and every desire and inclination proceeds from some cause, and that from another cause, in a con-

tinual chain whose first link is in the hand of God, the first of all causes—proceed from *necessity*. So that to him that could see the connection of those causes the *necessity* of all men's voluntary actions would appear manifest. And therefore God, that sees and disposes all things, sees also that the *liberty* of man in doing what he will is accompanied with the *necessity* of doing that which God will, and no more nor less. For though men may do many things which God does not command, nor is therefore author of them, yet they can have no passion nor appetite to anything of which appetite God's will is not the cause. And did not his will assure the *necessity* of man's will, and consequently of all that on man's will depends, the *liberty* of men would be a contradiction and impediment to the omnipotence and *liberty* of God. And this shall suffice, as to the matter in hand, of that natural *liberty* which only is properly called *liberty*.

Artificial bonds or covenants.

But as men, for the attaining of peace and conservation of themselves thereby, have made an artificial man, which we call a commonwealth, so also have they made artificial chains, called *civil laws,* which they themselves, by mutual covenants, have fastened at one end to the lips of that man or assembly to whom they have given the sovereign power, and at the other end to their own ears. These bonds, in their own nature but weak, may nevertheless be made to hold by the danger, though not by the difficulty, of breaking them.

Liberty of subjects consists in liberty from covenants.

In relation to these bonds only it is that I am to speak now of the *liberty* of *subjects*. For seeing there is no commonwealth in the world wherein there be rules enough set down for the regulating of all the actions and words of men, as being a thing impossible, it follows necessarily that in all kinds of actions by the laws pretermitted men have the liberty of doing what their own reasons shall suggest for the most profitable to themselves. For if we take liberty in the proper sense for corporal liberty—that is to say, freedom from chains and prison—it were very absurd for men to clamor as they do for the liberty they so manifestly enjoy. Again, if we take liberty for an exemption from laws, it is no less absurd for men to demand as they do that liberty by which all other men may be masters of their lives. And yet, as absurd as it is, this is it they demand, not knowing that the laws are of no power to protect them without a sword in the hands of a man or men to cause those laws to be put in execution. The liberty of a subject lies, therefore, only in those things which, in regulating their actions, the sovereign has pretermitted: such as is the liberty to buy and sell and otherwise contract with one another; to choose their own abode, their own diet, their own trade of life, and institute their children as they themselves think fit; and the like.

Liberty of the subject consistent with the unlimited power of the sovereign. Nevertheless we are not to understand that by such liberty the sovereign power of life and death is either abolished or limited. For it has been already shown that nothing the sovereign representative can do to a subject, on what pretense soever, can properly be called injustice or injury, because every subject is author of every act the sovereign does, so that he never wants right to anything otherwise than as he himself is the subject of God and bound thereby to observe the laws of nature. And therefore it may and does often happen in commonwealths that a subject may be put to death by the command of the sovereign power and yet neither do the other wrong—as when Jephtha caused his daughter to be sacrificed; [1] in which, and the like cases, he that so dies, had liberty to do the action for which he is nevertheless without injury put to death. And the same holds also in a sovereign prince that puts to death an innocent subject. For though the action be against the law of nature as being contrary to equity, as was the killing of Uriah by David,[2] yet it was not an injury to Uriah but to God. Not to Uriah, because the right to do what he pleased was given him by Uriah himself; and yet to God, because David was God's subject and prohibited all iniquity by the law of nature, which distinction David himself, when he repented the fact, evidently confirmed, saying, *To thee only have I sinned.*[3] In the same manner, the people of Athens, when they banished the most potent of their commonwealth for ten years, thought they committed no injustice; and

1 [Judg. 11.]
2 [II Sam. 11.]
3 [Ps. 51: 4.]

yet they never questioned what crime he had done, but what hurt he would do—nay, they commanded the banishment of they knew not whom, and, every citizen bringing his oystershell into the market place written with the name of him he desired should be banished, without actually accusing him, sometimes banished an Aristides for his reputation of justice, and sometimes a scurrilous jester, as Hyperbolus, to make a jest of it. And yet a man cannot say the sovereign people of Athens wanted right to banish them, or an Athenian the liberty to jest or to be just.[4]

The liberty which writers praise is the liberty of sovereigns, not of private men.

The liberty whereof there is so frequent and honorable mention in the histories and philosophy of the ancient Greeks and Romans, and in the writings and discourse of those that from them have received all their learning in the politics, is not the liberty of particular men but the liberty of the commonwealth—which is the same with that which every man then should have if there were no civil laws nor commonwealth at all. And the effects of it also be the same. For as among masterless men there is perpetual war of every man against his neighbor—no inheritance to transmit to the son nor to expect from the father, no propriety of goods or lands, no security, but a full and absolute liberty in every particular man—so in states and commonwealths not dependent on one another every commonwealth, not every man, has an absolute liberty to do what it shall judge—that is to say, what that man or assembly that represents it shall judge—most conducing to their benefit. But withal they live in the condition of a perpetual war and upon the confines of battle, with their frontiers armed and cannons planted against their neighbors round about. The Athenians and Romans were free—that is, free commonwealths; not that any particular men had the liberty to resist their own representative, but that their representative had the liberty to resist or invade other people. There is written on the turrets of the city of Lucca in great characters at this day the word LIBERTAS,

[4] [In the 5th century B.C., Athenians had the practice of expelling men who, though guilty of no crime, were considered dangerous to the state. Citizens inscribed the names of men they wanted expelled on pieces of broken pottery, *ostraca*. Aristides, an outstanding general and statesman, was ostracized in 483 B.C. but recalled two years later. The demagogue Hyperbolus was ostracized in 417 B.C.]

yet no man can thence infer that a particular man has more liberty or immunity from the service of the commonwealth there than in Constantinople. Whether a commonwealth be monarchical or popular, the freedom is still the same.

But it is an easy thing for men to be deceived by the specious name of liberty and, for want of judgment to distinguish, mistake that for their private inheritance and birthright which is the right of the public only. And when the same error is confirmed by the authority of men in reputation for their writings on this subject, it is no wonder if it produce sedition and change of government. In these western parts of the world, we are made to receive our opinions concerning the institution and rights of commonwealths from Aristotle, Cicero, and other men, Greeks and Romans that, living under popular states, derived those rights not from the principles of nature but transcribed them into their books out of the practice of their own commonwealths which were popular—as the grammarians describe the rules of language out of the practice of the time, or the rules of poetry out of the poems of Homer and Virgil. And because the Athenians were taught, to keep them from desire of changing their government, that they were freemen and all that lived under monarchy were slaves, therefore Aristotle puts it down in his *Politics* (lib. 6. cap. 2): *In democracy,* LIBERTY *is to be supposed; for it is commonly held that no man is* FREE *in any other government.* And as Aristotle, so Cicero and other writers have grounded their civil doctrine on the opinions of the Romans, who were taught to hate monarchy at first by them that, having deposed their sovereign, shared among them the sovereignty of Rome, and afterwards by their successors. And by reading of these Greek and Latin authors, men from their childhood have gotten a habit, under a false show of liberty, of favoring tumults and of licentious controlling the actions of their sovereigns and again of controlling those controllers, with the effusion of so much blood as I think I may truly say there was never anything so dearly bought as these western parts have bought the learning of the Greek and Latin tongues.

Liberty of subjects how to be measured. To come now to the particulars of the true liberty of a subject—that is to say, what are the things which, though commanded by the sovereign, he may nevertheless without injustice refuse to do—we are to consider what rights we pass away when we make a commonwealth, or, which is all one, what liberty we deny ourselves by owning all the actions, without exception, of the man or assembly we make our sovereign. For in the act of our *submission* consists both our *obligation* and our *liberty,* which must therefore be inferred by arguments taken from thence, there being no obligation on any man which arises not from some act of his own, for all men equally are by nature free. And because such arguments must either be drawn from the express words, *I authorize all his actions,* or from the intention of him that submits himself to his power, which intention is to be understood by the end for which he so submits, the obligation and liberty of the subject is to be derived either from those words or others equivalent, or else from the end of the institution of sovereignty —namely, the peace of the subjects within themselves and their defense against a common enemy.

Subjects have liberty to defend their own bodies, even against them that lawfully invade them. First, therefore, seeing sovereignty by institution is by covenant of every one to every one, and sovereignty by acquisition by covenants of the vanquished to the victor or child to the parent, it is manifest that every subject has liberty in all those things the right whereof cannot by covenant be transferred. I have shown before in the fourteenth chapter that covenants not to defend a man's own body are void. Therefore, *Are not bound to hurt themselves.* if the sovereign command a man, though justly condemned, to kill, wound, or maim himself, or not to resist those that assault him, or to abstain from the use of food, air, medicine, or any other thing without which he cannot live, yet has that man the liberty to disobey.

If a man be interrogated by the sovereign or his authority concerning a crime done by himself, he is not bound, without assurance of pardon, to confess it; because no man, as I have shown in the same chapter, can be obliged by covenant to accuse himself.

Again, the consent of a subject to sovereign power is contained in these words: *I authorize, or take upon me, all his actions;* in which there is no restriction at all of his own former natural liberty, for by allowing him to *kill me* I am not bound to kill myself when he commands me. It is one thing to say: *kill me, or my fellow, if you please;* another thing to say, *I will kill myself, or my fellow.* It follows therefore, that—

No man is bound by the words themselves either to kill himself or any other man, and consequently that the obligation a man may sometimes have, upon the command of the sovereign, to execute any dangerous or dishonorable office depends not on the words of our submission but on the intention, which is to be understood by the end thereof. When, therefore, our refusal to obey frustrates the end for which the sovereignty was ordained, then there is no liberty to refuse; otherwise there is.

Nor to warfare, unless they voluntarily undertake it. Upon this ground, a man that is commanded as a soldier to fight against the enemy, though his sovereign have right enough to punish his refusal with death, may nevertheless in many cases refuse, without injustice—as when he substitutes a sufficient soldier in his place, for in this case he deserts not the service of the commonwealth. And there is allowance to be made for natural timorousness, not only to women, of whom no such dangerous duty is expected, but also to men of feminine courage. When armies fight, there is on one side or both a running away; yet when they do it not out of treachery but fear, they are not esteemed to do it unjustly but dishonorably. For the same reason, to avoid battle is not injustice but cowardice. But he that enrolls himself a soldier, or takes impressed money, takes away the excuse of a timorous nature, and is obliged not only to go to the battle but also not to run from it without his captain's leave. And when the defense of the commonwealth requires at once the help of all that are able to bear arms, everyone is obliged; because otherwise the institution of the commonwealth, which they have not the purpose or courage to preserve, was in vain.

To resist the sword of the commonwealth in defense of another man, guilty or innocent, no man has liberty; because such liberty takes away from the sovereign the means of protecting us, and is therefore destructive of the very essence of government. But in case a great many men together have already resisted the sovereign power unjustly, or committed some capital crime for which every one of them expects death, whether have they not the liberty then to join together and assist and defend one another? Certainly they have, for they but defend their lives, which the guilty man may as well do as the innocent. There was indeed injustice in the first breach of their duty; their bearing of arms subsequent to it, though it be to maintain what they have done, is no new unjust act. And if it be only to defend their persons, it is not unjust at all. But the offer of pardon takes from them to whom it is offered the plea of self-defense, and makes their perseverance in assisting or defending the rest unlawful.

The greatest liberty of subjects depends on the silence of the law. As for other liberties, they depend on the silence of the law. In cases where the sovereign has prescribed no rule, there the subject has the liberty to do or forbear according to his own discretion. And therefore such liberty is in some places more and in some less, and in some times more, in other times less, according as they that have the sovereignty shall think most convenient. As, for example, there was a time when in England a man might enter into his own land and dispossess such as wrongfully possessed it by force. But in aftertimes that liberty of forcible entry was taken away by a statute made by the king in parliament. And in some places of the world men have the liberty of many wives; in other places such liberty is not allowed.

If a subject have a controversy with his sovereign—of debt, or of right of possession of lands or goods, or concerning any service required at his hands, or concerning any penalty, corporal or pecuniary, grounded on a precedent law—he has the same liberty to sue for his right as if it were against a subject, and before such judges as are appointed by the sovereign. For seeing the sovereign demands by force of a former law and not by virtue of his power, he declares thereby that he requires no more than shall appear to be due by that law. The suit, therefore, is not contrary to the will of the sovereign, and consequently the subject has the liberty to demand the hearing of his cause, and sentence according to that law. But if he demand or take anything by pretense of his power, there lies in that case no action of law; for all that is done by him in virtue of his power is done by the authority of every subject, and consequently he that brings an action against the sovereign brings it against himself.

If a monarch or sovereign assembly grant a liberty to all or any of his subjects, which grant standing he is disabled to provide for their safety, the grant is void unless he directly renounce or transfer the sovereignty to another. For in that he might openly, if it had been his will, and in plain terms have renounced or transferred it and did not, it is to be understood it was not his will but that the grant proceeds from ignorance of the repugnancy between such a liberty and the sovereign power; and therefore the sovereignty is still retained, and consequently all those powers which are necessary to the exercising thereof, such as are the power of war and peace, of judicature, of appointing officers and councilors, of levying money, and the rest named in the eighteenth chapter.

In what cases subjects are absolved of their obedience to their sovereign. The obligation of subjects to the sovereign is understood to last as long and no longer than the power lasts by which he is able to protect them. For the right men have by nature to protect themselves when none else can protect them can by no covenant be relinquished. The sovereignty is the soul of the commonwealth, which once departed from the body, the members do no more receive their motion from it. The end of obedience is protection, which, wheresoever a man sees it, either in his own or in another's sword, nature applies his obedience to it and his endeavor to maintain it. And though sovereignty, in the intention of them that make it, be immortal, yet is it in its own nature not only subject to violent death by foreign war, but also through the ignorance and passions of men, it has in it, from the very institution, many seeds of a natural mortality by intestine discord.

In case of captivity. If a subject be taken prisoner in war, or his person or his means of life be within the guards of the enemy, and has his life and corporal liberty given him on condition to be subject to the victor, he has liberty to accept the condition and, having accepted it, is the subject of him that took him, because he had no other way to preserve himself. The case is the same if he be detained on the same terms in a foreign country. But if a man be held in prison or bonds, or is not trusted with the liberty of his body, he cannot be understood to be bound by covenant to subjection; and therefore may, if he can, make his escape by any means whatsoever.

In case the sovereign cast off the government from himself and his heirs. If a monarch shall relinquish the sovereignty, both for himself and his heirs, his subjects return to the absolute liberty of nature; because, though nature may declare who are his sons and who are the nearest of his kin, yet it depends on his own will, as has been said in the precedent chapter, who shall be his heir. If, therefore, he will have no heir, there is no sovereignty nor subjection. The case is the same if he die without known kindred and without declaration of his heir. For then there can no heir be known, and consequently no subjection be due.

In case of banishment. If the sovereign banish his subject, during the banishment he is not subject. But he that is sent on a message or has leave to travel is still subject; but it is by contract between sovereigns, not by virtue of the covenant of subjection. For whosoever enters into another's dominion is subject to all the laws thereof unless he have a privilege by the amity of the sovereigns or by special license.

In case the sovereign render himself subject to another. If a monarch, subdued by war, render himself subject to the victor, his subjects are delivered from their former obligation and become obliged to the victor. But if he be held prisoner, or have not the liberty of his own body, he is not understood to have given away the right of sovereignty; and therefore his subjects are obliged to yield obedience to the magistrates formerly placed, governing not in their own name but in his. For, his right remaining, the question is only of the administration, that is to say, of the magistrates and officers, which, if he have not means to name, he is supposed to approve those which he himself had formerly appointed.

CHAPTER TWENTY-TWO

OF SYSTEMS SUBJECT, POLITICAL AND
PRIVATE

The divers sorts of systems of people. Having spoken of the generation, form, and power of a commonwealth, I am in order to speak next of the parts thereof. And first of systems, which re-

semble the similar parts or muscles of a body natural. By sys-
TEMS I understand any numbers of men joined in one interest
or one business. Of which some are *regular* and some *irregular*.
Regular are those where one man or assembly of men is constituted representative of the whole number. All other are *irregular*.

Of regular, some are *absolute* and *independent,* subject to
none but their own representative; such are only commonwealths of which I have spoken already in the five last precedent chapters. Others are dependent—that is to say, subordinate
to some sovereign power to which every one, as also their representative, is *subject*.

Of systems subordinate, some are *political* and some *private*.
Political, otherwise called *bodies politic* and *persons in law,* are
those which are made by authority from the sovereign power of
the commonwealth. *Private* are those which are constituted by
subjects among themselves or by authority from a stranger. For
no authority derived from foreign power, within the dominion
of another, is public there but private.

And of private systems, some are *lawful,* some *unlawful. Lawful* are those which are allowed by the commonwealth; all other
are *unlawful. Irregular* systems are those which, having no representative, consist only in concourse of people; which, if not
forbidden by the commonwealth nor made on evil design, such
as are conflux of people to markets or shows or any other harm-
less end, are lawful. But when the intention is evil or (if the
number be considerable) unknown, they are unlawful.

In all bodies politic the power of the representative is limited. In bodies politic, the power of the representative is always limited; and that which pre-
scribes the limits thereof is the power sovereign. For power unlimited is absolute sovereignty. And the sovereign in every commonwealth is the absolute representative of all the subjects; and therefore no other
can be representative of any part of them but so far forth as he
shall give leave. And to give leave to a body politic of subjects
to have an absolute representative to all intents and purposes
were to abandon the government of so much of the commonwealth and to divide the dominion, contrary to their peace and
defense; which the sovereign cannot be understood to do by any
grant that does not plainly and directly discharge them of their

subjection. For consequences of words are not the signs of his will when other consequences are signs of the contrary, but rather signs of error and misreckoning—to which all mankind is too prone.

The bounds of that power which is given to the representative of a body politic are to be taken notice of from two things. One is their writ, or letters from the sovereign; the other is the law of the commonwealth.

By letters patent. For though in the institution or acquisition of a commonwealth which is independent there needs no writing, because the power of the representative has there no other bounds but such as are set out by the unwritten law of nature, yet in subordinate bodies there are such diversities of limitation necessary concerning their businesses, times, and places as can neither be remembered without letters nor taken notice of unless such letters be patent, that they may be read to them, and withal sealed or testified with the seals or other permanent signs of the authority sovereign.

And the laws. And because such limitation is not always easy or perhaps possible to be described in writing, the ordinary laws common to all subjects must determine what the representative may lawfully do in all cases where the letters themselves are silent. And therefore,

When the representative is one man, his unwarranted acts are his own only. In a body politic, if the representative be one man, whatsoever he does in the person of the body which is not warranted in his letters nor by the laws is his own act and not the act of the body nor of any other member thereof besides himself, because further than his letters or the laws limit, he represents no man's person but his own. But what he does according to these is the act of every one, for of the act of the sovereign every one is author, because he is their representative unlimited; and the act of him that recedes not from the letters of the sovereign is the act of the sovereign, and therefore every member of the body is author of it.

When it is an assembly, it is the act of them that assented only. But if the representative be an assembly, whatsoever that assembly shall decree, not warranted by their letters or the laws, is the act of the assembly or body politic and the act of every one by whose vote the decree was made, but not the act of any man that, being present, voted to the contrary, nor of any man absent unless he voted it by procuration. It is the act of the assembly because voted by the major part; and if it be a crime, the assembly may be punished as far forth as it is capable, as by dissolution or forfeiture of their letters (which is to such artificial and fictitious bodies capital) or, if the assembly have a common stock wherein none of the innocent members have propriety, by pecuniary mulct. For from corporal penalties nature has exempted all bodies politic. But they that gave not their vote are therefore innocent, because the assembly cannot represent any man in things unwarranted by their letters, and consequently are not involved in their votes.

If the person of the body politic, being in one man, borrow money of a stranger—that is, of one that is not of the same body (for no letters need limit borrowing, seeing it is left to men's own inclinations to limit lending)—the debt is the representative's. For if he should have authority from his letters to make the members pay what he borrows, he should have by consequence the sovereignty of them; and therefore the grant were either void, as proceeding from error, commonly incident to human nature, and an insufficient sign of the will of the granter, or if it be avowed by him, then is the representer sovereign and falls not under the present question, which is only of bodies subordinate. No member, therefore, is obliged to pay the debt so borrowed but the representative himself, because he that lends it, being a stranger to the letters and to the qualification of the body, understands those only for his debtors that are engaged; and seeing the representer can engage himself and none else, has him only for debtor, who must therefore pay him, out of the common stock, if there be any, or, if there be none, out of his own estate.

When the representative is one man, if he borrow money, or owe it, by contract, he is liable only, the members not.

If he come into debt by contract, or mulct, the case is the same.

But when the representative is an assembly, and the debt to a stranger, all they and only they are responsible for the debt that gave their votes to the borrowing of it, or to the contract that made it due, or to the fact for which the mulct was imposed; because every one of those in voting did engage himself for the

When it is an assembly, they only are liable that have assented.

payment, for he that is author of the borrowing is obliged to the payment, even of the whole debt, though when paid by any one, he be discharged.

If the debt be to one of the assembly, the body only is obliged. But if the debt be to one of the assembly, the assembly only is obliged to the payment, out of their common stock if they have any; for having liberty of vote, if he vote the money shall be borrowed, he votes it shall be paid; if he vote it shall not be borrowed, or be absent, yet because in lending he votes the borrowing, he contradicts his former vote and is obliged by the latter, and becomes both borrower and lender, and consequently cannot demand payment from any particular man but from the common treasure only; which failing, he has no remedy nor complaint but against himself, that, being privy to the acts of the assembly and to their means to pay, and not being enforced, did nevertheless through his own folly lend his money.

Protestation against the decrees of bodies politic sometimes lawful, but against sovereign power never. It is manifest by this that in bodies politic, subordinate and subject to a sovereign power, it is sometimes not only lawful but expedient for a particular man to make open protestation against the decrees of the representative assembly and cause their dissent to be registered or to take witness of it, because otherwise they may be obliged to pay debts contracted and be responsible for crimes committed by other men. But in a sovereign assembly that liberty is taken away, both because he that protests there denies their sovereignty and also because whatsoever is commanded by the sovereign power is as to the subject, though not so always in the sight of God, justified by the command, for of such command every subject is the author.

Bodies politic for government of a province, colony, or town. The variety of bodies politic is almost infinite, for they are not only distinguished by the several affairs for which they are constituted, wherein there is an unspeakable diversity, but also by the times, places, and numbers subject to many limitations. And as to their affairs, some are ordained for government; as first, the government of a province may be committed to an assembly of men, wherein all resolutions shall depend on the votes of the major part; and then this assembly is a body politic,

and their power limited by commission. This word province signifies a charge or care of business which he whose business it is
commits to another man to be administered for and under him;
and therefore when in one commonwealth there be divers countries that have their laws distinct one from another or are far
distant in place, the administration of the government being
committed to divers persons, those countries where the sovereign is not resident but governs by commission are called provinces. But of the government of a province by an assembly residing in the province itself, there be few examples. The Romans, who had the sovereignty of many provinces, yet governed
them always by presidents and praetors, and not by assemblies,
as they governed the city of Rome and territories adjacent. In
like manner, when there were colonies sent from England to
plant Virginia and Sommer-islands,[1] though the governments of
them here were committed to assemblies in London, yet did
those assemblies never commit the government under them to
any assembly there, but did to each plantation send one governor. For though every man, where he can be present by nature, desires to participate of government, yet where they cannot be present they are by nature also inclined to commit the
government of their common interest rather to a monarchical
than a popular form of government; which is also evident in
those men that have great private estates, who, when they are
unwilling to take the pains of administering the business that
belongs to them, choose rather to trust one servant than an
assembly either of their friends or servants. But howsoever it
be in fact, yet we may suppose the government of a province or
colony committed to an assembly; and when it is, that which in
this place I have to say is this: that whatsoever debt is by that
assembly contracted, or whatsoever unlawful act is decreed, is
the act only of those that assented, and not of any that dissented
or were absent, for the reasons before alleged. Also, that an assembly residing out of the bounds of that colony whereof they

---

1 [The first permanent English settlement in Virginia was made at James-
town in 1607. The chief executive of the colony was a governor appointed by
the Virginia Company and, after 1624, by the king. Sommer-islands was the
early name of the Bermudas, derived from Sir George Somer, who established the first English settlement in the islands.]

have the government cannot execute any power over the persons or goods of any of the colony, to seize on them for debt or other duty, in any place without the colony itself, as having no jurisdiction nor authority elsewhere, but are left to the remedy which the law of the place allows them. And though the assembly have right to impose a mulct upon any of their members that shall break the laws they make, yet out of the colony itself they have no right to execute the same. And that which is said here of the rights of an assembly for the government of a province or a colony is applicable also to an assembly for the government of a town, a university, or a college, or a church, or for any other government over the persons of men.

And generally, in all bodies politic, if any particular member conceive himself injured by the body itself, the cognizance of his cause belongs to the sovereign and those the sovereign has ordained for judges in such causes, or shall ordain for that particular cause, and not to the body itself. For the whole body is in this case his fellow subject, which in a sovereign assembly is otherwise; for there, if the sovereign be not judge, though in his own cause, there can be no judge at all.

Bodies politic for ordering of trade. In a body politic for the well ordering of foreign traffic, the most commodious representative is an assembly of all the members—that is to say, such a one as every one that adventures his money may be present at all the deliberations and resolutions of the body if they will themselves. For proof whereof, we are to consider the end for which men that are merchants, and may buy and sell, export and import their merchandise, according to their own discretions, do nevertheless bind themselves up in one corporation. It is true there be few merchants that, with the merchandise they buy at home, can freight a ship to export it, or with that they buy abroad, to bring it home; and have therefore need to join together in one society, where every man may either participate of the gain according to the proportion of his adventure, or take his own and sell what he transports or imports at such prices as he thinks fit. But this is no body politic, there being no common representative to oblige them to any other law than that which is common to all other subjects. The end of their incorporating is to make their gain the greater, which is done two ways: by sole buying and sole selling, both at home and abroad. So that to grant to a company of merchants to be a corporation or body politic is to grant them a double monopoly, whereof one is to be sole buyers, another to be sole sellers. For when there is a company incorporate for any particular foreign country, they only export the commodities vendible in that country; which is sole buying at home and sole selling abroad. For at home there is but one buyer and abroad but one that sells, both which is gainful to the merchant, because thereby they buy at home at lower, and sell abroad at higher rates; and abroad there is but one buyer of foreign merchandise and but one that sells them at home, both which again are gainful to the adventurers.

Of this double monopoly one part is disadvantageous to the people at home, the other to foreigners. For at home, by their sole exportation, they set what price they please on the husbandry and handiworks of the people, and, by the sole importation, what price they please on all foreign commodities the people have need of—both which are ill for the people. On the contrary, by the sole selling of the native commodities abroad and sole buying the foreign commodities upon the place, they raise the price of those and abate the price of these to the disadvantage of the foreigner; for where but one sells the merchandise is the dearer, and where but one buys, the cheaper. Such corporations, therefore, are no other than monopolies, though they would be very profitable for a commonwealth if, being bound up into one body in foreign markets, they were at liberty at home every man to buy and sell at what price he could.

The end then of these bodies of merchants being not a common benefit to the whole body—which have in this case no common stock but what is deducted out of the particular adventures for building, buying, victualling, and manning of ships— but the particular gain of every adventurer, it is reason that every one be acquainted with the employment of his own—that is, every one be of the assembly that shall have the power to order the same—and be acquainted with their accounts. And therefore the representative of such a body must be an assembly, where every member of the body may be present at the consultations, if he will.

If a body politic of merchants contract a debt to a stranger by the act of their representative assembly, every member is liable by himself for the whole. For a stranger can take no notice of their private laws, but considers them as so many particular men, obliged every one to the whole payment till payment made by one discharges all the rest; but if the debt be to one of the company, the creditor is debtor for the whole to himself, and cannot therefore demand his debt, but only from the common stock, if there be any.

If the commonwealth impose a tax upon the body, it is understood to be laid upon every member proportionably to his particular adventure in the company. For there is in this case no other common stock but what is made of their particular adventures.

If a mulct be laid upon the body for some unlawful act, they only are liable by whose votes the act was decreed or by whose assistance it was executed; for in none of the rest is there any other crime but being of the body, which, if a crime, because the body was ordained by the authority of the commonwealth, is not his.

If one of the members be indebted to the body, he may be sued by the body; but his goods cannot be taken nor his person imprisoned by the authority of the body, but only by authority of the commonwealth; for if they can do it by their own authority, they can by their own authority give judgment that the debt is due, which is as much as to be judge in their own cause.

A body politic for counsel to be given to the sovereign. These bodies made for the government of men or of traffic be either perpetual or for a time prescribed by writing. But there be bodies also whose times are limited, and that only by the nature of their business. For example, if a sovereign monarch or a sovereign assembly shall think fit to give command to the towns and other several parts of their territory to send to him their deputies to inform him of the condition and necessities of the subjects, or to advise with him for the making of good laws, or for any other cause, as with one person representing the whole country, such deputies, having a place and time of meeting assigned them, are there and at that time a body politic representing every subject of that dominion; but it is only for such matters as shall be propounded unto them by that man or assembly that by the sovereign authority sent for them, and when it shall be declared that nothing more shall be propounded nor debated by them, the body is dissolved. For if they were the absolute representatives of the people, then were it the sovereign assembly; and so there would be two sovereign assemblies or two sovereigns over the same people, which cannot consist with their peace. And therefore where there is once a sovereignty, there can be no absolute representation of the people but by it. And for the limits of how far such a body shall represent the whole people, they are set forth in the writing by which they were sent for. For the people cannot choose their deputies to other intent than is in the writing directed to them from their sovereign expressed.

A regular private body, lawful, as a family. Private bodies regular and lawful are those that are constituted without letters or other written authority, saving the laws common to all other subjects. And because they be united in one person representative, they are held for regular: such as are all families, in which the father or master orders the whole family. For he obliges his children and servants as far as the law permits, though not further, because none of them are bound to obedience in those actions which the law has forbidden to be done. In all other actions, during the time they are under domestic government, they are subject to their fathers and masters as to their immediate sovereigns. For the father and master being before the institution of commonwealth absolute sovereigns in their own families, they lose afterward no more of their authority than the law of the commonwealth takes from them.

Private bodies regular, but unlawful. Private bodies regular but unlawful are those that unite themselves into one person representative without any public authority at all: such as are the corporations of beggars, thieves, and gypsies, the better to order their trade of begging and stealing; and the corporations of men that, by authority from any foreign person, unite themselves in another's dominion for the easier propagation of doctrines and for making a party against the power of the commonwealth.

Systems irregular, such as are private leagues. Irregular systems, in their nature but leagues or sometimes mere concourse of people without union to any particular design, not by obligation of one to another but proceeding only from a similitude of wills and inclinations, become lawful or unlawful according to the lawfulness or unlawfulness of every particular man's design therein; and his design is to be understood by the occasion.

The leagues of subjects, because leagues are commonly made for mutual defense, are in a commonwealth—which is no more than a league of all the subjects together—for the most part unnecessary, and savor of unlawful design; and are for that cause unlawful, and go commonly by the name of factions or conspiracies. For a league being a connection of men by covenants, if there be no power given to any one man or assembly, as in the condition of mere nature, to compel them to performance is so long only valid as there arises no just cause of distrust; and therefore leagues between commonwealths, over whom there is no human power established to keep them all in awe, are not only lawful but also profitable for the time they last. But leagues of the subjects of one and the same commonwealth, where every one may obtain his right by means of the sovereign power, are unnecessary to the maintaining of peace and justice, and, in case the design of them be evil or unknown to the commonwealth, unlawful. For all uniting of strength by private men is, if for evil intent, unjust; if for intent unknown, dangerous to the public and unjustly concealed.

Secret cabals. If the sovereign power be in a great assembly, and a number of men, part of the assembly, without authority consult apart to contrive the guidance of the rest, this is a faction or conspiracy unlawful, as being a fraudulent seducing of the assembly for their particular interest. But if he whose private interest is to be debated and judged in the assembly make as many friends as he can, in him it is no injustice, because in this case he is no part of the assembly. And though he hire such friends with money, unless there be an express law against it yet it is not injustice. For sometimes, as men's manners are, justice cannot be had without money; and every man may think his own cause just till it be heard and judged.

Feuds of private families. In all commonwealths, if private men entertain more servants than the government of his estate and lawful employment he has for them requires, it is faction and unlawful. For having the protection of the commonwealth, he needs not the defense of private force.

And whereas in nations not thoroughly civilized several numerous families have lived in continual hostility and invaded one another with private force, yet it is evident enough that they have done unjustly, or else they had no commonwealth.

Factions for government. And as factions for kindred, so also factions for government of religion, as of Papists, Protestants, etc., or of state, as patricians and plebeians of old time in Rome, and of aristocraticals and democraticals of old time in Greece, are unjust, as being contrary to the peace and safety of the people, and a taking of the sword out of the hand of the sovereign.

Concourse of people is an irregular system, the lawfulness or unlawfulness whereof depends on the occasion and on the number of them that are assembled. If the occasion be lawful and manifest, the concourse is lawful: as the usual meeting of men at church, or at a public show, in usual numbers —for if the numbers be extraordinarily great, the occasion is not evident, and consequently he that cannot render a particular and good account of his being among them is to be judged conscious of an unlawful and tumultuous design. It may be lawful for a thousand men to join to a petition to be delivered to a judge or magistrate; yet if a thousand men come to present it, it is a tumultuous assembly, because there needs but one or two for that purpose. But in such cases as these, it is not a set number that makes the assembly unlawful, but such a number as the present officers are not able to suppress and bring to justice.

When an unusual number of men assemble against a man whom they accuse, the assembly is an unlawful tumult because they may deliver their accusation to the magistrate by a few or by one man. Such was the case of St. Paul at Ephesus, where Demetrius and a great number of other men brought two of Paul's companions before the magistrate, saying with one voice, *Great is Diana of the Ephesians;* which was their way of demanding justice against them for teaching the people such doctrine as was against their religion and trade. The occasion here, considering the laws of that people, was just; yet was their assembly judged unlawful, and the magistrate reprehended them for it in these words (Acts 19: 38–40): *If Demetrius and the*

*other workmen can accuse any man of any thing, there be pleas
and deputies, let them accuse one another. And if you have any
other thing to demand, your case may be judged in an assembly
lawfully called. For we are in danger to be accused for this day's
sedition; because there is no cause by which any man can render
any reason of this concourse of people.* Where he calls an assembly, whereof men can give no just account, a sedition and such
as they could not answer for. And this is all I shall say concerning *systems* and assemblies of people, which may be compared,
as I said, to the similar parts of man's body: such as be lawful,
to the muscles; such as are unlawful, to wens, biles, and apostemes engendered by the unnatural conflux of evil humors.

CHAPTER TWENTY-THREE

OF THE PUBLIC MINISTERS OF
SOVEREIGN POWER

In the last chapter I have spoken of the similar parts of a commonwealth; in this I shall speak of the parts organical, which
are public ministers.

*Public minister,
who.*
       A PUBLIC MINISTER is he that by the sovereign,
whether a monarch or an assembly, is employed
in any affairs with authority to represent in
that employment the person of the commonwealth. And
whereas every man or assembly that has sovereignty represents
two persons—or, as the more common phrase is, has two capacities, one natural and another politic: as a monarch has the person not only of the commonwealth but also of a man; and a
sovereign assembly has the person not only of the commonwealth but also of the assembly—they that be servants to them in
their natural capacity are not public ministers, but those only
that serve them in the administration of the public business.
And therefore neither ushers nor sergeants nor other officers
that wait on the assembly for no other purpose but for the commodity of the men assembled in an aristocracy or democracy,

nor stewards, chamberlains, cofferers, or any other officers of the household of a monarch, are public ministers in a monarchy.

Ministers for the general adminis- tration. Of public ministers, some have charge committed to them of a general administration, either of the whole dominion or of a part thereof. Of the whole, as to a protector or regent, may be committed by the predecessor of an infant king, during his minority, the whole administration of his kingdom. In which case, every subject is so far obliged to obedience as the ordinances he shall make and the commands he shall give be in the king's name and not inconsistent with his sovereign power. Of a part or province, as when either a monarch or a sovereign assembly shall give the general charge thereof to a governor, lieutenant, prefect, or viceroy; and in this case also every one of that province is obliged to all he shall do in the name of the sovereign, and that not incompatible with the sovereign's right. For such protectors, viceroys, and governors have no other right but what depends on the sovereign's will; and no commission that can be given them can be interpreted for a declaration of the will to transfer the sovereignty without express and perspicuous words to that purpose. And this kind of public ministers resembles the nerves and tendons that move the several limbs of a body natural.

For special adminis- tration, as for economy. Others have special administration, that is to say, charges of some special business, either at home or abroad; as at home, first, for the economy of a commonwealth, they that have authority concerning the *treasure*—as tributes, impositions, rents, fines, or whatsoever public revenue, to collect, receive, issue, or take the accounts thereof—are public ministers: ministers, because they serve the person representative, and can do nothing against his command nor without his authority; public, because they serve him in his political capacity.

Secondly, they that have authority concerning the *militia*—to have the custody of arms, forts, ports; to levy, pay, or conduct soldiers; or to provide for any necessary thing for the use of war, either by land or sea—are public ministers. But a soldier without command, though he fight for the commonwealth, does not therefore represent the person of it, because there is none to represent it to. For every one that has command represents it to them only whom he commands.

For instruction of the people. They also that have authority to teach or to enable others to teach the people their duty to the sovereign power, and instruct them in the knowledge of what is just and unjust, thereby to render them more apt to live in godliness and in peace among themselves and resist the public enemy, are public ministers—ministers, in that they do it not by their own authority but by another's; and public, because they do it, or should do it, by no authority but that of the sovereign. The monarch or the sovereign assembly only has immediate authority from God to teach and instruct the people, and no man but the sovereign receives his power *Dei gratia* simply—that is to say, from the favor of none but God; all others receive theirs from the favor and providence of God and their sovereigns, as in a monarchy *Dei gratia et regis* or *Dei providentia et voluntate regis*.[1]

For judicature. They also to whom jurisdiction is given are public ministers. For in their seats of justice they represent the person of the sovereign, and their sentence is his sentence; for, as has been before declared, all judicature is essentially annexed to the sovereignty, and therefore all other judges are but ministers of him or them that have the sovereign power. And as controversies are of two sorts—namely, of *fact* and of *law*—so are judgments some of fact, some of law; and consequently in the same controversy there may be two judges, one of fact, another of law.

And in both these controversies, there may arise a controversy between the party judged and the judge; which because they be both subjects to the sovereign, ought in equity to be judged by men agreed on by consent of both, for no man can be judge in his own cause. But the sovereign is already agreed on for judge by them both, and is therefore either to hear the cause and determine it himself, or appoint for judge such as they shall both agree on. And this agreement is then understood to be made between them divers ways: as first, if the defendant be allowed to except against such of his judges whose interest makes him sus-

[1] [By the grace of God and the king; by the providence of God and the will of the king.]

pect them (for as to the complainant, he has already chosen his own judge), those which he excepts not against are judges he himself agrees on. Secondly, if he appeal to any other judge, he can appeal no further, for his appeal is his choice. Thirdly, if he appeal to the sovereign himself, and he by himself, or by delegates which the parties shall agree on, give sentence, that sentence is final, for the defendant is judged by his own judges—that is to say, by himself.

These properties of just and rational judicature considered, I cannot forbear to observe the excellent constitution of the courts of justice established both for Common and also for Public Pleas in England. By Common Pleas, I mean those where both the complainant and defendant are subjects; and by public, which are also called Pleas of the Crown, those where the complainant is the sovereign. For whereas there were two orders of men, whereof one was Lords, the other Commons, the Lords had this privilege: to have for judges in all capital crimes none but Lords, and of them as many as would be present; which being ever acknowledged as a privilege of favor, their judges were none but such as they had themselves desired. And in all controversies, every subject (as also in civil controversies the Lords) had for judges men of the country where the matter in controversy lay, against which he might make his exceptions till at last twelve men without exception being agreed on, they were judged by those twelve. So that having his own judges, there could be nothing alleged by the party why the sentence should not be final. These public persons, with authority from the sovereign power either to instruct or judge the people, are such members of the commonwealth as may fitly be compared to the organs of voice in a body natural.

For execution.   Public ministers are also those that have authority from the sovereign to procure the execution of judgments given, to publish the sovereign's commands, to suppress tumults, to apprehend and imprison malefactors, and other acts tending to the conservation of the peace. For every act they do by such authority is the act of the commonwealth; and their service, answerable to that of the hands in a body natural.

Public ministers abroad are those that represent the person of their own sovereign to foreign states. Such are ambassadors, messengers, agents, and heralds sent by public authority and on public business.

But such as are sent by authority only of some private party of a troubled state, though they be received, are neither public nor private ministers of the commonwealth, because none of their actions have the commonwealth for author. Likewise, an ambassador sent from a prince to congratulate, condole, or to assist at a solemnity, though the authority be public, yet because the business is private and belonging to him in his natural capacity, is a private person. Also if a man be sent into another country secretly to explore their counsels and strength, though both the authority and the business be public, yet because there is none to take notice of any person in him but his own, he is but a private minister; but yet a minister of the commonwealth, and may be compared to an eye in the body natural. And those that are appointed to receive the petitions or other informations of the people, and are as it were the public ear, are public ministers and represent their sovereign in that office.

Councilors without other employment than to advise are not public ministers. Neither a councilor nor a council of state, if we consider it with no authority of judicature or command, but only of giving advice to the sovereign when it is required, or of offering it when it is not required, is a public person. For the advice is addressed to the sovereign only, whose person cannot in his own presence be represented to him by another. But a body of councilors are never without some other authority, either of judicature or of immediate administration: as in a monarchy, they represent the monarch in delivering his commands to the public ministers; in a democracy, the council or senate propounds the result of their deliberations to the people as a council, but when they appoint judges, or hear causes, or give audience to ambassadors, it is in the quality of a minister of the people; and in an aristocracy, the council of state is the sovereign assembly itself, and gives counsel to none but themselves.

CHAPTER TWENTY-FOUR

OF THE NUTRITION AND PROCREATION
OF A COMMONWEALTH

The nourishment of a commonwealth consists in the commodities of sea and land: The NUTRITION of a commonwealth consists in the *plenty* and *distribution* of *materials* conducing to life; in *concoction* or *preparation;* and, when concocted, in the *conveyance* of it by convenient conduits to the public use.

As for the plenty of matter, it is a thing limited by nature to those commodities which from the two breasts of our common mother, land and sea, God usually either freely gives or for labor sells to mankind.

For the matter of this nutriment, consisting in animals, vegetals, and minerals, God has freely laid them before us in or near to the face of the earth, so there needs no more but the labor and industry of receiving them. Insomuch as plenty depends, next to God's favor, merely on the labor and industry of men.

This matter, commonly called commodities, is partly *native* and partly *foreign: native,* that which is to be had within the territory of the commonwealth; *foreign,* that which is imported from without. And because there is no territory under the dominion of one commonwealth, except it be of very vast extent, that produces all things needful for the maintenance and motion of the whole body, and few that produce not some thing more than necessary, the superfluous commodities to be had within become no more superfluous but supply these wants at home by importation of that which may be had abroad, either by exchange or by just war or by labor. For a man's labor also is a commodity exchangeable for benefit as well as any other thing; and there have been commonwealths that, having no more territory than has served them for habitation, have nevertheless not only maintained but also increased their power, partly by the labor of trading from one place to another, and partly by selling the manufactures whereof the materials were brought in from other places.

And the right distribution of them. The distribution of the materials of this nourishment is the constitution of *mine* and *thine* and *his*—that is to say, in one word, *propriety*— and belongs in all kinds of commonwealth to the sovereign power. For where there is no commonwealth, there is, as has been already shown, a perpetual war of every man against his neighbor; and therefore everything is his that gets it and keeps it by force, which is neither *propriety* nor *community*, but *uncertainty*. Which is so evident that even Cicero, a passionate defender of liberty, in a public pleading, attributes all propriety to the law civil. *Let the civil law, says he, be once abandoned or but negligently guarded, not to say oppressed, and there is nothing that any man can be sure to receive from his ancestor or leave to his children.* And again: *Take away the civil law, and no man knows what is his own and what another man's.*[1] Seeing therefore the introduction of *propriety* is an effect of commonwealth, which can do nothing but by the person that represents it, it is the act only of the sovereign; and consists in the laws, which none can make that have not the sovereign power. And this they well knew of old who called that νόμος—that is to say, *distribution*—which we call law; and defined justice by *distributing* to every man *his own.*

All private estates of land proceed originally from the arbitrary distribution of the sovereign. In this distribution, the first law is for division of the land itself, wherein the sovereign assigns to every man a portion according as he, and not according as any subject or any number of them, shall judge agreeable to equity and the common good. The children of Israel were a commonwealth in the wilderness, but wanted the commodities of the earth till they were masters of the Land of Promise; which afterward was divided among them, not by their own discretion, but by the discretion of Eleazar the priest and Joshua their general, who, when there were twelve tribes, making them thirteen by subdivision of the tribe of Joseph, made nevertheless but twelve portions of the land, and ordained for the tribe of Levi no land, but assigned them the tenth part of the whole fruits, which division was therefore arbitrary.[2] And though a people coming

[1] [Cicero, *De natura deorum* 3. 38; *De finibus* 5. 67, etc.]
[2] [Josh. 14:1-5.]

into possession of a land by war do not always exterminate the ancient inhabitants, as did the Jews, but leave to many or most or all of them their estates, yet it is manifest they hold them afterwards as of the victors' distribution, as the people of England held all theirs of William the Conqueror.

Propriety of a subject excludes not the dominion of the sovereign, but only of another subject. From whence we may collect that the propriety which a subject has in his lands consists in a right to exclude all other subjects from the use of them, and not to exclude their sovereign, be it an assembly or a monarch. For seeing the sovereign—that is to say, the commonwealth, whose person he represents—is understood to do nothing but in order to the common peace and security, this distribution of lands is to be understood as done in order to the same; and consequently, whatsoever distribution he shall make in prejudice thereof is contrary to the will of every subject that committed his peace and safety to his discretion and conscience, and therefore by the will of every one of them is to be reputed void. It is true that a sovereign monarch or the greater part of a sovereign assembly may ordain the doing of many things in pursuit of their passions contrary to their own consciences, which is a breach of trust and of the law of nature; but this is not enough to authorize any subject either to make war upon or so much as to accuse of injustice or any way to speak evil of their sovereign, because they have authorized all his actions and, in bestowing the sovereign power, made them their own. But in what cases the commands of sovereigns are contrary to equity and the law of nature is to be considered hereafter in another place.[3]

The public is not to be dieted. In the distribution of land, the commonwealth itself may be conceived to have a portion, and possess and improve the same by their representative; and that such portion may be made sufficient to sustain the whole expense to the common peace and defense necessarily required. Which were very true if there could be any representative conceived free from human passions and infirmities. But the nature of men being as it is, the setting forth of public land or of any certain revenue for the commonwealth is in vain, and tends to the dissolution of government and to the condition

3 [Chap. XXVI.]

of mere nature and war as soon as ever the sovereign power falls into the hands of a monarch or of an assembly that are either too negligent of money or too hazardous in engaging the public stock into a long or costly war. Commonwealths can endure no diet, for, seeing their expense is not limited by their own appetite but by external accidents and the appetites of their neighbors, the public riches cannot be limited by other limits than those which the emergent occasions shall require. And whereas in England there were by the Conqueror divers lands reserved to his own use besides forests and chases, either for his recreation or preservation of woods, and divers services reserved on the land he gave his subjects, yet it seems they were not reserved for his maintenance in his public but in his natural capacity. For he and his successors did for all that lay arbitrary taxes on all subjects' land when they judged it necessary. Or if those public lands and services were ordained as a sufficient maintenance of the commonwealth, it was contrary to the scope of the institution, being, as it appeared by those ensuing taxes, insufficient, and, as it appears by the late small revenue of the crown, subject to alienation and diminution. It is therefore in vain to assign a portion to the commonwealth, which may sell or give it away, and does sell and give it away when it is done by their representative.

The places and matter of traffic depend, as their distribution, on the sovereign. As the distribution of lands at home, so also to assign in what places and for what commodities the subject shall traffic abroad belongs to the sovereign. For if it did belong to private persons to use their own discretion therein, some of them would be drawn for gain both to furnish the enemy with means to hurt the commonwealth and hurt it themselves, by importing such things as, pleasing men's appetites, be nevertheless noxious or at least unprofitable to them. And therefore it belongs to the commonwealth—that is, to the sovereign only—to approve or disapprove both of the places and matter of foreign traffic.

The laws of transferring propriety belong also to the sovereign. Further, seeing it is not enough to the sustentation of a commonwealth that every man have a propriety in a portion of land or in some few commodities, or a natural property in some useful art—and there is no art in the world but is necessary either for the being or well-being almost of every particular man—it is necessary that men distribute that which they can spare, and transfer their propriety therein mutually one to another, by exchange and mutual contract. And therefore it belongs to the commonwealth—that is to say, to the sovereign—to appoint in what manner all kinds of contract between subjects —as buying, selling, exchanging, borrowing, lending, letting, and taking to hire—are to be made, and by what words and signs they shall be understood for valid. And for the matter and distribution of the nourishment to the several members of the commonwealth, thus much, considering the model of the whole work, is sufficient.

Money the blood of a commonwealth. By concoction, I understand the reducing of all commodities which are not presently consumed but reserved for nourishment in time to come to something of equal value, and withal so portable as not to hinder the motion of men from place to place; to the end a man may have in what place soever such nourishment as the place affords. And this is nothing else but gold and silver and money. For gold and silver, being, as it happens, almost in all countries of the world highly valued, is a commodious measure of the value of all things else between nations; and money, of what matter soever coined by the sovereign of a commonwealth, is a sufficient measure of the value of all things else between the subjects of that commonwealth. By the means of which measures, all commodities, movable and immovable, are made to accompany a man to all places of his resort, within and without the place of his ordinary residence; and the same passes from man to man within the commonwealth, and goes round about, nourishing, as it passes, every part thereof, in so much as this concoction is, as it were, the sanguification of the commonwealth, for natural blood is in like manner made of the fruits of the earth, and, circulating, nourishes by the way every member of the body of man.

And because silver and gold have their value from the matter itself, they have first this privilege: that the value of them cannot be altered by the power of one nor of a few commonwealths, as being a common measure of the commodities of all places. But base money may easily be enhanced or abased. Secondly, they have the privilege to make commonwealths move and stretch out their arms, when need is, into foreign countries, and supply not only private subjects that travel but also whole armies with provision. But that coin which is not considerable for the matter but for the stamp of the place, being unable to endure change of air, has its effect at home only; where also it is subject to the change of laws, and thereby to have the value diminished, to the prejudice many times of those that have it.

The conduits and way of money to the public use.
The conduits and ways by which it is conveyed to the public use are of two sorts: one, that conveys it to the public coffers; the other, that issues the same out again for public payments. Of the first sort are collectors, receivers, and treasurers; of the second are the treasurers again, and the officers appointed for payment of several public or private ministers. And in this also the artificial man maintains his resemblance with the natural, whose veins, receiving the blood from the several parts of the body, carry it to the heart, where, being made vital, the heart by the arteries sends it out again, to enliven and enable for motion all the members of the same.

The children of a commonwealth colonies.
The procreation or children of a commonwealth are those we call *plantations* or *colonies,* which are numbers of men sent out from the commonwealth, under a conductor or governor, to inhabit a foreign country either formerly void of inhabitants or made void then by war. And when a colony is settled, they are either a commonwealth of themselves, discharged of their subjection to their sovereign that sent them—as has been done by many commonwealths of ancient time, in which case the commonwealth from which they went was called their metropolis or mother, and requires no more of them than fathers require of the children whom they emancipate and make free from their domestic government, which is honor and friendship —or else they remain united to their metropolis, as were the colonies of the people of Rome, and then they are no commonwealths themselves but provinces and parts of the commonwealth that sent them. So that the right of colonies, saving honor and league with their metropolis, depends wholly on their license or letters by which their sovereign authorized them to plant.

CHAPTER TWENTY-FIVE

OF COUNSEL

Counsel, what.   How fallacious it is to judge of the nature of things by the ordinary and inconstant use of words appears in nothing more than in the confusion of counsels and commands arising from the imperative manner of speaking in them both, and in many other occasions besides. For the words *do this* are the words not only of him that commands but also of him that gives counsel and of him that exhorts; and yet there are but few that see not that these are very different things, or that cannot distinguish between them when they perceive who it is that speaks, and to whom the speech is directed, and upon what occasion. But finding those phrases in men's writings, and being not able or not willing to enter into a consideration of the circumstances, they mistake sometimes the precepts of counselors for the precepts of them that command, and sometimes the contrary, according as it best agrees with the conclusions they would infer or the actions they approve. To avoid which mistakes, and render to those terms of commanding, counseling, and exhorting their proper and distinct signification, I define them thus.

COMMAND is where a man says *do this* or *do not*
Differences between *this* without expecting other reason than the
command and
counsel.   will of him that says it. From this it follows manifestly that he that commands pretends thereby his own benefit, for the reason of his command is his own will only, and the proper object of every man's will is some good to himself.

COUNSEL is where a man says *do* or *do not this,* and deduces his reasons from the benefit that arrives by it to him to whom he says it. And from this it is evident that he that gives counsel pretends only, whatsoever he intends, the good of him to whom he gives it.

Therefore between counsel and command one great difference is that command is directed to a man's own benefit and counsel to the benefit of another man. And from this arises another difference: that a man may be obliged to do what he is commanded, as when he has covenanted to obey, but he cannot be obliged to do as he is counseled, because the hurt of not following it is his own; or if he should covenant to follow it, then is the counsel turned into the nature of a command. A third difference between them is that no man can pretend a right to be of another man's counsel, because he is not to pretend benefit by it to himself; but to demand right to counsel another argues a will to know his designs or to gain some other good to himself, which, as I said before, is of every man's will the proper object.

This also is incident to the nature of counsel: that whatsoever it be, he that asks it cannot in equity accuse or punish it; for to ask counsel of another is to permit him to give such counsel as he shall think best, and consequently he that gives counsel to his sovereign, whether a monarch or an assembly, when he asks it, cannot in equity be punished for it, whether the same be conformable to the opinion of the most or not, so it be to the proposition in debate. For if the sense of the assembly can be taken notice of before the debate be ended, they should neither ask nor take any further counsel; for the sense of the assembly is the resolution of the debate and end of all deliberation. And generally he that demands counsel is author of it and therefore cannot punish it; and what the sovereign cannot, no man else can. But if one subject gives counsel to another to do anything contrary to the laws, whether that counsel proceed from evil intention or from ignorance only, it is punishable by the commonwealth; because ignorance of the law is no good excuse where every man is bound to take notice of the laws to which he is subject.

Exhortation and dehortation, what. EXHORTATION and DEHORTATION is counsel accompanied with signs in him that gives it of vehement desire to have it followed; or to say it more briefly, *counsel vehemently pressed.* For he that exhorts does not deduce the consequences of what he advises to be done and tie himself therein to the rigor of true reasoning, but encourages him he counsels to action; as he that dehorts, deters him from it. And, therefore, they have in their speeches a regard to the common passions and opinions of men in deducing their reasons, and make use of similitudes, metaphors, examples, and other tools of oratory to persuade their hearers of the utility, honor, or justice of following their advice.

From whence may be inferred, first, that exhortation and dehortation is directed to the good of him that gives the counsel, not of him that asks it, which is contrary to the duty of a counselor, who, by the definition of counsel, ought to regard not his own benefit but his whom he advises. And that he directs his counsel to his own benefit is manifest enough by the long and vehement urging or by the artificial giving thereof, which, being not required of him and consequently proceeding from his own occasions, is directed principally to his own benefit and but accidentally to the good of him that is counseled, or not at all.

Secondly, that the use of exhortation and dehortation lies only where a man is to speak to a multitude; because when the speech is addressed to one, he may interrupt him and examine his reasons more rigorously than can be done in a multitude, which are too many to enter into dispute and dialogue with him that speaks indifferently to them all at once.

Thirdly, that they that exhort and dehort where they are required to give counsel are corrupt counselors and, as it were, bribed by their own interest. For though the counsel they give be never so good, yet he that gives it is no more a good counselor than he that gives a just sentence for a reward is a just judge. But where a man may lawfully command, as a father in his family or a leader in an army, his exhortations and dehortations are not only lawful but also necessary and laudable. But then they are no more counsels but commands, which, when they are for execution of sour labor, sometimes necessity and always humanity requires to be sweetened in the delivery by encouragement, and in the tune and phrase of counsel rather than in harsher language of command.

Examples of the difference between command and counsel we may take from the forms of speech that express them in Holy Scripture. *Have no other Gods but me; make to thyself no graven image; take not God's name in vain; sanctify the sabbath; honor thy parents; kill not; steal not,* etc.,[1] are commands,

1 [Exod. 20:1-17; Deut. 5:6-21.]

because the reason for which we are to obey them is drawn from the will of God our king, whom we are obliged to obey. But these words, *Sell all thou hast; give it to the poor; and follow me*,[2] are counsel, because the reason for which we are to do so is drawn from our own benefit, which is this: that we shall have *treasure in Heaven*. These words, *Go into the village over against you, and you shall find an ass tied, and her colt; loose her, and bring her to me*,[3] are a command, for the reason of their fact is drawn from the will of their Master; but these words, *Repent and be baptized in the name of Jesus*,[4] are counsel, because the reason why we should so do tends not to any benefit of God Almighty, who shall still be king in what manner soever we rebel, but of ourselves, who have no other means of avoiding the punishment hanging over us for our sins.

Differences of fit and unfit counselors. As the difference of counsel from command has been now deduced from the nature of counsel, consisting in a deducing of the benefit or hurt that may arise to him that is to be counseled by the necessary or probable consequences of the action he propounds, so may also the differences between *apt* and *inept* counselors be derived from the same. For experience being but memory of the consequences of like actions formerly observed, and counsel but the speech whereby that experience is made known to another, the virtues and defects of counsel are the same with the virtues and defects intellectual; and to the person of a commonwealth, his counselors serve him in the place of memory and mental discourse. But with this resemblance of the commonwealth to a natural man there is one dissimilitude joined of great importance; which is, that a natural man receives his experience from the natural objects of sense, which work upon him without passion or interest of their own, whereas they that give counsel to the representative person of a commonwealth may have, and have often, their particular ends and passions that render their counsels always suspected and many times unfaithful. And therefore we may set down for the first condition of a good

2 [Matt. 19:21; Mark 10:21; Luke 18:22.]
3 [Matt. 21:2; Mark 11:2; Luke 19:30.]
4 [Acts 2:38.]

counselor *that his ends and interests be not inconsistent with the ends and interests of him he counsels.*

Secondly, because the office of a counselor, when an action comes into deliberation, is to make manifest the consequences of it in such manner as he that is counseled may be truly and evidently informed, he ought to propound his advice in such form of speech as may make the truth most evidently appear— that is to say, with as firm ratiocination, as significant and proper language, and as briefly as the evidence will permit. And therefore *rash and unevident inferences*—such as are fetched only from examples or authority of books, and are not arguments of what is good or evil but witnesses of fact or of opinion —*obscure, confused, and ambiguous expressions, also all metaphorical speeches tending to the stirring up of passion* (because such reasoning and such expressions are useful only to deceive, or to lead him we counsel toward other ends than his own) *are repugnant to the office of a counselor.*

Thirdly, because the ability of counseling proceeds from experience and long study, and no man is presumed to have experience in all those things that to the administration of a great commonwealth are necessary to be known, *no man is presumed to be a good counselor but in such business as he has not only been much versed in but has also much meditated on and considered.* For seeing the business of a commonwealth is this: to preserve the people in peace at home and defend them against foreign invasion, we shall find it requires great knowledge of the disposition of mankind, of the rights of government, and of the nature of equity, law, justice, and honor, not to be attained without study; and of the strength, commodities, places, both of their own country and their neighbors; as also of the inclinations and designs of all nations that may any way annoy them. And this is not attained to without much experience. Of which things, not only the whole sum but every one of the particulars requires the age and observation of a man in years and of more than ordinary study. The wit required for counsel, as I have said before (chap. VIII), is judgment. And the differences of men in that point come from different education, of some to one kind of study or business, and of others to another. When for the doing of anything there be infallible rules, as in engines and edifices the rules of geometry, all the experience of the world cannot equal his counsel that has learned or found out the rule. And when there is no such rule, he that has most experience in that particular kind of business has therein the best judgment and is the best counselor.

Fourthly, to be able to give counsel to a commonwealth in a business that has reference to another commonwealth, *it is necessary to be acquainted with the intelligences and letters* that come from thence, *and with all the records of treaties and other transactions of state* between them; which none can do but such as the representative shall think fit. By which we may see that they who are not called to counsel can have no good counsel in such cases to obtrude.

Fifthly, supposing the number of counselors equal, a man is better counseled by hearing them apart than in an assembly, and that for many causes. First, in hearing them apart, you have the advice of every man; but in an assembly many of them deliver their advice with *aye* or *no,* or with their hands or feet, not moved by their own sense but by the eloquence of another, or for fear of displeasing some that have spoken, or the whole assembly, by contradiction, or for fear of appearing duller in apprehension than those that have applauded the contrary opinion. Secondly, in an assembly of many there cannot choose but be some whose interests are contrary to that of the public; and these their interests make passionate, and passion eloquent, and eloquence draws others into the same advice. For the passions of men, which asunder are moderate as the heat of one brand, in an assembly are like many brands that inflame one another, especially when they blow one another with orations, to the setting of the commonwealth on fire under pretense of counseling it. Thirdly, in hearing every man apart, one may examine, when there is need, the truth or probability of his reasons and of the grounds of the advice he gives by frequent interruptions and objections; which cannot be done in an assembly, where, in every difficult question, a man is rather astonied and dazzled with the variety of discourse upon it than informed of the course he ought to take. Besides, there cannot be an assembly of many called together for advice wherein there be not some that have the ambition to be thought eloquent and also learned in the politics, and give not their advice with care of the business propounded but of the applause of their motley orations, made of the divers colored threads or shreds of authors; which is an impertinence at least, that takes away the time of serious consultation and, in the secret way of counseling apart, is easily avoided. Fourthly, in deliberations that ought to be kept secret, whereof there be many occasions in public business, the counsels of many, and especially in assemblies, are dangerous; and therefore great assemblies are necessitated to commit such affairs to lesser numbers, and of such persons as are most versed and in whose fidelity they have most confidence.

To conclude, who is there that so far approves the taking of counsel from a great assembly of counselors that wishes for or would accept of their pains when there is a question of marrying his children, disposing of his hands, governing his household, or managing his private estate, especially if there be among them such as wish not his prosperity? A man that does his business by the help of many and prudent counselors, with every one consulting apart in his proper element, does it best, as he that uses able seconds at tennis play placed in their proper stations. He does next best that uses his own judgment only, as he that has no second at all. But he that is carried up and down to his business in a framed counsel, which cannot move but by the plurality of consenting opinions, the execution whereof is commonly, out of envy or interest, retarded by the part dissenting, does it worst of all, and like one that is carried to the ball, though by good players, yet in a wheelbarrow or other frame, heavy of itself and retarded also by the inconcurrent judgments and endeavors of them that drive it; and so much the more as they be more that set their hands to it, and most of all when there is one or more among them that desire to have him lose. And though it be true that many eyes see more than one, yet it is not to be understood of many counselors but then only when the final resolution is in one man. Otherwise, because many eyes see the same thing in divers lines, and are apt to look asquint toward their private benefit, they that desire not to miss their mark, though they look about with two eyes, yet they never aim but with one; and therefore no great popular commonwealth was ever kept up but either by a foreign enemy that united them, or by the reputation of some eminent man among them, or by the secret counsel of a few, or by the mutual fear of equal factions, and not by the open consultations of the assembly. And as for very little commonwealths, be they popular or monarchical, there is no human wisdom can uphold them longer than the jealousy lasts of their potent neighbors.

CHAPTER TWENTY-SIX

OF CIVIL LAWS

Civil law, what.   By CIVIL LAWS I understand the laws that men are therefore bound to observe because they are members, not of this or that commonwealth in particular, but of a commonwealth. For the knowledge of particular laws belongs to them that profess the study of the laws of their several countries, but the knowledge of civil law in general to any man. The ancient law of Rome was called their *civil law* from the word *civitas,* which signifies a commonwealth; and those countries which, having been under the Roman empire and governed by that law, retain still such part thereof as they think fit call that part the civil law to distinguish it from the rest of their own civil laws. But that is not it I intend to speak of here, my design being not to show what is law here and there, but what is law; as Plato, Aristotle, Cicero, and divers others have done without taking upon them the profession of the study of the law.

And first it is manifest that law in general is not counsel but command; nor a command of any man to any man, but only of him whose command is addressed to one formerly obliged to obey him. And as for civil law, it adds only the name of the person commanding, which is *persona civitatis,* the person of the commonwealth.

Which considered, I define civil law in this manner. CIVIL LAW *is to every subject those rules which the commonwealth has commanded him, by word, writing, or other sufficient sign of the will, to make use of for the distinction of right and wrong— that is to say, of what is contrary and what is not contrary to the rule.*

In which definition there is nothing that is not at first sight evident. For every man sees that some laws are addressed to all the subjects in general, some to particular provinces, some to particular vocations, and some to particular men: and are therefore laws to every of those to whom the command is directed and to none else. As also, that laws are the rules of just and unjust, nothing being reputed unjust that is not contrary to some law. Likewise that none can make laws but the commonwealth, because our subjection is to the commonwealth only; and that commands are to be signified by sufficient signs, because a man knows not otherwise how to obey them. And therefore, whatsoever can from this definition by necessary consequence be deduced, ought to be acknowledged for truth. Now I deduce from it this that follows.

The sovereign is legislator. 1. The legislator in all commonwealths is only the sovereign, be he one man, as in a monarchy, or one assembly of men, as in a democracy or aristocracy. For the legislator is he that makes the law. And the commonwealth only prescribes and commands the observation of those rules which we call law; therefore the commonwealth is the legislator. But the commonwealth is no person, nor has capacity to do anything but by the representative—that is, the sovereign—and therefore the sovereign is the sole legislator. For the same reason, none can abrogate a law made but the sovereign, because a law is not abrogated but by another law that forbids it to be put in execution.

And not subject to civil law. 2. The sovereign of a commonwealth, be it an assembly or one man, is not subject to the civil laws. For having power to make and repeal laws, he may when he pleases free himself from that subjection by repealing those laws that trouble him and making of new; and consequently he was free before. For he is free that can be free when he will; nor is it possible for any person to be bound to himself, because he that can bind can release, and therefore he that is bound to himself only is not bound.

Use, a law not by virtue of time, but of the sovereign's consent. 3. When long use obtains the authority of a law, it is not the length of time that makes the authority but the will of the sovereign signified by his silence, for silence is sometimes an argument of consent; and it is no longer law than the sovereign shall be silent therein. And therefore if the sovereign shall have a question of right grounded not upon his present will but upon the laws formerly made, the length of time shall bring no prejudice to his right, but the question shall be judged by equity. For many unjust actions and unjust sentences go uncontrolled a longer time than any man can remember. And our lawyers account no customs law but such as are reasonable, and that evil customs are to be abolished. But the judgment of what is reasonable and of what is to be abolished belongs to him that makes the law, which is the sovereign assembly or monarch.

The law of nature and the civil law contain each other. 4. The law of nature and the civil law contain each other and are of equal extent. For the laws of nature—which consist in equity, justice, gratitude, and other moral virtues on these depending—in the condition of mere nature, as I have said before in the end of the fifteenth chapter, are not properly laws but qualities that dispose men to peace and obedience. When a commonwealth is once settled, then are they actually laws and not before, as being then the commands of the commonwealth and therefore also civil laws; for it is the sovereign power that obliges men to obey them. For in the differences of private men, to declare what is equity, what is justice, and what is moral virtue, and to make them binding, there is need of the ordinances of sovereign power, and punishments to be ordained for such as shall break them; which ordinances are therefore part of the civil law. The law of nature, therefore, is a part of the civil law in all commonwealths of the world. Reciprocally also, the civil law is a part of the dictates of nature. For justice—that is to say, performance of covenant, and giving to every man his own—is a dictate of the law of nature. But every subject in a commonwealth has covenanted to obey the civil law: either one with another, as when they assemble to make a common representative, or with the representative itself one by one when, subdued by the sword, they promise obedience that they may receive life; and therefore obedience to the civil law is part also of the law of nature. Civil and natural law are not different kinds but different parts of law, whereof one part, being written, is called civil, the other unwritten, natural. But the right of nature—that is, the natural liberty of man—may by the civil law be abridged and restrained; nay, the end of making laws is no other but such restraint, without the which there cannot possibly be any peace. And law was brought into the world for nothing else but to limit the natural liberty of particular men in such manner as they might not hurt but assist one another and join together against a common enemy.

Provincial laws are not made by custom, but by the sovereign power.

5. If the sovereign of one commonwealth subdue a people that have lived under other written laws and afterwards govern them by the same laws by which they were governed before, yet those laws are the civil laws of the victor and not of the vanquished commonwealth. For the legislator is he, not by whose authority the laws were first made, but by whose authority they now continue to be laws. And therefore where there be divers provinces within the dominion of a commonwealth, and in those provinces diversity of laws, which commonly are called the customs of each several province, we are not to understand that such customs have their force only from length of time, but that they were anciently laws written or otherwise made known for the constitutions and statutes of their sovereigns, and are now laws, not by virtue of the prescription of time, but by the constitutions of their present sovereigns. But if an unwritten law, in all the provinces of a dominion, shall be generally observed, and no iniquity appear in the use thereof, that law can be no other but a law of nature, equally obliging all mankind.

Some foolish opinions of lawyers concerning the making of laws.

6. Seeing then all laws, written and unwritten, have their authority and force from the will of the commonwealth—that is to say, from the will of the representative, which in a monarchy is the monarch and in other commonwealths the sovereign assembly—a man may wonder from whence proceed such opinions as are found in the books of lawyers of eminence in several commonwealths directly or by consequence making the legislative power depend on private men or subordinate judges. As for example, *that the common law has no controller but the parliament,* which is true only where a parliament has the sovereign power and cannot be assembled nor dissolved but by their own discretion. For if there be a right in any else to dissolve them, there is a right also to control them, and consequently to control their controllings. And if there be no such right, then the controller of laws is not *parliamentum,* but *rex*

in parliamento. And where a parliament is sovereign, if it should assemble never so many or so wise men from the countries subject to them, for whatsoever cause, yet there is no man will believe that such an assembly has thereby acquired to themselves a legislative power. *Item,* that the two arms of a commonwealth are *force and justice: the first whereof is in the king, the other deposited in the hands of the parliament.* As if a commonwealth could consist where the force were in any hand which justice had not the authority to command and govern.

7. That law can never be against reason, our lawyers are agreed; and that not the letter—that is, every construction of it —but that which is according to the intention of the legislator is the law. And it is true; but the doubt is of whose reason it is that shall be received for law. It is not meant of any private reason, for then there would be as much contradiction in the laws as there is in the Schools; nor yet, as Sir Edward

Sir Edw. Coke upon Littleton, lib. 2, ch. 6, fol. 97, b.

Coke makes it, an *artificial perfection of reason, gotten by long study, observation, and experience,* as his was. For it is possible long study may increase and confirm erroneous sentences; and where men build on false grounds, the more they build the greater is the ruin; and of those that study and observe with equal time and diligence, the reasons and resolutions are and must remain discordant; and therefore it is not that *juris prudentia,* or wisdom of subordinate judges, but the reason of this our artificial man, the commonwealth, and his command that makes law; and the commonwealth being in their representative but one person, there cannot easily arise any contradiction in the laws, and when there does, the same reason is able, by interpretation or alteration, to take it away. In all courts of justice, the sovereign, which is the person of the commonwealth, is he that judges; the subordinate judge ought to have regard to the reason which moved his sovereign to make such law that his sentence may be according thereunto, which then is his sovereign's sentence; otherwise it is his own, and an unjust one.

8. From this—that the law is a command, and

Law made, if not also made known, is no law.

a command consists in declaration or manifestation of the will of him that commands, by voice, writing, or some other sufficient argument of the same—we may understand that the command of the commonwealth is law only to those that have means to take notice of it. Over natural fools, children, or madmen there is no law, no more than over brute beasts; nor are they capable of the title of just or unjust, because they had never power to make any covenant or to understand the consequences thereof, and consequently never took upon them to authorize the actions of any sovereign, as they must do that make to themselves a commonwealth. And as those from whom nature or accident has taken away the notice of all laws in general, so also every man from whom any accident, not proceeding from his own default, has taken away the means to take notice of any particular law is excused if he observe it not; and to speak properly, that law is no law to him. It is therefore necessary to consider in this place what arguments and signs be sufficient for the knowledge of what is the law—that is to say, what is the will of the sovereign, as well in monarchies as in other forms of government.

Unwritten laws are all of them laws of nature.
And first, if it be a law that obliges all the subjects without exception, and is not written nor otherwise published in such places as they may take notice thereof, it is a law of nature. For whatsoever men are to take knowledge of for law, not upon other men's words but every one from his own reason, must be such as is agreeable to the reason of all men, which no law can be but the law of nature. The laws of nature, therefore, need not any publishing nor proclamation, as being contained in this one sentence approved by all the world: *Do not that to another which you think unreasonable to be done by another to yourself.*

Secondly, if it be a law that obliges only some condition of men or one particular man, and be not written nor published by word, then also it is a law of nature, and known by the same arguments and signs that distinguish those in such a condition from other subjects. For whatsoever law is not written or some way published by him that makes it law can be known no way but by the reason of him that is to obey it, and is therefore also a law not only civil but natural. For example, if the sovereign employ a public minister without written instructions what to do, he is obliged to take for instructions the dictates of reason: as if he make a judge, the judge is to take notice that his sentence ought to be according to the reason of his sovereign,

which being always understood to be equity, he is bound to it
by the law of nature; or if an ambassador, he is, in all things not
contained in his written instructions, to take for instruction
that which reason dictates to be most conducing to his sovereign's interests; and so of all other ministers of the sovereignty,
public and private. All which instructions of natural reason
may be comprehended under one name of *fidelity,* which is a
branch of natural justice.

The law of nature excepted, it belongs to the essence of all
other laws to be made known to every man that shall be obliged
to obey them, either by word, or writing, or some other act
known to proceed from the sovereign authority. For the will of
another cannot be understood but by his own word or act, or
by conjecture taken from his scope and purpose; which in the
person of the commonwealth is to be supposed always consonant to equity and reason. And in ancient time, before letters
were in common use, the laws were many times put into verse,
that the rude people, taking pleasure in singing or reciting
them, might the more easily retain them in memory. And for
the same reason Solomon (Prov. 7: 3) advises a man to bind the
ten commandments upon his ten fingers. And for the law which
Moses gave to the people of Israel at the renewing of the covenant (Deut. 11: 19), he bids them to teach it their children by
discoursing of it both at home and upon the way, at going to
bed and at rising from bed, and to write it upon the posts and
doors of their houses; and (Deut. 31: 12) to assemble the people
—man, woman, and child—to hear it read.

Nothing is law where the legislator cannot be known. Nor is it enough the law be written and published, but also that there be manifest signs
that it proceeds from the will of the sovereign.
For private men, when they have or think
they have force enough to secure their unjust designs and con-
voy them safely to their ambitious ends, may publish for laws
what they please, without or against the legislative authority.
There is therefore requisite not only a declaration of the law,
but also sufficient signs of the author and authority. The author
or legislator is supposed in every commonwealth to be evident
because he is the sovereign who, having been constituted by the
consent of everyone, is supposed by everyone to be sufficiently
known. And though the ignorance and security of men be such,

for the most part, as that, when the memory of the first constitution of their commonwealth is worn out, they do not consider by whose power they used to be defended against their
enemies, and to have their industry protected, and to be righted
when injury is done them; yet because no man that considers
can make question of it, no excuse can be derived from the ignorance of where the sovereignty is placed. And it is a dictate of
natural reason, and consequently an evident law of nature, that
no man ought to weaken that power, the protection whereof he
has himself demanded or wittingly received against others.
Therefore, of who is sovereign no man, but by his own fault
(whatsoever evil men suggest), can make any doubt. The difficulty consists in the evidence of the authority derived from him,
the removing whereof depends on the knowledge of the public
registers, public counsels, public ministers, and public seals

Difference between verifying and authorizing.
by which all laws are sufficiently verified—
verified, I say, not authorized, for the verification is but the testimony and record, not the
authority of the law, which consists in the
command of the sovereign only.

The law verified by the subordinate judge.
If, therefore, a man have a question of injury
depending on the law of nature—that is to
say, on common equity—the sentence of the
judge that by commission has authority to
take cognizance of such causes is a sufficient verification of
the law of nature in that individual case. For though the
advice of one that professes the study of the law be useful for the avoiding of contention, yet it is but advice; it
is the judge must tell men what is law upon the hearing
of the controversy.

By the public registers.
But when the question is of injury or crime
upon a written law, every man by recourse to
the registers, by himself or others, may, if he
will, be sufficiently informed before he do such injury or commit the crime, whether it be an injury or not; nay, he ought to
do so, for when a man doubts whether the act he goes about be
just or unjust, and may inform himself if he will, the doing is
unlawful. In like manner, he that supposes himself injured in a
case determined by the written law, which he may, by himself
or others, see and consider, if he complain before he consults

with the law, he does unjustly and betrays a disposition rather to vex other men than to demand his own right.

By letters patent and public seal. If the question be of obedience to a public officer, to have seen his commission with the public seal and heard it read, or to have had the means to be informed of it if a man would, is a sufficient verification of his authority. For every man is obliged to do his best endeavor to inform himself of all written laws that may concern his own future actions.

The interpretation of the law depends on the sovereign power. The legislator known, and the laws, either by writing or by the light of nature, sufficiently published, there wants yet another very material circumstance to make them obligatory. For it is not the letter but the intendment or meaning—that is to say, the authentic interpretation of the law (which is the sense of the legislator)—in which the nature of the law consists; and therefore the interpretation of all laws depends on the authority sovereign, and the interpreters can be none but those which the sovereign, to whom only the subject owes obedience, shall appoint. For else, by the craft of an interpreter, the law may be made to bear a sense contrary to that of the sovereign, by which means the interpreter becomes the legislator.

All laws need interpretation. All laws, written and unwritten, have need of interpretation. The unwritten law of nature, though it be easy to such as without partiality and passion make use of their natural reason, and therefore leaves the violators thereof without excuse, yet considering there be very few, perhaps none, that in some cases are not blinded by self-love or some other passion, it is now become of all laws the most obscure and has consequently the greatest need of able interpreters. The written laws, if they be short, are easily misinterpreted from the divers significations of a word or two; if long, they be more obscure by the divers significations of many words: insomuch as no written law, delivered in few or many words, can be well understood without a perfect understanding of the final causes for which the law was made, the knowledge of which final causes is in the legislator. To him, therefore, there cannot be any knot in the law insoluble, either by finding out the ends to undo it by, or else by making what ends he will—as Alexander did with his sword in the Gordian knot [1]—by the legislative power, which no other interpreter can do.

The authentical in-terpretation of law is not that of writers. The interpretation of the laws of nature, in a commonwealth, depends not on the books of moral philosophy. The authority of writers, without the authority of the commonwealth, makes not their opinions law, be they never so true. That which I have written in this treatise concerning the moral virtues, and of their necessity for the procuring and maintaining peace, though it be evident truth, is not therefore presently law but because in all commonwealths in the world it is part of the civil law. For though it be naturally reasonable, yet it is by the sovereign power that it is law; otherwise, it were a great error to call the laws of nature unwritten law, whereof we see so many volumes published and in them so many contradictions of one another and of themselves.

The interpreter of the law is the judge giving sentence viva voce *in every particular case.* The interpretation of the law of nature is the sentence of the judge constituted by the sovereign authority to hear and determine such controversies as depend thereon, and consists in the application of the law to the present case. For in the act of judicature, the judge does no more but consider whether the demand of the party be consonant to natural reason and equity; and the sentence he gives is therefore the interpretation of the law of nature, which interpretation is authentic not because it is his private sentence but because he gives it by authority of the sovereign, whereby it becomes the sovereign's sentence, which is law for that time to the parties pleading.

The sentence of a judge does not bind him, or another judge to give like sentence in like cases ever after. But because there is no judge subordinate nor sovereign but may err in a judgment of equity, if afterward in another like case he find it more consonant to equity to give a contrary sentence, he is obliged to do it. No man's error becomes his own law nor obliges him to persist in it. Neither, for the same reason, becomes it a law to other

1 [At the ancient city of Gordium, in Phrygia, Alexander the Great was shown a large, involved knot. According to a local oracle, the man who untied the Gordian knot would rule all Asia. Alexander cut through the knot with his sword.]

judges, though sworn to follow it. For though a wrong sentence given by authority of the sovereign, if he know and allow it, in such laws as are mutable, be a constitution of a new law in cases in which every little circumstance is the same, yet in laws immutable, such as are the laws of nature, they are no laws to the same or other judges in the like cases for ever after. Princes succeed one another; and one judge passeth, another cometh; nay, heaven and earth shall pass, but not one tittle of the law of nature shall pass, for it is the eternal law of God.[2] Therefore all the sentences of precedent judges that have ever been cannot altogether make a law contrary to natural equity; nor any examples of former judges can warrant an unreasonable sentence or discharge the present judge of the trouble of studying what is equity, in the case he is to judge, from the principles of his own natural reason. For example sake, it is against the law of nature *to punish the innocent;* and innocent is he that acquits himself judicially and is acknowledged for innocent by the judge. Put the case now that a man is accused of a capital crime and, seeing the power and malice of some enemy and the frequent corruption and partiality of judges, runs away for fear of the event, and afterwards is taken and brought to a legal trial, and makes it sufficiently appear he was not guilty of the crime and, being thereof acquitted, is nevertheless condemned to lose his goods: this is a manifest condemnation of the innocent. I say, therefore, that there is no place in the world where this can be an interpretation of a law of nature, or be made a law by the sentences of precedent judges that had done the same. For he that judged it first judged unjustly, and no injustice can be a pattern of judgment to succeeding judges. A written law may forbid innocent men to fly, and they may be punished for flying; but that flying for fear of injury should be taken for presumption of guilt after a man is already absolved of the crime judicially is contrary to the nature of a presumption, which has no place after judgment given. Yet this is set down by a great lawyer for the common law of England. *If a man,* says he, *that is innocent be accused of felony, and for fear flies for the same, albeit he judicially acquits himself of the felony, yet if it be*

2 [Cf. Eccles. 1:4; Matt. 5:18; Luke 16:17.]

found that he fled for the felony, he shall, notwithstanding his innocency, forfeit all his goods, chattels, debts, and duties. For as to the forfeiture of them, the law will admit no proof against the presumption in law grounded upon his flight. Here you see *an innocent man judicially acquitted, notwithstanding his innocency,* when no written law forbade him to fly, after his acquittal, *upon a presumption in law,* condemned to lose all the goods he has. If the law ground upon his flight a presumption of the fact, which was capital, the sentence ought to have been capital; if the presumption were not of the fact, for what then ought he to lose his goods? This therefore is no law of England; nor is the condemnation grounded upon a presumption of law but upon the presumption of the judges. It is also against law to say that no proof shall be admitted against a presumption of law. For all judges, sovereign and subordinate, if they refuse to hear proof, refuse to do justice; for though the sentence be just, yet the judges that condemn without hearing the proofs offered are unjust judges, and their presumption is but prejudice, which no man ought to bring with him to the seat of justice, whatsoever precedent judgments or examples he shall pretend to follow. There be other things of this nature wherein men's judgments have been perverted by trusting to precedents; but this is enough to show that though the sentence of the judge be a law to the party pleading, yet it is no law to any judge that shall succeed him in that office.

In like manner, when question is of the meaning of written laws, he is not the interpreter of them that writes a commentary upon them. For commentaries are commonly more subject to cavil than the text, and therefore need other commentaries; and so there will be no end of such interpretation. And therefore, unless there be an interpreter authorized by the sovereign, from which the subordinate judges are not to recede, the interpreter can be no other than the ordinary judges, in the same manner as they are in cases of the unwritten law; and their sentences are to be taken by them that plead for laws in that particular case but not to bind other judges in like cases to give like judgments. For a judge may err in the interpretation even of written laws, but no error of a subordinate judge can change the law, which is the general sentence of the sovereign.

*The difference be-
tween the letter
and sentence
of the law.*
In written laws, men use to make a difference between the letter and the sentence of the law; and when by the letter is meant whatsoever can be gathered from the bare words, it is well distinguished. For the significations of almost all words are, either in themselves or in the metaphorical use of them, ambiguous, and may be drawn in argument to make many senses; but there is only one sense of the law. But if by the letter be meant the literal sense, then the letter and the sentence or intention of the law is all one. For the literal sense is that which the legislator intended should by the letter of the law be signified. Now the intention of the legislator is always supposed to be equity, for it were a great contumely for a judge to think otherwise of the sovereign. He ought, therefore, if the word of the law do not fully authorize a reasonable sentence, to supply it with the law of nature; or if the case be difficult, to respite judgment till he have received more ample authority. For example, a written law ordains that he which is thrust out of his house by force shall be restored by force: it happens that a man by negligence leaves his house empty and returning is kept out by force, in which case there is no special law ordained. It is evident that this case is contained in the same law, for else there is no remedy for him at all, which is to be supposed against the intention of the legislator. Again, the word of the law commands to judge according to the evidence: a man is accused falsely of a fact which the judge himself saw done by another and not by him that is accused. In this case neither shall the letter of the law be followed to the condemnation of the innocent, nor shall the judge give sentence against the evidence of the witnesses, because the letter of the law is to the contrary, but procure of the sovereign that another be made judge and himself witness. So that the incommodity that follows the bare words of a written law may lead him to the intention of the law, whereby to interpret the same the better; though no incommodity can warrant a sentence against the law. For every judge of right and wrong is not judge of what is commodious or incommodious to the commonwealth.

*The abilities re-
quired in a judge.*
The abilities required in a good interpreter of the law—that is to say, in a good judge—are not the same with those of an advocate, namely, the study of the laws. For a judge, as he ought to take notice of

the fact from none but the witnesses, so also he ought to take notice of the law from nothing but the statutes and constitutions
of the sovereign, alleged in the pleading or declared to him by
some that have authority from the sovereign power to declare
them; and need not take care beforehand what he shall judge,
for it shall be given him what he shall say concerning the fact by
witnesses, and what he shall say in point of law from those that
shall in their pleadings show it and by authority interpret it
upon the place. The Lords of Parliament in England were
judges, and most difficult causes have been heard and determined by them, yet few of them were much versed in the study
of the laws and fewer had made profession of them; and though
they consulted with lawyers that were appointed to be present
there for that purpose, yet they alone had the authority of giving sentence. In like manner, in the ordinary trials of right,
twelve men of the common people are the judges, and give sentence, not only of the fact but of the right; and pronounce simply for the complainant or for the defendant—that is to say, are
judges, not only of the fact but also of the right; and in a question of crime, not only determine whether done or not done,
but also whether it be *murder, homicide, felony, assault,* and
the like, which are determinations of law; but because they are
not supposed to know the law of themselves, there is one that
has authority to inform them of it in the particular case they
are to judge of. But yet if they judge not according to that he
tells them, they are not subject thereby to any penalty, unless
it be made appear that they did it against their consciences or
had been corrupted by reward.

The things that make a good judge or good interpreter of the
laws are, first, *a right understanding* of that principal law of nature called *equity,* which, depending not on the reading of
other men's writings but on the goodness of a man's own natural reason and meditation, is presumed to be in those most that
have had most leisure and had the most inclination to meditate
thereon. Secondly, *contempt of unnecessary riches and preferments.* Thirdly, *to be able in judgment to divest himself of all
fear, anger, hatred, love, and compassion.* Fourthly, and lastly,
*patience to hear; diligent attention in hearing; and memory to
retain, digest, and apply what he has heard.*

Divisions of law. The difference and division of the laws has been made in divers manners according to the different methods of those men that have written of them. For it is a thing that depends not on nature but on the scope of the writer, and is subservient to every man's proper method. In the Institutions of Justinian [3] we find seven sorts of civil laws:

1. *The edicts, constitutions,* and *epistles of the prince,* that is, of the emperor, because the whole power of the people was in him. Like these are the proclamations of the kings of England.

2. *The decrees of the whole people of Rome,* comprehending the senate, when they were put to the question by the *senate.* These were laws at first by the virtue of the sovereign power residing in the people; and such of them as by the emperors were not abrogated remained laws by the authority imperial. For all laws that bind are understood to be laws by his authority that has power to repeal them. Somewhat like to these laws are the Acts of Parliament in England.

3. *The decrees of the common people,* excluding the senate, when they were put to the question by the *tribune* of the people. For such of them as were not abrogated by the emperors remained laws by the authority imperial. Like to these were the orders of the House of Commons in England.

4. *Senatus consulta,* the *orders of the senate,* because when the people of Rome grew so numerous as it was inconvenient to assemble them, it was thought fit by the emperor that men should consult the senate instead of the people; and these have some resemblance with the acts of council.

5. *The edicts of praetors,* and in some cases of *aediles,* such as are the chief justices in the courts of England.

6. *Responsa prudentum,* which were the sentences and opinions of those lawyers to whom the emperor gave authority to interpret the law and to give answer to such as in matter of law demanded their advice, which answers the judges in giving

[3] [The greatest achievement of the reign of Justinian, Eastern Roman Emperor from 527 to 565, was the codification of Roman law in the *Corpus Juris Civilis,* of which the *Institutes* was one part. Justinian's code was intensively studied in the late middle ages and early modern times and influenced development of local (national) law throughout Europe.]

judgment were obliged by the constitutions of the emperor to observe, and should be like the reports of cases judged if other judges be by the law of England bound to observe them. For the judges of the common law of England are not properly judges but *juris consulti*, of whom the judges, who are either the lords or twelve men of the country, are in point of law to ask advice.

7. Also *unwritten customs*, which in their own nature are an imitation of law, by the tacit consent of the emperor, in case they be not contrary to the law of nature, are very laws.

Another division of law.

Another division of laws is into *natural* and *positive*. *Natural* are those which have been laws from all eternity, and are called not only *natural* but also *moral* laws, consisting in the moral virtues, as justice, equity, and all habits of the mind that conduce to peace and charity; of which I have already spoken in the fourteenth and fifteenth chapters.

Positive are those which have not been from eternity but have been made laws by the will of those that have had the sovereign power over others, and are either written or made known to men by some other argument of the will of their legislator.

Again, of positive laws some are *human,* some *divine;* and of human positive laws, some are *distributive,* some *penal. Distributive* are those that determine the rights of the subjects, declaring to every man what it is by which he acquires and holds a propriety in lands or goods, and a right or liberty of action; and these speak to all the subjects. *Penal* are those which declare what penalty shall be inflicted on those that violate the law, and speak to the ministers and officers ordained for execution. For though everyone ought to be informed of the punishments ordained beforehand for their transgression, nevertheless the command is not addressed to the delinquent, who cannot be supposed will faithfully punish himself, but to public ministers appointed to see the penalty executed. And these penal laws are for the most part written together with the laws distributive, and are sometimes called judgments. For all laws are general judgments or sentences of the legislator, as also every particular judgment is a law to him whose case is judged.

Divine positive laws (for natural laws, being

eternal and universal, are all divine) are those which being the commandments of God, not from all eternity, nor universally addressed to all men, but only to a certain people or to certain persons, are declared for such by those whom God has authorized to declare them. But this authority of man to declare what be these positive laws of God, how can it be known? God may command a man by a supernatural way to deliver laws to other men. But because it is of the essence of law that he who is to be obliged be assured of the authority of him that declares it, which we cannot naturally take notice to be from God, *how can a man without supernatural revelation be assured of the revelation received by the declarer?* and *how can he be bound to obey them?* For the first question, how a man can be assured of the revelation of another without a revelation particularly to himself, it is evidently impossible. For though a man may be induced to believe such revelation from the miracles they see him do, or from seeing the extraordinary sanctity of his life, or from seeing the extraordinary wisdom or extraordinary felicity of his actions, all which are marks of God's extraordinary favor, yet they are not assured evidences of special revelation. Miracles are marvelous works; but that which is marvelous to one may not be so to another. Sanctity may be feigned, and the visible felicities of this world are most often the work of God by natural and ordinary causes. And therefore no man can infallibly know by natural reason that another has had a supernatural revelation of God's will, but only a belief; everyone, as the signs thereof shall appear greater or lesser, a firmer or a weaker belief.

But for the second, how can he be bound to obey them, it is not so hard. For if the law declared be not against the law of nature, which is undoubtedly God's law, and he undertake to obey it, he is bound by his own act—bound, I say, to obey it, but not bound to believe it, for men's belief and interior cogitations are not subject to the commands but only to the operation of God, ordinary or extraordinary. Faith of supernatural law is not a fulfilling but only an assenting to the same, and not a duty that we exhibit to God but a gift which God freely gives to whom he pleases; as also unbelief is not a breach of any of his laws, but a rejection of them all, except the laws natural. But this that I say will be made yet clearer by the examples and testimonies concerning this point in Holy Scripture. The covenant God made with Abraham, in a supernatural manner, was thus (Gen. 17:10): *This is the covenant which thou shalt observe between me and thee and thy seed after thee.* Abraham's seed had not this revelation, nor were yet in being; yet they are a party to the covenant, and bound to obey what Abraham should declare to them for God's law; which they could not be but in virtue of the obedience they owed to their parents, who, if they be subject to no other earthly power, as here in the case of Abraham, have sovereign power over their children and servants. Again, where God says to Abraham: *In thee shall all nations of the earth be blessed; for I know thou wilt command thy children, and thy house after thee to keep the way of the Lord, and to observe righteousness and judgment,*[4] it is manifest the obedience of his family, who had no revelation, depended on their former obligation to obey their sovereign. At Mount Sinai Moses only went up to God; the people were forbidden to approach on pain of death; yet they were bound to obey all that Moses declared to them for God's law. Upon what ground, but on this submission of their own: *Speak thou to us, and we will hear thee; but let not God speak to us, lest we die?* [5] By which two places it sufficiently appears that in a commonwealth a subject that has no certain and assured revelation particularly to himself concerning the will of God is to obey for such the command of the commonwealth; for if men were at liberty to take for God's commandments their own dreams and fancies, or the dreams and fancies of private men, scarce two men would agree upon what is God's commandment, and yet in respect of them every man would despise the commandments of the commonwealth. I conclude, therefore, that in all things not contrary to the moral law—that is to say, to the law of nature—all subjects are bound to obey that for divine law which is declared to be so by the laws of the commonwealth. Which also is evident to any man's reason, for whatsoever is not against the law of nature may be made law in the name of them that have the sovereign

4 [Gen. 18:18-19.]
5 [Exod. 20:19.]

power, and there is no reason men should be the less obliged by it when it is propounded in the name of God. Besides, there is no place in the world where men are permitted to pretend other commandments of God than are declared for such by the commonwealth. Christian states punish those that revolt from the Christian religion, and all other states those that set up any religion by them forbidden. For in whatsoever is not regulated by the commonwealth, it is equity, which is the law of nature and therefore an eternal law of God, that every man equally enjoy his liberty.

Another division of laws. There is also another distinction of laws, into *fundamental* and *not fundamental;* but I could never see in any author what a fundamental law signifies. Nevertheless, one may very reasonably distinguish laws in that manner.

A fundamental law, what. For a fundamental law in every commonwealth is that which, being taken away, the commonwealth fails and is utterly dissolved, as a building whose foundation is destroyed. And therefore a fundamental law is that by which subjects are bound to uphold whatsoever power is given to the sovereign, whether a monarch or a sovereign assembly, without which the commonwealth cannot stand, such as is the power of war and peace, of judicature, of election of officers, and of doing whatsoever he shall think necessary for the public good. Not fundamental is that the abrogating whereof draws not with it the dissolution of the commonwealth, such as are the laws concerning controversies between subject and subject. Thus much of the division of laws.

Difference between law and right. I find the words *lex civilis* and *jus civile*—that is to say, *law* and *right civil*—promiscuously used for the same thing, even in the most learned authors, which nevertheless ought not to be so. For *right* is *liberty,* namely that liberty which the civil law leaves us; but *civil law* is an *obligation,* and takes from us the liberty which the law of nature gave us. Nature gave a right to every man to secure himself by his own strength, and to invade a suspected neighbor by way of prevention; but the civil law takes away that liberty in all cases where the protection of the law may be safely stayed for. Insomuch as *lex* and *jus* are as different as *obligation* and *liberty.*

Likewise *laws* and *charters* are taken promiscu-
And between a law and a charter. ously for the same thing. Yet charters are dona-
tions of the sovereign, and not laws, but exemp-
tions from law. The phrase of a law is *jubeo, injungo, I command* and *enjoin;* the phrase of a charter is *dedi, concessi, I
have given, I have granted;* but what is given or granted to a
man is not forced upon him by a law. A law may be made to
bind all the subjects of a commonwealth; a liberty or charter
is only to one man or some one part of the people. For to say all
the people of a commonwealth have liberty in any case whatsoever is to say that in such case there has been no law made, or
else, having been made, is now abrogated.

CHAPTER TWENTY-SEVEN

OF CRIMES, EXCUSES, AND EXTENUATIONS

Sin, what.   A SIN is not only a transgression of a law but
also any contempt of the legislator. For such contempt is a
breach of all his laws at once. And therefore may consist, not
only in the *commission* of a fact, or in speaking of words by the
laws forbidden, or in the *omission* of what the law commands,
but also in the *intention* or purpose to transgress. For the purpose to break the law is some degree of contempt of him to
whom it belongs to see it executed. To be delighted in the imagination only of being possessed of another man's goods, servants,
or wife, without any intention to take them from him by force
or fraud, is no breach of the law that says *Thou shalt not covet;* [1]
nor is the pleasure a man may have in imagining or dreaming
of the death of him from whose life he expects nothing but damage and displeasure a sin, but the resolving to put some act in
execution that tends thereto. For to be pleased in the fiction of
that which would please a man if it were real is a passion so ad-
herent to the nature both of man and every other living creature
as to make it a sin were to make sin of being a man. The consid-

[1] [Exod. 20:17; Deut. 5:21.]

eration of this has made me think them too severe, both to themselves and others, that maintain that the first motions of the
mind, though checked with the fear of God, be sins.[2] But I confess it is safer to err on that hand than on the other.

A crime, what.

A CRIME is a sin consisting in the committing,
by deed or word, of that which the law forbids,
or the omission of what it has commanded. So that every crime
is a sin, but not every sin a crime. To intend to steal or kill is a
sin, though it never appear in word or fact, for God that seeth
the thoughts of man [3] can lay it to his charge; but till it appear
by something done or said, by which the intention may be ar-
gued by a human judge, it has not the name of crime; which distinction the Greeks observed in the words ἁμάρτημα and ἔγκλημα
or αἰτία, whereof the former, which is translated *sin,* signifies any
swerving from the law whatsoever, but the two latter, which are
translated *crime,* signify that sin only whereof one man may accuse another. But of intentions which never appear by any outward act there is no place for human accusation. In like manner
the Latins by *peccatum,* which is *sin,* signify all manner of deviation from the law; but by *crimen,* which word they derive from
cerno, which signifies *to perceive,* they mean only such sins as
may be made appear before a judge, and therefore are not mere
intentions.

*Where no civil law
is, there is no crime.*

From this relation of sin to the law, and of
crime to the civil law, may be inferred, first,
that where law ceases, sin ceases. But because
the law of nature is eternal, violation of covenants, ingratitude,
arrogance, and all facts contrary to any moral virtue can never
cease to be sin. Secondly, that the civil law ceasing, crimes cease,
for there being no other law remaining but that of nature, there
is no place for accusation, every man being his own judge and
accused only by his own conscience and cleared by the upright-
ness of his own intention. When, therefore, his intention is
right, his fact is no sin; if otherwise, his fact is sin but not crime.
Thirdly, that when the sovereign power ceases, crime also
ceases, for where there is no such power there is no protection to
be had from the law, and therefore everyone may protect himself by his own power; for no man in the institution of sovereign

2 [Cf. Matt. 5:27-28.]
3 [Ps. 94:11.]

power can be supposed to give away the right of preserving his own body, for the safety whereof all sovereignty was ordained. But this is to be understood only of those that have not themselves contributed to the taking away of the power that protected them, for that was a crime from the beginning.

Ignorance of the law of nature excuses no man.

The source of every crime is some defect of the understanding or some error in reasoning or some sudden force of the passions. Defect in the understanding is *ignorance;* in reasoning, *erroneous opinion.* Again, ignorance is of three sorts: of the *law,* and of the *sovereign,* and of the *penalty.* Ignorance of the law of nature excuses no man, because every man that has attained to the use of reason is supposed to know he ought not to do to another what he would not have done to himself. Therefore into what place soever a man shall come, if he do anything contrary to that law, it is a crime. If a man come from the Indies hither, and persuade men here to receive a new religion, or teach them anything that tends to disobedience of the laws of this country, though he be never so well persuaded of the truth of what he teaches, he commits a crime and may be justly punished for the same, not only because his doctrine is false but also because he does that which he would not approve in another, namely, that coming from hence, he should endeavor to alter the religion there. But ignorance of the civil law shall excuse a man in a strange country till it be declared to him, because till then no civil law is binding.

Ignorance of the civil law excuses sometimes.

In the like manner, if the civil law of a man's own country be not so sufficiently declared as he may know it if he will, nor the action against the law of nature, the ignorance is a good excuse; in other cases ignorance of the civil law excuses not.

Ignorance of the sovereign excuses not.

Ignorance of the sovereign power in the place of a man's ordinary residence excuses him not, because he ought to take notice of the power by which he has been protected there.

Ignorance of the penalty excuses not.

Ignorance of the penalty, where the law is declared, excuses no man, for in breaking the law, which without a fear of penalty to follow were not a law but vain words, he undergoes the penalty, though he know not what it is; because whosoever voluntarily does any action accepts all the known consequences of it; but punishment is a known consequence of the violation of the laws in every commonwealth; which punishment, if it be determined already by the law, he is subject to that; if not, then he is subject to arbitrary punishment. For it is reason that he which does injury, without other limitation than that of his own will, should suffer punishment without other limitation than that of his will whose law is thereby violated.

Punishments declared before the fact excuse from greater punishments after it. But when a penalty is either annexed to the crime in the law itself or has been usually inflicted in the like cases, there the delinquent is excused from a greater penalty. For the punishment foreknown, if not great enough to deter men from the action, is an invitement to it, because when men compare the benefit of their injustice with the harm of their punishment, by necessity of nature they choose that which appears best for themselves; and therefore when they are punished more than the law had formerly determined, or more than others were punished for the same crime, it is the law that tempted and deceives them.

Nothing can be made a crime by a law made after the fact. No law made after a fact done can make it a crime, because if the fact be against the law of nature the law was before the fact, and a positive law cannot be taken notice of before it be made and therefore cannot be obligatory. But when the law that forbids a fact is made before the fact be done, yet he that does the fact is liable to the penalty ordained after, in case no lesser penalty were made known before, neither by writing nor by example, for the reason immediately before alleged.

False principles of right and wrong causes of crime. From defect in reasoning—that is to say, from error—men are prone to violate the laws three ways. First, by presumption of false principles: as when men, from having observed how in all places and in all ages unjust actions have been authorized by the force and victories of those who have committed them, and that, potent men breaking through the cobweb laws of their country, the weaker sort and those that have failed in their enterprises have been esteemed the only criminals, have thereupon taken for principles and grounds of their reasoning *that justice is but*

*a vain word, that whatsoever a man can get by his own industry
and hazard is his own, that the practice of all nations cannot be
unjust, that examples of former times are good arguments of
doing the like again,* and many more of that kind; which being
granted, no act in itself can be a crime but must be made so, not
by the law, but by the success of them that commit it; and the
same fact be virtuous or vicious as fortune pleases, so that what
Marius makes a crime, Sulla shall make meritorious, and Caesar, the same laws standing, turn again into a crime, to the perpetual disturbance of the peace of the commonwealth.[4]

*False teachers mis-
interpreting the law
of nature.*
Secondly, by false teachers, that either misin-
terpret the law of nature, making it thereby
repugnant to the law civil, or by teaching for
laws such doctrines of their own or traditions
of former times as are inconsistent with the duty of a subject.

*And false inferences
from true princi-
ples, by teachers.*
Thirdly, by erroneous inferences from true
principles, which happens commonly to men
that are hasty and precipitate in concluding
and resolving what to do: such as are they that
have both a great opinion of their own understanding and believe that things of this nature require not time and study but
only common experience and a good natural wit, whereof no
man thinks himself unprovided; whereas the knowledge of right
and wrong, which is no less difficult, there is no man will pretend to without great and long study. And of those defects in
reasoning, there is none that can excuse, though some of them
may extenuate, a crime in any man that pretends to the administration of his own private business, much less in them that undertake a public charge, because they pretend to the reason
upon the want whereof they would ground their excuse.

By their passions.
Of the passions that most frequently are the
causes of crime, one is vainglory, or a foolish
overrating of their own worth—as if difference of worth were an
effect of their wit or riches or blood or some other natural qual-

[4] [The rivalry for power of Gaius Marius (157-86 B.C.) and Lucius Cornelius Sulla (138-78 B.C.) inaugurated the series of civil wars and military dic-
tatorships which destroyed the Roman republic. The ablest of the dictators
was Julius Caesar (102-44 B.C.), whose career was ended by his assassination.
His heir Augustus finally pacified the state and firmly established the princi-
pate or empire.]

ity, not depending on the will of those that have the sovereign authority. From whence proceeds a presumption that the punishments ordained by the laws, and extended generally to all subjects, ought not to be inflicted on them with the same rigor they are inflicted on poor, obscure, and simple men, comprehended under the name of the *vulgar*.

Presumption of riches.

Therefore it happens commonly that such as value themselves by the greatness of their wealth adventure on crimes upon hope of escaping punishment by corrupting public justice or obtaining pardon by money or other rewards.

And friends.

And that such as have multitude of potent kindred, and popular men that have gained reputation among the multitude, take courage to violate the laws from a hope of oppressing the power to whom it belongs to put them in execution.

Wisdom.

And that such as have a great and false opinion of their own wisdom take upon them to reprehend the actions and call in question the authority of them that govern, and so to unsettle the laws with their public discourse as that nothing shall be a crime but what their own designs require should be so. It happens also to the same men to be prone to all such crimes as consist in craft and in deceiving of their neighbors, because they think their designs are too subtle to be perceived. These, I say, are effects of a false presumption of their own wisdom. For of them that are the first movers in the disturbance of commonwealth, which can never happen without a civil war, very few are left alive long enough to see their new designs established, so that the benefit of their crimes redounds to posterity and such as would least have wished it, which argues they were not so wise as they thought they were. And those that deceive upon hope of not being observed do commonly deceive themselves, the darkness in which they believe they lie hidden being nothing else but their own blindness; and are no wiser than children that think all hid by hiding their own eyes.

And generally all vainglorious men, unless they be withal timorous, are subject to anger, as being more prone than others to interpret for contempt the ordinary liberty of conversation; and there are few crimes that may not be produced by anger.

As for the passions of hate, lust, ambition, and
Hatred, lust, ambi- covetousness, what crimes they are apt to pro-
tion, covetousness,
causes of crime. duce is so obvious to every man's experience
and understanding as there needs nothing to
be said of them, saving that they are infirmities so annexed to the
nature both of man and all other living creatures as that their
effects cannot be hindered but by extraordinary use of reason or
a constant severity in punishing them. For in those things men
hate they find a continual and unavoidable molestation,
whereby either a man's patience must be everlasting, or he must
be eased by removing the power of that which molests him. The
former is difficult; the latter is many times impossible without
some violation of the law. Ambition and covetousness are passions also that are perpetually incumbent and pressing, whereas
reason is not perpetually present to resist them; and therefore
whensoever the hope of impunity appears, their effects proceed.
And for lust, what it wants in the lasting it has in the vehemence, which suffices to weigh down the apprehension of all easy
or uncertain punishments.

Of all passions, that which inclines men least to
Fear sometimes break the laws is fear. Nay, excepting some
cause of crime, as
when the danger generous natures, it is the only thing, when
is neither present there is apparence of profit or pleasure by
nor corporeal. breaking the laws, that makes men keep them.
And yet in many cases a crime may be committed through fear.

For not every fear justifies the action it produces, but the fear
only of corporeal hurt, which we call *bodily fear* and from
which a man cannot see how to be delivered but by the action.
A man is assaulted, fears present death, from which he sees not
how to escape but by wounding him that assaults him; if he
wound him to death, this is no crime, because no man is supposed at the making of a commonwealth to have abandoned the
defense of his life or limbs where the law cannot arrive time
enough to his assistance. But to kill a man because from his actions or his threatenings I may argue he will kill me when he
can, seeing I have time and means to demand protection from
the sovereign power, is a crime. Again, a man receives words of
disgrace or some little injuries for which they that made the laws
had assigned no punishment, nor thought it worthy of a man

that has the use of reason to take notice of, and is afraid, unless he revenge it, he shall fall into contempt and consequently be obnoxious to the like injuries from others; and to avoid this, breaks the law and protects himself for the future by the terror of his private revenge. This is a crime, for the hurt is not corporeal but phantastical and, though in this corner of the world made sensible by a custom not many years since begun among young and vain men, so light as a gallant man and one that is assured of his own courage cannot take notice of. Also a man may stand in fear of spirits, either through his own superstition or through too much credit given to other men that tell him of strange dreams and visions, and thereby be made believe they will hurt him for doing or omitting divers things which nevertheless to do or omit is contrary to the laws; and that which is so done or omitted is not to be excused by this fear, but is a crime. For, as I have shown before in the second chapter, dreams be naturally but the fancies remaining in sleep after the impressions our senses had formerly received waking, and, when men are by any accident unassured they have slept, seem to be real visions; and therefore he that presumes to break the law upon his own or another's dream or pretended vision, or upon other fancy of the power of invisible spirits, than is permitted by the commonwealth, leaves the law of nature, which is a certain offense, and follows the imagery of his own or another private man's brain, which he can never know whether it signifies anything or nothing, nor whether he that tells his dream say true or lie; which if every private man should have leave to do, as they must by the law of nature if anyone have it, there could no law be made to hold, and so all commonwealth would be dissolved.

Crimes not equal. From these different sources of crimes it appears already that all crimes are not, as the Stoics of old time maintained, of the same alloy. There is place not only for EXCUSE, by which that which seemed a crime is proved to be none at all, but also for EXTENUATION, by which the crime that seemed great is made less. For though all crimes do equally deserve the name of injustice, as all deviation from a straight line is equally crookedness—which the Stoics rightly observed—yet it does not follow that all crimes are equally unjust, no more than that all crooked lines are equally crooked—which the Stoics not observing, held it as great a crime to kill a hen against the law as to kill one's father.

Total excuses. That which totally excuses a fact and takes away from it the nature of a crime can be none but that which at the same time takes away the obligation of the law. For the fact committed once against the law, if he that committed it be obliged to the law, can be no other than a crime.

The want of means to know the law totally excuses. For the law whereof a man has no means to inform himself is not obligatory. But the want of diligence to inquire shall not be considered as a want of means, nor shall any man that pretends to reason enough for the government of his own affairs be supposed to want means to know the laws of nature, because they are known by the reason he pretends to; only children and madmen are excused from offenses against the law natural.

Where a man is captive or in the power of the enemy (and he is then in the power of the enemy when his person or his means of living is so), if it be without his own fault, the obligation of the law ceases; because he must obey the enemy or die, and consequently such obedience is no crime, for no man is obliged, when the protection of the law fails, not to protect himself by the best means he can.

If a man, by the terror of present death, be compelled to do a fact against the law, he is totally excused, because no law can oblige a man to abandon his own preservation. And supposing such a law were obligatory, yet a man would reason thus: *If I do it not, I die presently; if I do it, I die afterwards; therefore by doing it, there is time of life gained;* nature therefore compels him to the fact.

When a man is destitute of food or other thing necessary for his life, and cannot preserve himself any other way but by some fact against the law—as if in a great famine he take the food by force or stealth which he cannot obtain for money nor charity, or in defense of his life snatch away another man's sword—he is totally excused, for the reason next before alleged.

Excuses against the author. Again, facts done against the law by the authority of another are by that authority excused against the author, because no man ought to accuse his own fact in another that is but his instrument; but it is not excused against a third person thereby injured, because in the violation of the law both the author and actor are criminals. From hence it follows that when that man or assembly that has the sovereign power commands a man to do that which is contrary to a former law, the doing of it is totally excused; for he ought not to condemn it himself because he is the author, and what cannot justly be condemned by the sovereign cannot justly be punished by any other. Besides, when the sovereign commands anything to be done against his own former law, the command, as to that particular fact, is an abrogation of the law.

If that man or assembly that has the sovereign power disclaim any right essential to the sovereignty, whereby there accrues to the subject any liberty inconsistent with the sovereign power— that is to say, with the very being of a commonwealth—if the subject shall refuse to obey the command in anything contrary to the liberty granted, this is nevertheless a sin, and contrary to the duty of the subject; for he ought to take notice of what is inconsistent with the sovereignty, because it was erected by his own consent and for his own defense, and that such liberty as is inconsistent with it was granted through ignorance of the evil consequence thereof. But if he not only disobey, but also resist a public minister in the execution of it, then it is a crime, because he might have been righted, without any breach of the peace, upon complaint.

The degrees of crime are taken on divers scales, and measured, first, by the malignity of the source or cause; secondly, by the contagion of the example; thirdly, by the mischief of the effect; and fourthly, by the concurrence of times, places, and persons.

Presumption of power aggravates. The same fact done against the law, if it proceed from presumption of strength, riches, or friends to resist those that are to execute the law, is a greater crime than if it proceed from hope of not being discovered or of escape by flight; for presumption of impunity by force is a root from whence springs, at all times and upon all temptations, a contempt of all laws, whereas in the latter case the apprehension of danger that makes a man fly renders him more obedient for the future. A crime which we know to be so is greater than the same crime proceeding from a false persuasion that it is lawful; for he that commits it against his own conscience presumes on his force or other power, which encourages him to commit the same again, but he that does it by error, after the error is shown him, is conformable to the law.

Evil teachers extenuate. He whose error proceeds from the authority of a teacher or an interpreter of the law publicly authorized is not so faulty as he whose error proceeds from a peremptory pursuit of his own principles and reasoning; for what is taught by one that teaches by public authority the commonwealth teaches, and has a resemblance of law till the same authority controls it, and in all crimes that contain not in them a denial of the sovereign power, nor are against an evident law, excuses totally; whereas he that grounds his actions on his private judgment ought, according to the rectitude or error thereof, to stand or fall.

Examples of impunity extenuate. The same fact, if it have been constantly punished in other men, is a greater crime than if there have been many precedent examples of impunity. For those examples are so many hopes of impunity given by the sovereign himself; and because he which furnishes a man with such a hope and presumption of mercy as encourages him to offend has his part in the offense, he cannot reasonably charge the offender with the whole.

Premeditation aggravates. A crime arising from a sudden passion is not so great as when the same arises from long meditation, for in the former case there is a place for extenuation in the common infirmity of human nature; but he that does it with premeditation has used circumspection and cast his eye on the law, on the punishment, and on the consequence thereof to human society, all which, in committing the crime, he has contemned and postposed to his own appetite. But there is no suddenness of passion sufficient for a total excuse, for all the time between the first knowing of the law and the commission of the fact shall be taken for a time of deliberation, because he ought by meditation of the law to rectify the irregularity of his passions.

Where the law is publicly and with assiduity before all the people read and interpreted, a fact done against it is a greater crime than where men are left without such instruction, to inquire of it with difficulty, uncertainty, and interruption of their callings, and be informed by private men; for in this case, part of the fault is discharged upon common infirmity, but in the former there is apparent negligence, which is not without some contempt of the sovereign power.

Those facts which the law expressly condemns *Tacit approbation of the sovereign extenuates.* but the lawmaker, by other manifest signs of his will, tacitly approves are less crimes than the same facts condemned both by the law and lawmaker. For seeing the will of the lawmaker is a law, there appear in this case two contradictory laws, which would totally excuse if men were bound to take notice of the sovereign's approbation by other arguments than are expressed by his command. But because there are punishments consequent not only to the transgression of his law but also to the observing of it, he is in part a cause of the transgression and therefore cannot reasonably impute the whole crime to the delinquent. For example, the law condemns duels, the punishment is made capital; on the contrary part, he that refuses duel is subject to contempt and scorn, without remedy, and sometimes by the sovereign himself thought unworthy to have any charge or preferment in war. If thereupon he accept duel, considering all men lawfully endeavor to obtain the good opinion of them that have the sovereign power, he ought not in reason to be rigorously punished, seeing part of the fault may be discharged on the punisher; which I say, not as wishing liberty of private revenges or any other kind of disobedience, but a care in governors not to countenance anything obliquely which directly they forbid. The examples of princes to those that see them are, and ever have been, more potent to govern their actions than the laws themselves. And though it be our duty to do not what they do but what they say, yet will that duty never be performed till it please God to give man an extraordinary and supernatural grace to follow that precept.

Again, if we compare crimes by the mischief of *Comparison of crimes from their effects.* their effects, first, the same fact, when it redounds to the damage of many, is greater than when it redounds to the hurt of few. And therefore, when a fact hurts not only in the present but also, by example, in the future, it is a greater crime than if it hurt only in the present; for the former is a fertile crime, and multiplies to the hurt of many; the latter is barren. To maintain doctrines contrary to the religion established in the commonwealth is a greater fault in an authorized preacher than in a private person; so also is it to live profanely, incontinently, or do any irreligious act whatsoever. Likewise in a professor of the law, to maintain any point or do any act that tends to the weakening of the sovereign power is a greater crime than in another man; also in a man that has such reputation for wisdom as that his counsels are followed or his actions imitated by many, his fact against the law is a greater crime than the same fact in another: for such men not only commit crime, but teach it for law to all other men. And generally all crimes are the greater by the scandal they give—that is to say, by becoming stumbling blocks to the weak, that look not so much upon the way they go in as upon the light that other men carry before them.

Laesa Majestas. Also facts of hostility against the present state of the commonwealth are greater crimes than the same acts done to private men, for the damage extends itself to all: such are the betraying of the strengths or revealing of the secrets of the commonwealth to an enemy; also all attempts upon the representative of the commonwealth, be it a monarch or an assembly; and all endeavors by word or deed to diminish the authority of the same, either in the present time or in succession—which crimes the Latins understand by *crimina laesae majestatis,* and consist in design or act contrary to a fundamental law.

Bribery and false testimony. Likewise those crimes which render judgments of no effect are greater crimes than injuries done to one or a few persons; as to receive money to give false judgment or testimony is a greater crime than otherwise to deceive a man of the like or a greater sum, because not only he has wrong that falls by such judgments, but all judgments are rendered useless, and occasion ministered to force and private revenges.

Depeculation. Also robbery and depeculation of the public treasure or revenues is a greater crime than the robbing or defrauding of a private man, because to rob the public is to rob many at once.

Counterfeiting
authority.

Also the counterfeit usurpation of public ministry, the counterfeiting of public seals or public coin, than counterfeiting of a private man's person or his seal, because the fraud thereof extends to the damage of many.

Crimes against pri-
vate men compared.

Of facts against the law done to private men, the greater crime is that where the damage in the common opinion of men is most sensible. And therefore—

To kill against the law is a greater crime than any other injury, life preserved.

And to kill with torment, greater than simply to kill.

And mutilation of a limb, greater than the spoiling a man of his goods.

And the spoiling a man of his goods by terror of death or wounds, than by clandestine surreption.

And by clandestine surreption, than by consent fraudulently obtained.

And the violation of chastity by force, greater than by flattery.

And of a woman married, than of a woman not married.

For all these things are commonly so valued, though some men are more and some less sensible of the same offense. But the law regards not the particular but the general inclination of mankind.

And therefore the offense men take from contumely, in words or gesture, when they produce no other harm than the present grief of him that is reproached, has been neglected in the laws of the Greeks, Romans, and other both ancient and modern commonwealths, supposing the true cause of such grief to consist, not in the contumely, which takes no hold upon men conscious of their own virtue, but in the pusillanimity of him that is offended by it.

Also a crime against a private man is much aggravated by the person, time, and place. For to kill one's parent is a greater crime than to kill another, for the parent ought to have the honor of a sovereign, though he surrendered his power to the civil law, because he had it originally by nature. And to rob a poor man is a greater crime than to rob a rich man, because it is to the poor a more sensible damage.

And a crime committed in the time or place appointed for devotion is greater than if committed at another time or place, for it proceeds from a greater contempt of the law.

Many other cases of aggravation and extenuation might be added, but by these I have set down it is obvious to every man to take the altitude of any other crime proposed.

Public crimes, what. Lastly, because in almost all crimes there is an injury done not only to some private men but also to the commonwealth, the same crime, when the accusation is in the name of the commonwealth, is called public crime, and when in the name of a private man, a private crime; and the pleas according thereunto called public, *judicia publica,* Pleas of the Crown, or Private Pleas. As in an accusation of murder, if the accuser be a private man, the plea is a Private Plea; if the accuser be the sovereign, the plea is a Public Plea.

CHAPTER TWENTY-EIGHT

OF PUNISHMENTS AND REWARDS

The definition of punishment. A PUNISHMENT *is an evil inflicted by public authority on him that has done or omitted that which is judged by the same authority to be a transgression of the law; to the end that the will of men may thereby the better be disposed to obedience.*

Right to punish, whence derived. Before I infer anything from this definition, there is a question to be answered of much importance—which is, by what door the right or authority of punishing in any case came in. For by that which has been said before, no man is supposed bound by covenant not to resist violence, and consequently it cannot be intended that he gave any right to another to lay violent hands upon his person. In the making of a commonwealth, every man gives away the right of defending another, but not of defending himself.

Also he obliges himself to assist him that has the sovereignty in the punishing of another, but of himself not. But to covenant to assist the sovereign in doing hurt to another, unless he that so covenants have a right to do it himself, is not to give him a right to punish. It is manifest therefore that the right which the commonwealth—that is, he or they that represent it—has to punish is not grounded on any concession or gift of the subjects. But I have also shown formerly that before the institution of commonwealth every man had a right to everything and to do whatsoever he thought necessary to his own preservation, subduing, hurting, or killing any man in order thereunto. And this is the foundation of that right of punishing which is exercised in every commonwealth. For the subjects did not give the sovereign that right, but only in laying down theirs strengthened him to use his own as he should think fit for the preservation of them all; so that it was not given but left to him, and to him only, and (excepting the limits set him by natural law) as entire as in the condition of mere nature and of war of every one against his neighbor.

Private injuries and revenges no punishments.

From the definitions of punishment, I infer, first, that neither private revenges nor injuries of private men can properly be styled punishment, because they proceed not from public authority.

Nor denial of preferment;

Secondly, that to be neglected and unpreferred by the public favor is not a punishment, because no new evil is thereby on any man inflicted—he is only left in the estate he was in before.

Nor pain inflicted without public hearing;

Thirdly, that the evil inflicted by public authority without precedent public condemnation is not to be styled by the name of punishment but of a hostile act, because the fact for which a man is punished ought first to be judged by public authority to be a transgression of the law.

Nor pain inflicted by usurped power;

Fourthly, that the evil inflicted by usurped power, and judges without authority from the sovereign, is not punishment but an act of hostility, because the acts of power usurped have not for author the person condemned and therefore are not acts of public authority.

Nor pain inflicted without respect to the future good.

Fifthly, that all evil which is inflicted without intention or possibility of disposing the delinquent or, by his example, other men to obey the laws is not punishment but an act of hostility, because without such an end no hurt done is contained under that name.

Natural evil consequences no punishments.

Sixthly, whereas to certain actions there be annexed by nature divers hurtful consequences—as when a man in assaulting another is himself slain or wounded, or when he falls into sickness by the doing of some unlawful act—such hurt, though in respect of God, who is the author of nature, it may be said to be inflicted and therefore a punishment divine, yet it is not contained in the name of punishment in respect of men, because it is not inflicted by the authority of man.

Hurt inflicted, if less than the benefit of transgressing, is not punishment.

Seventhly, if the harm inflicted be less than the benefit or contentment that naturally follows the crime committed, that harm is not within the definition, and is rather the price or redemption than the punishment of a crime; because it is of the nature of punishment to have for end the disposing of men to obey the law, which end, if it be less than the benefit of the transgression, it attains not, but works a contrary effect.

Where the punishment is annexed to the law, a greater hurt is not punishment but hostility.

Eighthly, if a punishment be determined and prescribed in the law itself, and after the crime committed there be a greater punishment inflicted, the excess is not punishment but an act of hostility. For seeing the aim of punishment is not a revenge but terror, and the terror of a great punishment unknown is taken away by the declaration of a less, the unexpected addition is no part of the punishment. But where there is no punishment at all determined by the law, there whatsoever is inflicted has the nature of punishment. For he that goes about the violation of a law wherein no penalty is determined expects an indeterminate—that is to say, an arbitrary—punishment.

Hurt inflicted for a fact done before the law no punishment.

Ninthly, harm inflicted for a fact done before there was a law that forbade it is not punishment but an act of hostility; for before the law there is no transgression of the law; but punishment supposes a fact judged to have been a transgression of the law; therefore harm inflicted before the law made is not punishment but an act of hostility.

The representative of the commonwealth unpunishable.

Tenthly, hurt inflicted on the representative of the commonwealth is not punishment but an act of hostility, because it is of the nature of punishment to be inflicted by public authority, which is the authority only of the representative itself.

Hurt to revolted subjects is done by right of war, not by way of punishment.

Lastly, harm inflicted upon one that is a declared enemy falls not under the name of punishment, because seeing they were either never subject to the law and therefore cannot transgress it, or having been subject to it and professing to be no longer so by consequence deny they can transgress it, all the harms that can be done them must be taken as acts of hostility. But in declared hostility, all infliction of evil is lawful. From whence it follows that if a subject shall by fact or word wittingly and deliberately deny the authority of the representative of the commonwealth (whatsoever penalty has been formerly ordained for treason) he may lawfully be made to suffer whatsoever the representative will. For in denying subjection, he denies such punishment as by the law has been ordained, and therefore suffers as an enemy of the commonwealth —that is, according to the will of the representative. For the punishments set down in the law are to subjects, not to enemies; such as are they that having been by their own acts subjects, deliberately revolting, deny the sovereign power.

The first and most general distribution of punishments is into *divine* and *human*. Of the former I shall have occasion to speak in a more convenient place hereafter.[1]

Human are those punishments that be inflicted by the commandment of man; and are either *corporal* or *pecuniary* or *ignominy* or *imprisonment* or *exile* or mixed of these.

[1] [In Part III, "Of a Christian Commonwealth," not included in the present edition.]

Punishments corporal.   *Corporal punishment* is that which is inflicted on the body directly, and according to the intention of him that inflicts it: such as are stripes, or wounds, or deprivation of such pleasures of the body as were before lawfully enjoyed.

Capital.   And of these, some be *capital*, some *less* than capital. Capital is the infliction of death, and that either simply or with torment. Less than capital are stripes, wounds, chains, and any other corporal pain not in its own nature mortal. For if upon the infliction of a punishment death follow not in the intention of the inflictor, the punishment is not to be esteemed capital, though the harm prove mortal by an accident not to be foreseen—in which case death is not inflicted but hastened.

Pecuniary punishment is that which consists not only in the deprivation of a sum of money, but also of lands or any other goods which are usually bought and sold for money. And in case the law that ordains such a punishment be made with design to gather money from such as shall transgress the same, it is not properly a punishment but the price of privilege and exemption from the law, which does not absolutely forbid the fact but only to those that are not able to pay the money—except where the law is natural or part of religion, for in that case it is not an exemption from the law but a transgression of it. As where a law exacts a pecuniary mulct of them that take the name of God in vain, the payment of the mulct is not the price of a dispensation to swear but the punishment of the transgression of a law indispensable. In like manner if the law impose a sum of money to be paid to him that has been injured, this is but a satisfaction for the hurt done him and extinguishes the accusation of the party injured, not the crime of the offender.

Ignominy.   *Ignominy* is the infliction of such evil as is made dishonorable, or the deprivation of such good as is made honorable, by the commonwealth. For there be some things honorable by nature, as the effects of courage, magnanimity, strength, wisdom, and other abilities of body and mind; others made honorable by the commonwealth, as badges, titles, offices, or any other singular mark of the sovereign's favor. The former, though they may fail by nature or accident, cannot be taken away by a law, and therefore the loss of them is not punishment. But the latter may be taken away by the public authority that made them honorable and are properly punishments; such are degrading men condemned of their badges, titles, and offices, or declaring them incapable of the like in time to come.

Imprisonment. *Imprisonment* is when a man is by public authority deprived of liberty, and may happen from two divers ends, whereof one is the safe custody of a man accused, the other is the inflicting of pain on a man condemned. The former is not punishment, because no man is supposed to be punished before he be judicially heard and declared guilty. And therefore whatsoever hurt a man is made to suffer by bonds or restraint before his cause be heard, over and above that which is necessary to assure his custody, is against the law of nature. But the latter is punishment, because evil and inflicted by public authority for somewhat that has by the same authority been judged a transgression of the law. Under this word *imprisonment* I comprehend all restraint of motion caused by an external obstacle, be it a house, which is called by the general name of a prison; or an island, as when men are said to be confined to it; or a place where men are set to work, as in old time men have been condemned to quarries and in these times to galleys; or be it a chain, or any other such impediment.

Exile. *Exile* (banishment) is when a man is for a crime condemned to depart out of the dominion of the commonwealth or out of a certain part thereof; and during a prefixed time, or forever, not to return into it; and seems not in its own nature, without other circumstances, to be a punishment but rather an escape, or a public commandment to avoid punishment by flight. And Cicero says there was never any such punishment ordained in the city of Rome, but calls it a refuge of men in danger. For if a man banished be nevertheless permitted to enjoy his goods and the revenue of his lands, the mere change of air is no punishment, nor does it tend to that benefit of the commonwealth for which all punishments are ordained— that is to say, to the forming of men's wills to the observation of the law—but many times to the damage of the commonwealth. For a banished man is a lawful enemy of the commonwealth that banished him as being no more a member of the same. But if he be withal deprived of his lands or goods, then the punishment lies not in the exile but is to be reckoned among punishments pecuniary.

The punishment of innocent subjects is contrary to the law of nature.

All punishments of innocent subjects, be they great or little, are against the law of nature; for punishment is only for transgression of the law, and therefore there can be no punishment of the innocent. It is therefore a violation, first, of that law of nature which forbids all men, in their revenges, to look at anything but some future good, for there can arrive no good to the commonwealth by punishing the innocent. Secondly, of that which forbids ingratitude, for seeing all sovereign power is originally given by the consent of every one of the subjects, to the end they should as long as they are obedient be protected thereby, the punishment of the innocent is a rendering of evil for good. And thirdly, of the law that commands equity—that is to say, an equal distribution of justice—which in punishing the innocent is not observed.

But the harm done to innocents in war not so.

But the infliction of what evil soever on an innocent man that is not a subject, if it be for the benefit of the commonwealth and without violation of any former covenant, is no breach of the law of nature. For all men that are not subjects are either enemies or else they have ceased from being so by some precedent covenants. But against enemies whom the commonwealth judges capable to do them hurt, it is lawful by the original right of nature to make war, wherein the sword judges not, nor does the victor make distinction of nocent and innocent as to the time past nor has other respect of mercy than as it conduces to

Nor that which is done to declared rebels.

the good of his own people. And upon this ground it is that also in subjects who deliberately deny the authority of the commonwealth established, the vengeance is lawfully extended, not only to the fathers, but also to the third and fourth generation not yet in being and consequently innocent of the fact for which they are afflicted; because the nature of this offense consists in the renouncing of subjection, which is a relapse into the condition of war commonly called rebellion, and they that so

offend suffer not as subjects but as enemies. For *rebellion* is but
war renewed.

REWARD is either of *gift* or by *contract*. When
Reward is either salary or grace. by contract, it is called *salary* and *wages,* which
is benefit due for service performed or prom-
ised. When of gift, it is benefit proceeding from the *grace* of
them that bestow it, to encourage or enable men to do them
service. And therefore when the sovereign of a commonwealth
appoints a salary to any public office, he that receives it is bound
in justice to perform his office; otherwise, he is bound only in
honor to acknowledgment and an endeavor of requital. For
though men have no lawful remedy when they be commanded
to quit their private business to serve the public without reward or salary, yet they are not bound thereto by the law of nature nor by the institution of the commonwealth unless the
service cannot otherwise be done; because it is supposed the sovereign may make use of all their means, insomuch as the most
common soldier may demand the wages of his warfare as a debt.

The benefits which a sovereign bestows on a
Benefits bestowed for fear are not rewards. subject for fear of some power and ability he
has to do hurt to the commonwealth are not
properly rewards; for they are not salaries, because there is in this case no contract supposed, every man being
obliged already not to do the commonwealth disservice; nor are
they graces, because they be extorted by fear, which ought not
to be incident to the sovereign power; but are rather sacrifices
which the sovereign, considered in his natural person and not
in the person of the commonwealth, makes for the appeasing the
discontent of him he thinks more potent than himself; and encourage not to obedience, but on the contrary to the continuance and increasing of further extortion.

And whereas some salaries are certain and pro-
Salaries certain and casual. ceed from the public treasure, and others uncertain and casual, proceeding from the execu-
tion of the office for which the salary is ordained, the latter is in
some cases hurtful to the commonwealth, as in the case of judicature. For where the benefit of the judges and ministers of a
court of justice arises from the multitude of causes that are
brought to their cognizance, there must needs follow two inconveniences: one is the nourishing of suits, for the more suits, the

greater benefit; and another that depends on that which is contention about jurisdiction, each court drawing to itself as many causes as it can. But in offices of execution there are not those inconveniences, because their employment cannot be increased by any endeavor of their own. And thus much shall suffice for the nature of punishment and reward, which are, as it were, the nerves and tendons that move the limbs and joints of a commonwealth.

Hitherto I have set forth the nature of man, whose pride and other passions have compelled him to submit himself to government; together with the great power of his governor, whom I compared to *Leviathan,* taking that comparison out of the two last verses of the one-and-fortieth of Job, where God, having set forth the great power of *Leviathan,* calls him King of the Proud. *There is nothing,* says he, *on earth to be compared with him. He is made so as not to be afraid. He seeth every high thing below him, and is king of all the children of pride.* But because he is mortal and subject to decay, as all other earthly creatures are, and because there is that in heaven, though not on earth, that he should stand in fear of, and whose laws he ought to obey, I shall in the next following chapters speak of his diseases and the causes of his mortality and of what laws of nature he is bound to obey.

CHAPTER TWENTY-NINE

OF THOSE THINGS THAT WEAKEN OR TEND TO THE DISSOLUTION OF A COMMONWEALTH

Dissolution of commonwealths proceeds from their imperfect institution. Though nothing can be immortal which mortals make, yet if men had the use of reason they pretend to their commonwealths might be secured at least from perishing by internal diseases. For by the nature of their institution they are designed to live as long as mankind, or as the laws of nature, or as justice itself, which gives them life. Therefore when they come to be dissolved, not by external violence but intestine disorder, the fault is not in men as they are the *matter* but as they are the *makers* and orderers of them. For men, as they become at last weary of irregular jostling and hewing one another and desire with all their hearts to conform themselves into one firm and lasting edifice, so for want both of the art of making fit laws to square their actions by, and also of humility and patience to suffer the rude and cumbersome points of their present greatness to be taken off, they cannot without the help of a very able architect be compiled into any other than a crazy building, such as, hardly lasting out their own time, must assuredly fall upon the heads of their posterity.

Among the *infirmities,* therefore, of a commonwealth, I will reckon in the first place those that arise from an imperfect institution and resemble the diseases of a natural body which proceed from a defectuous procreation.

Of which this is one: *that a man, to obtain a kingdom, is sometimes content with less power than to the peace and defense of the commonwealth is necessarily required.* From whence it comes to pass that when the exercise of the power laid by is for the public safety to be resumed, it has the resemblance of an unjust act, which disposes great numbers of men, when occasion is presented, to rebel; in the same manner as the bodies of children, gotten by diseased parents, are subject either to untimely death or to purge the ill quality derived from their vicious conception by breaking out into biles and scabs. And when kings deny themselves some such necessary power, it is not always, though sometimes, out of ignorance of what is necessary to the office they undertake, but many times out of a hope to recover the same again at their pleasure. Wherein they reason not well, because such as will hold them to their promises shall be maintained against them by foreign commonwealths, who in order to the good of their own subjects let slip few occasions to *weaken* the estate of their neighbors. So was Thomas Becket, archbishop of Canterbury, supported against Henry the Second by the Pope, the subjection of ecclesiastics to the commonwealth having been dispensed with by William the Conqueror at his reception when he took an oath not to infringe the liberty of

Want of absolute power.

the church. And so were the barons, whose power was by William Rufus, to have their help in transferring the succession from his elder brother to himself, increased to a degree inconsistent with the sovereign power, maintained in their rebellion against King John by the French.

Nor does this happen in monarchy only. For whereas the style of the ancient Roman commonwealth was *The Senate and People of Rome,* neither senate nor people pretended to the whole power; which first caused the seditions of Tiberius Gracchus, Caius Gracchus, Lucius Saturninus, and others, and afterwards the wars between the senate and the people under Marius and Sulla, and again under Pompey and Caesar, to the extinction of their democracy and the setting up of monarchy.

The people of Athens bound themselves but from one only action, which was that no man on pain of death should propound the renewing of the war for the island of Salamis; and yet thereby—if Solon had not caused to be given out he was mad, and afterwards in gesture and habit of a madman, and in verse, propounded it to the people that flocked about him—they had had an enemy perpetually in readiness, even at the gates of their city; such damage or shifts are all commonwealths forced to, that have their power never so little limited.

Private judgment of good and evil. In the second place, I observe the *diseases* of a commonwealth that proceed from the poison of seditious doctrines, whereof one is *that every private man is judge of good and evil actions.* This is true in the condition of mere nature, where there are no civil laws; and also under civil government in such cases as are not determined by the law. But otherwise, it is manifest that the measure of good and evil actions is the civil law, and the judge the legislator, who is always representative of the commonwealth. From this false doctrine, men are disposed to debate with themselves and dispute the commands of the commonwealth, and afterwards to obey or disobey them as in their private judgments they shall think fit, whereby the commonwealth is distracted and *weakened.*

Erroneous conscience. Another doctrine repugnant to civil society is *that whatsoever a man does against his conscience is sin;* and it depends on the presumption of making himself judge of good and evil. For a man's conscience and his judgment is the same thing, and as the judgment, so also the conscience may be erroneous. Therefore, though he that is subject to no civil law sins in all he does against his conscience because he has no other rule to follow but his own reason, yet it is not so with him that lives in a commonwealth, because the law is the public conscience by which he has already undertaken to be guided. Otherwise in such diversity as there is of private consciences, which are but private opinions, the commonwealth must needs be distracted, and no man dare to obey the sovereign power further than it shall seem good in his own eyes.

It has been also commonly taught *that faith and sanctity are not to be attained by study and reason, but by supernatural inspiration or infusion.* Which granted, I see not why any man should render a reason of his faith, or why every Christian should not be also a prophet, or why any man should take the law of his country rather than his own inspiration for the rule of his action. And thus we fall again in the fault of taking upon us to judge of good and evil, or to make judges of it such private men as pretend to be supernaturally inspired, to the dissolution of all civil government. Faith comes by hearing, and hearing by those accidents which guide us into the presence of them that speak to us; which accidents are all contrived by God Almighty, and yet are not supernatural but only, for the great number of them that concur to every effect, unobservable. Faith and sanctity are indeed not very frequent, but yet they are not miracles, but brought to pass by education, discipline, correction, and other natural ways by which God works them in his elect at such times as he thinks fit. And these three opinions, pernicious to peace and government, have in this part of the world proceeded chiefly from the tongues and pens of unlearned divines, who, joining the words of Holy Scripture together otherwise than is agreeable to reason, do what they can to make men think that sanctity and natural reason cannot stand together.

Pretense of inspiration.

A fourth opinion repugnant to the nature of a commonwealth is this: *that he that has the sovereign power is subject to the civil laws.* It is true that sovereigns are all subject to the laws of nature, because such laws be divine and cannot by any man

Subjecting the sovereign power to civil laws.

or commonwealth be abrogated. But to those laws which the sovereign himself—that is, which the commonwealth—makes he is not subject. For to be subject to laws is to be subject to the commonwealth—that is, to the sovereign representative—that is, to himself, which is not subjection but freedom from the laws. Which error, because it sets the laws above the sovereign, sets also a judge above him and a power to punish him, which is to make a new sovereign, and again for the same reason a third to punish the second, and so continually without end to the confusion and dissolution of the commonwealth.

Attributing of abso-lute propriety to subjects.

A fifth doctrine that tends to the dissolution of a commonwealth is *that every private man has an absolute propriety in his goods such as excludes the right of the sovereign.* Every man has indeed a propriety that excludes the right of every other subject, and he has it only from the sovereign power, without the protection whereof every other man should have equal right to the same. But if the right of the sovereign also be excluded, he cannot perform the office they have put him into, which is to defend them both from foreign enemies and from the injuries of one another; and consequently there is no longer a commonwealth.

And if the propriety of subjects exclude not the right of the sovereign representative to their goods, much less to their offices of judicature or execution in which they represent the sovereign himself.

Dividing of the sovereign power.

There is a sixth doctrine plainly and directly against the essence of a commonwealth, and it is this: *that the sovereign power may be divided.* For what is it to divide the power of a commonwealth but to dissolve it, for powers divided mutually destroy each other. And for these doctrines men are chiefly beholding to some of those that, making profession of the laws, endeavor to make them depend upon their own learning and not upon the legislative power.

Imitation of neighbor nations.

And as false doctrine, so also oftentimes the example of different government in a neighboring nation disposes men to alteration of the form already settled. So the people of the Jews were stirred up to reject God and to call upon the prophet Samuel for a king after the manner of the nations;[1] so also the lesser cities of Greece were continually disturbed with seditions of the aristocratical and democratical factions, one part of almost every commonwealth desiring to imitate the Lacedemonians, the other, the Athenians. And I doubt not but many men have been contented to see the late troubles in England[2] out of an imitation of the Low Countries, supposing there needed no more to grow rich than to change, as they had done, the form of their government.[3] For the constitution of man's nature is of itself subject to desire novelty. When, therefore, they are provoked to the same by the neighborhood also of those that have been enriched by it, it is almost impossible for them not to be content with those that solicit them to change, and love the first beginnings though they be grieved with the continuance of disorder, like hotbloods that, having gotten the itch, tear themselves with their own nails till they can endure the smart no longer.

Imitation of the Greeks and Romans. And as to rebellion in particular against monarchy, one of the most frequent causes of it is the reading of the books of policy and histories of the ancient Greeks and Romans, from which young men and all others that are unprovided of the antidote of solid reason, receiving a strong and delightful impression of the great exploits of war achieved by the conductors of their armies, receive withal a pleasing idea of all they have done besides, and imagine their great prosperity not to have proceeded from the emulation of particular men but from the virtue of their popular form of government, not considering the frequent seditions and civil wars produced by the imperfection of their policy. From the reading, I say, of such books, men have undertaken to

---

1 [I Sam. 8:4-7.]

2 [Reference is to the Civil War. Cf. Editor's Introduction.]

3 [Prompted by a variety of religious, economic, and particularistic motives, the provinces of the Low Countries revolted in 1572 against their overlord, Philip II of Spain. The northern provinces, of which Holland was the chief, succeeded in 1579 in establishing themselves as an independent republic. In Hobbes's time, the Dutch republic was enjoying its golden age. Engaged in constant warfare, it was one of the great powers of Europe, maintaining a powerful navy and carving out an extensive colonial empire. Its commercial prosperity was unequaled, and it was also the center of a flourishing intellectual and artistic life.]

kill their kings, because the Greek and Latin writers, in their books and discourses of policy, make it lawful and laudable for any man so to do, provided before he do it he call him tyrant. For they say not *regicide*—that is, killing a king—but *tyrannicide*—that is, killing of a tyrant—is lawful. From the same books, they that live under a monarch conceive an opinion that the subjects in a popular commonwealth enjoy liberty but that in a monarchy they are all slaves. I say, they that live under a monarchy conceive such an opinion, not they that live under a popular government, for they find no such matter. In sum, I cannot imagine how anything can be more prejudicial to a monarchy than the allowing of such books to be publicly read without present applying such correctives of discreet masters as are fit to take away their venom; which venom I will not doubt to compare to the biting of a mad dog, which is a disease the physicians call *hydrophobia* or *fear of water*. For as he that is so bitten has a continual torment of thirst and yet abhors water, and is in such an estate as if the poison endeavored to convert him into a dog, so when a monarchy is once bitten to the quick by those democratical writers that continually snarl at that estate, it wants nothing more than a strong monarch, which nevertheless, out of a certain *tyrannophobia* or fear of being strongly governed, when they have him they abhor.

As there have been doctors that hold there be three souls in a man, so there be also that think there may be more souls—that is, more sovereigns—than one in a commonwealth, and set up a *supremacy* against the *sovereignty, canons* against *laws,* and a *ghostly authority* against the *civil,* working on men's minds with words and distinctions that of themselves signify nothing but betray by their obscurity that there walks, as some think, invisibly another kingdom—as it were, a kingdom of fairies—in the dark. Now seeing it is manifest that the civil power and the power of the commonwealth is the same thing, and that supremacy and the power of making canons and granting faculties implies a commonwealth, it follows that where one is sovereign, another supreme, where one can make laws and another make canons, there must needs be two commonwealths of one and the same subjects, which is a kingdom divided in itself, and cannot stand. For notwithstanding the insignificant distinction of *temporal* and *ghostly*, they are still two kingdoms and every subject is subject to two masters. For seeing the *ghostly* power challenges the right to declare what is sin, it challenges by consequence to declare what is law, sin being nothing but the transgression of the law; and again, the civil power challenging to declare what is law, every subject must obey two masters who both will have their commands be observed as law, which is impossible. Or, if it be but one kingdom, either the *civil*, which is the power of the commonwealth, must be subordinate to the *ghostly*, and then there is no sovereignty but the *ghostly*, or the *ghostly* must be subordinate to the *temporal*, and then there is no *supremacy* but the *temporal*. When, therefore, these two powers oppose one another, the commonwealth cannot but be in great danger of civil war and dissolution. For the *civil* authority being more visible, and standing in the clearer light of natural reason, cannot choose but draw to it in all times a very considerable part of the people; and the *spiritual*, though it stand in the darkness of School distinctions and hard words, yet because the fear of darkness and ghosts is greater than other fears, cannot want a party sufficient to trouble and sometimes to destroy a commonwealth. And this is a disease which not unfitly may be compared to the epilepsy or falling sickness, which the Jews took to be one kind of possession by spirits in the body natural. For as in this disease there is an unnatural spirit or wind in the head that obstructs the roots of the nerves and, moving them violently, takes away the motion which naturally they should have from the power of the soul in the brain and thereby causes violent and irregular motions—which men call convulsions—in the parts, insomuch as he that is seized therewith falls down sometimes into the water and sometimes into the fire, as a man deprived of his senses; so also in the body politic, when the spiritual power moves the members of a commonwealth by the terror of punishments and hope of rewards—which are the nerves of it—otherwise than by the civil power—which is the soul of the commonwealth—they ought to be moved, and by strange and hard words suffocates their understanding, it must needs thereby distract the people and either overwhelm the commonwealth with oppression or cast it into the fire of a civil war.

Mixed government. Sometimes also in the merely civil government there be more than one soul: as when the power of levying money, which is the nutritive faculty, has depended on a general assembly; the power of conduct and command, which is the motive faculty, on one man; and the power of making laws, which is the rational faculty, on the accidental consent not only of those two but also of a third; this endangers the commonwealth, sometimes for want of consent to good laws, but most often for want of such nourishment as is necessary to life and motion. For although few perceive that such government is not government but division of the commonwealth into three factions, and call it mixed monarchy, yet the truth is that it is not one independent commonwealth but three independent factions, nor one representative person but three. In the kingdom of God, there may be three persons independent without breach of unity in God that reigns; but where men reign, that be subject to diversity of opinions, it cannot be so. And therefore if the king bear the person of the people, and the general assembly bear also the person of the people, and another assembly bear the person of a part of the people, they are not one person nor one sovereign, but three persons and three sovereigns.

To what disease in the natural body of man I may exactly compare this irregularity of a commonwealth I know not. But I have seen a man that had another man growing out of his side, with a head, arms, breast, and stomach of his own; if he had had another man growing out of his other side, the comparison might then have been exact.

Want of money. Hitherto I have named such diseases of a commonwealth as are of the greatest and most present danger. There be other not so great which nevertheless are not unfit to be observed. At first, the difficulty of raising money for the necessary uses of the commonwealth, especially in the approach of war. This difficulty arises from the opinion that every subject has a propriety in his lands and goods exclusive of the sovereign's right to the use of the same. From whence it comes to pass that the sovereign power, which foresees the necessities and dangers of the commonwealth, finding the passage of money to the public treasury obstructed by the tenacity of the people, whereas it ought to extend itself to encounter and prevent such dangers in their beginnings, contracts itself as long as it can, and when it cannot longer, struggles with the people by stratagems of law to obtain little sums, which not sufficing, he is fain at last violently to open the way for present supply or perish; and being put often to these extremities, at last reduces the people to their due temper, or else the commonwealth must perish. Insomuch as we may compare this distemper very aptly to an ague, wherein the fleshy parts being congealed or by venomous matter obstructed, the veins which by their natural course empty themselves into the heart are not, as they ought to be, supplied from the arteries, whereby there succeeds at first a cold contraction and trembling of the limbs, and afterward a hot and strong endeavor of the heart, to force a passage for the blood; and before it can do that, contents itself with the small refreshments of such things as cool for a time till, if nature be strong enough, it break at last the contumacy of the parts obstructed and dissipates the venom into sweat; or, if nature be too weak, the patient dies.

Monopolies, and abuses of publicans. Again, there is sometimes in a commonwealth a disease which resembles the pleurisy; and that is when the treasure of the commonwealth, flowing out of its due course, is gathered together in too much abundance in one or a few private men by monopolies or by farms of the public revenues; in the same manner as the blood in a pleurisy, getting into the membrane of the breast, breeds there an inflammation accompanied with a fever and painful stitches.

Popular men. Also, the popularity of a potent subject, unless the commonwealth have very good caution of his fidelity, is a dangerous disease; because the people, which should receive their motion from the authority of the sovereign, by the flattery and by the reputation of an ambitious man are drawn away from their obedience to the laws to follow a man of whose virtues and designs they have no knowledge. And this is commonly of more danger in a popular government than in a monarchy, because an army is of so great force and multitude as it may easily be made believe they are the people. By this means it was that Julius Caesar, who was set up by the people against the senate, having won to himself the affections of his army, made himself master both of senate and people. And this pro-

ceeding of popular and ambitious men is plain rebellion, and
may be resembled to the effects of witchcraft.

*Excessive greatness
of a town, multitude
of corporations.*
Another infirmity of a commonwealth is the
immoderate greatness of a town, when it is
able to furnish out of its own circuit the number and expense of a great army; as also the
great number of corporations, which are as it were many lesser
commonwealths in the bowels of a greater, like worms in the entrails of a natural man. To which may be
*Liberty of disputing
against sovereign
power.*
added the liberty of disputing against absolute
power by pretenders to political prudence,
which, though bred for the most part in the
lees of the people, yet animated by false doctrines are perpetually meddling with the fundamental laws to the molestation of
the commonwealth, like the little worms which physicians call
ascarides.

We may further add the insatiable appetite, or βουλιμία, of
enlarging dominion, with the incurable *wounds* thereby many
times received from the enemy, and the *wens* of ununited conquests which are many times a burden and with less danger
lost than kept; as also the *lethargy* of ease and *consumption* of
riot and vain expense.

*Dissolution of the
commonwealth.*
Lastly, when in a war foreign or intestine the
enemies get a final victory so as, the forces of
the commonwealth keeping the field no longer,
there is no further protection of subjects in their loyalty, then
is the commonwealth DISSOLVED and every man at liberty to protect himself by such courses as his own discretion shall suggest
unto him. For the sovereign is the public soul, giving life and
motion to the commonwealth; which expiring, the members are
governed by it no more than the carcase of a man by his departed though immortal soul. For though the right of a sovereign monarch cannot be extinguished by the act of another, yet
the obligation of the members may. For he that wants protection may seek it anywhere, and when he has it is obliged, without fraudulent pretense of having submitted himself out of
fear, to protect his protection as long as he is able. But when the
power of an assembly is once suppressed, the right of the same
perishes utterly; because the assembly itself is extinct, and consequently there is no possibility for the sovereignty to re-enter.

CHAPTER THIRTY

OF THE OFFICE OF THE SOVEREIGN
REPRESENTATIVE

The procuration of The office of the sovereign, be it a monarch or
the good of the an assembly, consists in the end for which he
people. was trusted with the sovereign power, namely,
the procuration of *the safety of the people;* to which he is
obliged by the law of nature, and to render an account thereof
to God, the author of that law, and to none but him. But by
safety here is not meant a bare preservation but also all other
contentments of life which every man by lawful industry, without danger or hurt to the commonwealth, shall acquire to himself.

By instruction And this is intended should be done, not by
and laws. care applied to individuals further than their
protection from injuries when they shall com-
plain, but by a general providence contained in public instruction, both of doctrine and example, and in the making and
executing of good laws, to which individual persons may apply
their own cases.

Against the duty of And because, if the essential rights of sover-
a sovereign to relin- eignty, specified before in the eighteenth chap-
quish any essential ter, be taken away, the commonwealth is
right of sovereignty: thereby dissolved and every man returns into
the condition and calamity of a war with every other man,
which is the greatest evil that can happen in this life, it is the
office of the sovereign to maintain those rights entire, and consequently against his duty, first, to transfer to another or to lay
from himself any of them. For he that deserts the means deserts
the ends; and he deserts the means that, being the sovereign, acknowledges himself subject to the civil laws and renounces the
power of supreme judicature, or of making war or peace by his
own authority, or of judging of the necessities of the commonwealth, or of levying money and soldiers when and as much as
in his own conscience he shall judge necessary, or of making of-

ficers and ministers both of war and peace, or of appointing
teachers and examining what doctrines are conformable or contrary to the defense, peace, and good of the people. Secondly, it
is against his duty to let the people be ignorant

Or not to see the
people taught the
grounds of them.

or misinformed of the grounds and reasons of
those his essential rights, because thereby men
are easy to be seduced and drawn to resist him
when the commonwealth shall require their use and exercise.

And the grounds of these rights have the rather need to be
diligently and truly taught, because they cannot be maintained
by any civil law or terror of legal punishment. For a civil law
that shall forbid rebellion (and such is all resistance to the essential rights of the sovereignty) is not, as a civil law, any obligation, but by virtue only of the law of nature that forbids the
violation of faith; which natural obligation if men know not,
they cannot know the right of any law the sovereign makes.
And for the punishment, they take it but for an act of hostility
which, when they think they have strength enough, they will
endeavor by acts of hostility to avoid.

As I have heard some say that justice is but a

Objection of those
that say there are
no principles of
reason for absolute
sovereignty.

word without substance, and that whatsoever a
man can by force or art acquire to himself, not
only in the condition of war but also in a commonwealth, is his own, which I have already
showed to be false, so there be also that maintain that there are
no grounds nor principles of reason to sustain those essential
rights which make sovereignty absolute. For if there were, they
would have been found out in some place or other; whereas we
see there has not hitherto been any commonwealth where those
rights have been acknowledged or challenged. Wherein they
argue as ill as if the savage people of America should deny there
were any grounds or principles of reason so to build a house as
to last as long as the materials because they never yet saw any so
well built. Time and industry produce every day new knowledge. And as the art of well building is derived from principles
of reason, observed by industrious men that had long studied
the nature of materials and the divers effects of figure and proportion long after mankind began, though poorly, to build, so,
long time after men have begun to constitute commonwealths,

imperfect and apt to relapse into disorder, there may principles of reason be found out by industrious meditation to make their constitution, excepting by external violence, everlasting. And such are those which I have in this discourse set forth; which whether they come not into the sight of those that have power to make use of them, or be neglected by them or not, concerns my particular interests at this day very little. But supposing that these of mine are not such principles of reason, yet I am sure they are principles from authority of Scripture, as I shall make it appear when I shall come to speak of the kingdom of God administered by Moses over the Jews, his peculiar people by covenant.[1]

Objection from the incapacity of the vulgar. But they say again that though the principles be right, yet common people are not of capacity enough to be made to understand them. I should be glad that the rich and potent subjects of a kingdom or those that are accounted the most learned were no less incapable than they. But all men know that the obstructions to this kind of doctrine proceed not so much from the difficulty of the matter as from the interest of them that are to learn. Potent men digest hardly anything that sets up a power to bridle their affections, and learned men anything that discovers their errors and thereby lessens their authority; whereas the common people's minds, unless they be tainted with dependence on the potent or scribbled over with the opinions of their doctors, are like clean paper, fit to receive whatsoever by public authority shall be imprinted in them. Shall whole nations be brought to *acquiesce* in the great mysteries of the Christian religion which are above reason, and millions of men be made believe that the same body may be in innumerable places at one and the same time, which is against reason; and shall not men be able, by their teaching and preaching, protected by the law, to make that received which is so consonant to reason that any unprejudicated man needs no more to learn it than to hear it? I conclude, therefore, that in the instruction of the people in the essential rights which are the natural and fundamental laws of sovereignty there is no difficulty, while a sovereign has his

---

1 [In Part III, "Of a Christian Commonwealth," not included in the present edition.]

power entire, but what proceeds from his own fault or the fault of those whom he trusts in the administration of the commonwealth; and consequently, it is his duty to cause them so to be instructed, and not only his duty but his benefit also, and security against the danger that may arrive to himself in his natural person from rebellion.

Subjects are to be taught not to effect change of government: And, to descend to particulars, the people are to be taught, first, that they ought not to be in love with any form of government they see in their neighbor nations more than with their own, nor, whatsoever present prosperity they behold in nations that are otherwise governed than they, to desire change. For the prosperity of a people ruled by an aristocratical or democratical assembly comes not from aristocracy nor from democracy but from the obedience and concord of the subjects; nor do the people flourish in a monarchy because one man has the right to rule them but because they obey him. Take away in any kind of state the obedience and consequently the concord of the people, and they shall not only not flourish but in short time be dissolved. And they that go about by disobedience to do no more than reform the commonwealth shall find they do thereby destroy it; like the foolish daughters of Pelius in the fable, which, desiring to renew the youth of their decrepit father, did by the counsel of Medea cut him in pieces and boil him together with strange herbs, but made not of him a new man. This desire of change is like the breach of the first of God's commandments, for there God says *Non habebis Deos alienos*—Thou shalt not have the Gods of other nations [2]—and in another place concerning *kings* that they are *Gods*.[3]

Nor adhere, against the sovereign, to popular men; Secondly, they are to be taught that they ought not to be led with admiration of the virtue of any of their fellow subjects, how high soever he stand or how conspicuously soever he shine in the commonwealth; nor of any assembly, except the sovereign assembly, so as to defer to them any obedience or honor appropriate to the sovereign only, whom, in their particular stations, they represent; nor to receive any influence from them but such

[2] [Exod. 20:3; Deut. 5:7.]

[3] [The reference is to the ancient origins of the belief in the divine right of kings.]

as is conveyed by them from the sovereign authority. For that sovereign cannot be imagined to love his people as he ought that is not jealous of them but suffers them by the flattery of popular men to be seduced from their loyalty, as they have often been, not only secretly, but openly, so as to proclaim marriage with them *in facie ecclesiae* [4] by preachers and by publishing the same in the open streets—which may fitly be compared to the violation of the second of the ten commandments.[5]

Nor to dispute the sovereign power. Thirdly, in consequence to this, they ought to be informed how great a fault it is to speak evil of the sovereign representative, whether one man or an assembly of men; or to argue and dispute his power; or any way to use his name irreverently, whereby he may be brought into contempt with his people, and their obedience, in which the safety of the commonwealth consists, slackened. Which doctrine the third commandment by resemblance points to.[6]

And to have days set apart to learn their duty; Fourthly, seeing people cannot be taught this, nor when it is taught remember it, nor after one generation past so much as know in whom the sovereign power is placed, without setting apart from their ordinary labor some certain times in which they may attend those that are appointed to instruct them, it is necessary that some such times be determined wherein they may assemble together and, after prayers and praises given to God, the sovereign of sovereigns, hear those their duties told them, and the positive laws, such as generally concern them all, read and expounded, and be put in mind of the authority that makes them laws. To this end had the Jews every seventh day a sabbath, in which the law was read and expounded, and in the solemnity whereof they were put in mind: that their king was God; that having created the world in six days, he rested the seventh day; and by their resting on it from their labor, that that God was their king which redeemed them from their servile and painful labor in Egypt and gave them a time, after they

---

4 [This refers to the Church's doctrine that a marriage, to be valid, must be solemnized by ecclesiastical rites.]

5 [Exod. 20:4-5; Deut. 5:8-10.]

6 [Exod. 20:7; Deut. 5:11.]

had rejoiced in God, to take joy also in themselves by lawful recreation.[7] So that the first table of the commandments is spent all in setting down the sum of God's absolute power—not only as God but as king by pact, in peculiar, of the Jews; and may therefore give light to those that have sovereign power conferred on them by the consent of men to see what doctrine they ought to teach their subjects.

And to honor their parents;   And because the first instruction of children depends on the care of their parents, it is necessary that they should be obedient to them while they are under their tuition; and not only so, but that also afterwards, as gratitude requires, they acknowledge the benefit of their education by external signs of honor. To which end they are to be taught that originally the father of every man was also his sovereign lord, with power over him of life and death; and that the fathers of families, when by instituting a commonwealth they resigned that absolute power, yet it was never intended they should lose the honor due unto them for their education. For to relinquish such right was not necessary to the institution of sovereign power, nor would there be any reason why any man should desire to have children or take the care to nourish and instruct them if they were afterwards to have no other benefit from them than from other men. And this accords with the fifth commandment.[8]

And to avoid doing of injury;   Again, every sovereign ought to cause justice to be taught, which, consisting in taking from no man what is his, is as much as to say, to cause men to be taught not to deprive their neighbors, by violence or fraud, of anything which by the sovereign authority is theirs. Of things held in propriety, those that are dearest to a man are his own life and limbs; and in the next degree, in most men, those that concern conjugal affection; and after them, riches and means of living. Therefore the people are to be taught to abstain from violence of one another's person by private revenges; from violation of conjugal honor; and from forcible rapine and fraudulent surreption of one another's goods. For

---

[7] [Exod. 20:8-11; Deut. 5:13-15.]
[8] [Exod. 20:12; Deut. 5:16.]

which purpose also it is necessary they be showed the evil consequences of false judgment, by corruption either of judges or
witnesses, whereby the distinction of propriety is taken away
and justice becomes of no effect—all which things are intimated
in the sixth, seventh, eighth, and ninth commandments.[9]

And to do all this sincerely from the heart. Lastly, they are to be taught that not only the
unjust facts but the designs and intentions to
do them, though by accident hindered, are injustice, which consists in the pravity of the will
as well as in the irregularity of the act. And this is the intention
of the tenth commandment [10] and the sum of the second table,
which is reduced all to this one commandment of mutual charity, *thou shalt love thy neighbor as thyself,*[11] as the sum of the
first table is reduced to *the love of God,* whom they had then
newly received as their king.

The use of universities. As for the means and conduits by which the
people may receive this instruction, we are to
search by what means so many opinions con-
trary to the peace of mankind, upon weak and false principles,
have nevertheless been so deeply rooted in them. I mean those
which I have in the precedent chapter specified: as that men
shall judge of what is lawful and unlawful, not by the law itself,
but by their own consciences—that is to say, by their own private judgments; that subjects sin in obeying the commands of
the commonwealth unless they themselves have first judged
them to be lawful; that their propriety in their riches is such as
to exclude the dominion which the commonwealth has over the
same; that it is lawful for subjects to kill such as they call tyrants; that the sovereign power may be divided, and the like
which come to be instilled into the people by this means. They
whom necessity or covetousness keeps attent on their trades and
labor, and they on the other side whom superfluity or sloth carries after their sensual pleasures—which two sorts of men take
up the greatest part of mankind—being diverted from the deep
meditation which the learning of truth not only in the matter
of natural justice but also of all other sciences necessarily re-

9 [Exod. 20:13-16; Deut. 5:17-20.]
10 [Exod. 20:17; Deut. 5:21.]
11 [Lev. 19:18.]

quires, receive the notions of their duty chiefly from divines in the pulpit and partly from such of their neighbors or familiar acquaintance as, having the faculty of discoursing readily and plausibly, seem wiser and better learned in cases of law and conscience than themselves. And the divines and such others as make show of learning derive their knowledge from the universities and from the schools of law, or from the books which by men eminent in those schools and universities have been published. It is therefore manifest that the instruction of the people depends wholly on the right teaching of youth in the universities. But are not, may some man say, the universities of England learned enough already to do that? or is it you will undertake to teach the universities? Hard questions. Yet to the first I doubt not to answer that till toward the latter end of Henry the Eighth the power of the Pope was always upheld against the power of the commonwealth principally by the universities; [12] and that the doctrines maintained by so many preachers against the sovereign power of the king, and by so many lawyers and others that had their education there, is a sufficient argument that, though the universities were not authors of those false doctrines, yet they knew not how to plant the true. For in such a contradiction of opinions, it is most certain that they have not been sufficiently instructed; and it is no wonder if they yet retain a relish of that subtle liquor wherewith they were first seasoned against the civil authority. But to the latter question, it is not fit nor needful for me to say either aye or no, for any man that sees what I am doing may easily perceive what I think.

The safety of the people requires further from him or them that have the sovereign power that justice be equally administered to all degrees of people; that is, that as well the rich and mighty as poor and obscure persons may be righted of the injuries done them, so as the great may have no greater hope of impunity when they do violence, dishonor, or any injury to the meaner sort than when one of these does the like to one of them; for in this consists equity, to which, as being a precept of

12 [For political and personal reasons, Henry VIII (1491-1547) in 1532 led England out of the Roman communion, Parliament declaring the king supreme head of church and state. Hobbes refers to the widespread opposition which these acts encountered, especially among the universities which, through their preferred position, became a center of resistance.]

the law of nature, a sovereign is as much subject as any of the meanest of his people. All breaches of the law are offenses against the commonwealth, but there be some that are also against private persons. Those that concern the commonwealth only may without breach of equity be pardoned; for every man may pardon what is done against himself, according to his own discretion. But an offense against a private man cannot in equity be pardoned without the consent of him that is injured, or reasonable satisfaction.

The inequality of subjects proceeds from the acts of sovereign power, and therefore has no more place in the presence of the sovereign—that is to say, in a court of justice—than the inequality between kings and their subjects in the presence of the King of kings. The honor of great persons is to be valued for their beneficence and the aids they give to men of inferior rank, or not at all. And the violences, oppressions, and injuries they do are not extenuated but aggravated by the greatness of their persons because they have least need to commit them. The consequences of this partiality toward the great proceed in this manner. Impunity makes insolence; insolence, hatred; and hatred, an endeavor to pull down all oppressing and contumelious greatness, though with the ruin of the commonwealth.

Equal taxes. To equal justice appertains also the equal imposition of taxes, the equality whereof depends not on the equality of riches but on the equality of the debt that every man owes to the commonwealth for his defense. It is not enough for a man to labor for the maintenance of his life, but also to fight, if need be, for the securing of his labor. They must either do as the Jews did after their return from captivity, in reedifying the temple, build with one hand and hold the sword in the other,[13] or else they must hire others to fight for them. For the impositions that are laid on the people by the sovereign power are nothing else but the wages due to them that hold the public sword to defend private men in the exercise of their several trades and callings. Seeing then the benefit that every one receives thereby is the enjoyment of life, which is equally dear to poor and rich, the debt which a poor man owes them that defend his life is the same which a rich man owes for the defense

13 [Neh. 4:17.]

of his, saving that the rich, who have the service of the poor, may be debtors not only for their own persons but for many more. Which considered, the equality of imposition consists rather in the equality of that which is consumed than of the riches of the persons that consume the same. For what reason is there that he which labors much and, sparing the fruits of his labor, consumes little should be more charged than he that, living idly, gets little and spends all he gets, seeing the one has no more protection from the commonwealth than the other? But when the impositions are laid upon those things which men consume, every man pays equally for what he uses; nor is the commonwealth defrauded by the luxurious waste of private men.

Public charity. And whereas many men, by accident inevitable, become unable to maintain themselves by their labor, they ought not to be left to the charity of private persons but to be provided for, as far forth as the necessities of nature require, by the laws of the commonwealth. For as it is uncharitableness in any man to neglect the impotent, so it is in the sovereign of a commonwealth to expose them to the hazard of such uncertain charity.

Prevention of idleness. But for such as have strong bodies, the case is otherwise: they are to be forced to work; and to avoid the excuse of not finding employment, there ought to be such laws as may encourage all manner of arts —as navigation, agriculture, fishing—and all manner of manufacture that requires labor. The multitude of poor and yet strong people still increasing, they are to be transplanted into countries not sufficiently inhabited, where nevertheless they are not to exterminate those they find there but constrain them to inhabit closer together, and not to range a great deal of ground to snatch what they find but to court each little plot with art and labor to give them their sustenance in due season. And when all the world is overcharged with inhabitants, then the last remedy of all is war, which provides for every man by victory or death.

Good laws, what. To the care of the sovereign belongs the making of good laws. But what is a good law? By a good law I mean not a just law, for no law can be unjust. The law is made by the sovereign power, and all that is done by such power is warranted and owned by every one of the people; and that which every man will have so, no man can say is unjust. It is in the laws of a commonwealth as in the laws of gaming: whatsoever the gamesters all agree on is injustice to none of them. A good law is that which is *needful* for the *good of the people,* and withal *perspicuous.*

Such as are necessary. For the use of laws, which are but rules authorized, is not to bind the people from all voluntary actions but to direct and keep them in such a motion as not to hurt themselves by their own impetuous desires, rashness, or indiscretion—as hedges are set, not to stop travelers, but to keep them in their way. And therefore a law that is not needful, having not the true end of a law, is not good. A law may be conceived to be good when it is for the benefit of the sovereign though it be not necessary for the people; but it is not so. For the good of the sovereign and people cannot be separated. It is a weak sovereign that has weak subjects, and a weak people whose sovereign wants power to rule them at his will. Unnecessary laws are not good laws but traps for money, which, where the right of sovereign power is acknowledged, are superfluous, and where it is not acknowledged, insufficient to defend the people.

Such as are perspicuous. The perspicuity consists not so much in the words of the law itself as in a declaration of the causes and motives for which it was made. That is it that shows us the meaning of the legislator; and the meaning of the legislator known, the law is more easily understood by few than many words. For all words are subject to ambiguity, and therefore multiplication of words in the body of the law is multiplication of ambiguity; besides, it seems to imply, by too much diligence, that whosoever can evade the words is without the compass of the law. And this is a cause of many unnecessary processes. For when I consider how short were the laws of ancient times and how they grew by degrees still longer, methinks I see a contention between the penners and pleaders of the law, the former seeking to circumscribe the latter and the latter to evade their circumscriptions, and that the pleaders have got the victory. It belongs therefore to the office of a legislator (such as is in all commonwealths the supreme representative, be it one man or an assembly) to make the reason perspicuous why the law was made, and the body of the law itself as short but in as proper and significant terms as may be.

Punishments.   It belongs also to the office of the sovereign to make a right application of punishments and rewards. And seeing the end of punishing is not revenge and discharge of choler but correction, either of the offender or of others by his example, the severest punishments are to be inflicted for those crimes that are of most danger to the public: such as are those which proceed from malice to the government established; those that spring from contempt of justice; those that provoke indignation in the multitude; and those which, unpunished, seem authorized, as when they are committed by sons, servants, or favorites of men in authority. For indignation carries men not only against the actors and authors of injustice, but against all power that is likely to protect them: as in the case of Tarquin, when for the insolent act of one of his sons he was driven out of Rome and the monarchy itself dissolved.[14] But crimes of infirmity—such as are those which proceed from great provocation, from great fear, great need, or from ignorance, whether the fact be a great crime or not—there is place many times for lenity without prejudice to the commonwealth; and lenity, when there is such place for it, is required by the law of nature. The punishment of the leaders and teachers in a commotion, not the poor seduced people, when they are punished, can profit the commonwealth by their example. To be severe to the people is to punish that ignorance which may in great part be imputed to the sovereign, whose fault it was that they were no better instructed.

Rewards.   In like manner it belongs to the office and duty of the sovereign to apply his rewards always so as there may arise from them benefit to the commonwealth, wherein consists their use and end; and is then done when they that have well served the commonwealth are, with as little expense of the common treasure as is possible, so well recompensed as others thereby may be encouraged both to serve the

[14] [According to legend, Tarquin, the last Roman king, was driven from the city (510 B.C.) by a popular rising after his son had raped—and thereby occasioned the suicide of—the virtuous Lucretia (Livy 1).]

same as faithfully as they can and to study the arts by which they may be enabled to do it better. To buy with money or preferment from a popular ambitious subject to be quiet and desist from making ill impressions in the minds of the people has nothing of the nature of reward (which is ordained not for disservice, but for service past), nor a sign of gratitude, but of fear; nor does it tend to the benefit but to the damage of the public. It is a contention with ambition like that of Hercules with the monster Hydra, which having many heads, for every one that was vanquished there grew up three. For in like manner, when the stubbornness of one popular man is overcome with reward there arise many more, by the example, that do the same mischief in hope of like benefit; and as all sorts of manufacture, so also malice increases by being vendible. And though sometimes a civil war may be deferred by such ways as that, yet the danger grows still the greater and the public ruin more assured. It is therefore against the duty of the sovereign, to whom the public safety is committed, to reward those that aspire to greatness by disturbing the peace of their country, and not rather to oppose the beginnings of such men with a little danger than after a longer time with greater.

Counselors. Another business of the sovereign is to choose good counselors; I mean such whose advice he is to take in the government of the commonwealth. For this word counsel, *consilium,* corrupted from *considium,* is of a large signification and comprehends all assemblies of men that sit together, not only to deliberate what is to be done hereafter, but also to judge of facts past and of law for the present. I take it here in the first sense only, and in this sense there is no choice of counsel neither in a democracy nor aristocracy, because the persons counseling are members of the person counseled. The choice of counselors, therefore, is proper to monarchy, in which the sovereign that endeavors not to make choice of those that in every kind are the most able discharges not his office as he ought to do. The most able counselors are they that have least hope of benefit by giving evil counsel and most knowledge of those things that conduce to the peace and defense of the commonwealth. It is a hard matter to know who expects benefit from public troubles, but the signs that guide to a just suspicion is the soothing of the people in their unreasonable or irremediable grievances by men whose estates are not sufficient to discharge their accustomed expenses and may easily be observed by anyone whom it concerns to know it. But to know who has most knowledge of the public affairs is yet harder, and they that know them need them a great deal the less. For to know who knows the rules almost of any art is a great degree of the knowledge of the same art, because no man can be assured of the truth of another's rules but he that is first taught to understand them. But the best signs of knowledge of any art are much conversing in it and constant good effects of it. Good counsel comes not by lot nor by inheritance, and therefore there is no more reason to expect good advice from the rich or noble in matter of state than in delineating the dimensions of a fortress, unless we shall think there needs no method in the study of the politics as there does in the study of geometry, but only to be lookers-on, which is not so. For the politics is the harder study of the two. Whereas in these parts of Europe it has been taken for a right of certain persons to have place in the highest council of state by inheritance; it is derived from the conquests of the ancient Germans, wherein many absolute lords, joining together to conquer other nations, would not enter into the confederacy without such privileges as might be marks of difference in time following between their posterity and the posterity of their subjects; which privileges, being inconsistent with the sovereign power, by the favor of the sovereign they may seem to keep, but contending for them as their right they must needs by degrees let them go, and have at last no further honor than adheres naturally to their abilities.

And how able soever be the counselors in any affair, the benefit of their counsel is greater when they give every one his advice and the reasons of it apart than when they do it in an assembly by way of orations, and when they have premeditated than when they speak on the sudden; both because they have more time to survey the consequences of action, and are less subject to be carried away to contradiction through envy, emulation, or other passions arising from the difference of opinion.

The best counsel in those things that concern not other nations but only the ease and benefit the subjects may enjoy by laws that look only inward is to be taken from the general informations and complaints of the people of each province, who are best acquainted with their own wants and ought, therefore, when they demand nothing in derogation of the essential rights of sovereignty, to be diligently taken notice of. For without those essential rights, as I have often before said, the commonwealth cannot at all subsist.

Commanders. A commander of an army in chief, if he be not popular, shall not be beloved nor feared as he ought to be by his army and consequently cannot perform that office with good success. He must therefore be industrious, valiant, affable, liberal, and fortunate that he may gain an opinion both of sufficiency and of loving his soldiers. This is popularity, and breeds in the soldiers both desire and courage to recommend themselves to his favor; and protects the severity of the general in punishing, when need is, the mutinous or negligent soldiers. But this love of soldiers, if caution be not given of the commander's fidelity, is a dangerous thing to sovereign power, especially when it is in the hands of an assembly not popular. It belongs therefore to the safety of the people both that they be good conductors and faithful subjects to whom the sovereign commits his armies.

But when the sovereign himself is popular—that is, reverenced and beloved of his people—there is no danger at all from the popularity of a subject. For soldiers are never so generally unjust as to side with their captain, though they love him, against their sovereign, when they love not only his person but also his cause. And therefore those who by violence have at any time suppressed the power of their lawful sovereign, before they could settle themselves in his place have been always put to the trouble of contriving their titles to save the people from the shame of receiving them. To have a known right to sovereign power is so popular a quality as he that has it needs no more, for his own part, to turn the hearts of his subjects to him but that they see him able absolutely to govern his own family; nor, on the part of his enemies, but a disbanding of their armies. For the greatest and most active part of mankind has never hitherto been well contented with the present.

Concerning the offices of one sovereign to another, which are comprehended in that law which is commonly called the *law of nations,* I need not say anything in this place because the law of nations and the law of nature is the same thing. And every sovereign has the same right in procuring the safety of his people that any particular man can have in procuring the safety of his own body. And the same law that dictates to men that have no civil government what they ought to do and what to avoid in regard of one another dictates the same to commonwealths— that is, to the consciences of sovereign princes and sovereign assemblies, there being no court of natural justice but in the conscience only, where not man but God reigns, whose laws, such of them as oblige all mankind, in respect of God as he is the author of nature are *natural,* and in respect of the same God as he is King of kings are *laws.* But of the kingdom of God as King of kings and as King also of a peculiar people, I shall speak in the rest of this discourse.

CHAPTER THIRTY-ONE

OF THE KINGDOM OF GOD BY NATURE

The scope of the following chapters. That the condition of mere nature—that is to say, of absolute liberty such as is theirs that neither are sovereigns nor subjects—is anarchy and the condition of war; that the precepts by which men are guided to avoid that condition are the laws of nature; that a commonwealth without sovereign power is but a word without substance and cannot stand; that subjects owe to sovereigns simple obedience in all things wherein their obedience is not repugnant to the laws of God—I have sufficiently proved in that which I have already written. There wants only, for the entire knowledge of civil duty, to know what are those laws of God. For without that, a man knows not, when he is commanded anything by the civil power, whether it be contrary to the law of God or not; and so either by too much civil obedience offends the Divine Majesty, or through fear of offending God transgresses the commandments of the commonwealth. To avoid both these rocks, it is necessary to know what are the laws divine. And seeing the knowledge of all law depends on the knowledge of the sovereign power, I shall say something in that which follows of the KINGDOM OF GOD.

Who are subjects in the kingdom of God.

God is king, let the earth rejoice, says the Psalmist (97: 1). And again (Ps. 99: 1) *God is king, though the nations be angry; and he that sitteth on the cherubim, though the earth be moved.* Whether men will or not, they must be subject always to the divine power. By denying the existence or providence of God, men may shake off their ease but not their yoke. But to call this power of God, which extends itself not only to man but also to beasts and plants and bodies inanimate, by the name of kingdom is but a metaphorical use of the word. For he only is properly said to reign that governs his subjects by his word, and by promise of rewards to those that obey it and by threatening them with punishment that obey it not. Subjects therefore in the kingdom of God are not bodies inanimate nor creatures irrational, because they understand no precepts as his; nor atheists, nor they that believe not that God has any care of the actions of mankind, because they acknowledge no word for his nor have hope of his rewards or fear of his threatenings. They therefore that believe there is a God that governs the world, and has given precepts and propounded rewards and punishments to mankind, are God's subjects; all the rest are to be understood as enemies.

A threefold word of God, reason, revelation, prophecy.

To rule by words requires that such words be manifestly made known, for else they are no laws; for to the nature of laws belongs a sufficient and clear promulgation such as may take away the excuse of ignorance, which in the laws of men is but of one only kind, and that is proclamation or promulgation by the voice of man. But God declares his laws three ways: by the dictates of *natural reason,* by *revelation,* and by the *voice* of some *man* to whom, by the operation of miracles, he procures credit with the rest. From hence there arises a triple word of God: *rational, sensible,* and *prophetic;* to which corresponds a triple hearing: *right reason, sense supernatural,* and *faith.* As for sense supernatural, which consists in revelation or inspiration, there have not been any universal laws so given, because God speaks not in that manner but to particular persons, and to divers men divers things.

A twofold kingdom of God, natural and prophetic. From the difference between the other two kinds of God's word, *rational* and *prophetic,* there may be attributed to God a twofold kingdom, *natural* and *prophetic:* natural, wherein he governs as many of mankind as acknowledge his providence by the natural dictates of right reason; and prophetic, wherein having chosen out one peculiar nation, the Jews, for his subjects, he governed them, and none but them, not only by natural reason but by positive laws, which he gave them by the mouths of his holy prophets. Of the natural kingdom of God I intend to speak in this chapter.

The right of God's sovereignty is derived from his omnipotence. The right of nature whereby God reigns over men and punishes those that break his laws is to be derived, not from his creating them—as if he required obedience as of gratitude for his benefits—but from his *irresistible power.* I have formerly shown how the sovereign right arises from pact; to show how the same right may arise from nature requires no more but to show in what case it is never taken away. Seeing all men by nature had right to all things, they had right every one to reign over all the rest. But because this right could not be obtained by force, it concerned the safety of every one, laying by that right, to set up men with sovereign authority, by common consent, to rule and defend them; whereas if there had been any man of power irresistible, there had been no reason why he should not by that power have ruled and defended both himself and them according to his own discretion. To those therefore whose power is irresistible, the dominion of all men adheres naturally by their excellence of power; and consequently it is from that power that the kingdom over men, and the right of afflicting men at his pleasure, belongs naturally to God Almighty—not as creator and gracious, but as omnipotent. And though punishment be due for sin only, because by that word is understood affliction for sin, yet the right of afflicting is not always derived from men's sin but from God's power.

Sin not the cause of all affliction. This question, *why evil men often prosper and good men suffer adversity,* has been much disputed by the ancients, and is the same with this of ours, *by what right God dispenses the prosperities and adversities of this life;* and is of that difficulty as it has shaken the faith not only of the vulgar but of philosophers and, which is more, of the saints concerning the Divine Providence. *How good,* says David (Ps. 73: 1-3), *is the God of Israel to those that are upright in heart; and yet my feet were almost gone, my treadings had well-nigh slipt; for I was grieved at the wicked, when I saw the ungodly in such prosperity.* And Job, how earnestly does he expostulate with God for the many afflictions he suffered, notwithstanding his righteousness? This question in the case of Job is decided by God himself, not by arguments derived from Job's sin, but his own power. For whereas the friends of Job drew their arguments from his affliction to his sin, and he defended himself by the conscience of his innocence, God himself takes up the matter, and having justified the affliction by arguments drawn from his power, such as this (Job 38:4): *Where wast thou when I laid the foundations of the earth?* and the like, both approved Job's innocence and reproved the erroneous doctrine of his friends. Conformable to this doctrine is the sentence of our Saviour concerning the man that was born blind in these words: *Neither hath this man sinned, nor his fathers; but that the works of God might be made manifest in him.*[1] And though it be said *that death entered into the world by sin*[2] (by which is meant that if Adam had never sinned he had never died, that is, never suffered any separation of his soul from his body), it follows not thence that God could not justly have afflicted him though he had not sinned, as well as he afflicts other living creatures that cannot sin.

Divine laws. Having spoken of the right of God's sovereignty as grounded only on nature, we are to consider next what are the Divine laws or dictates of natural reason; which laws concern either the natural duties of one man to another, or the honor naturally due to our Divine Sovereign. The first are the same laws of nature of which I have spoken

[1] [John 9:3.]
[2] [Rom. 5:12.]

already in the fourteenth and fifteenth chapters of this treatise, namely, equity, justice, mercy, humility, and the rest of the moral virtues. It remains therefore that we consider what precepts are dictated to men by their natural reason only, without other word of God, touching the honor and worship of the Divine Majesty.

Honor and worship, what. Honor consists in the inward thought and opinion of the power and goodness of another; and therefore to honor God is to think as highly of his power and goodness as is possible. And of that opinion, the external signs appearing in the words and actions of men are called *worship,* which is one part of that which the Latins understand by the word *cultus.* For *cultus* signifies properly and constantly that labor which a man bestows on anything with a purpose to make benefit by it. Now those things whereof we make benefit are either subject to us, and the profit they yield follows the labor we bestow upon them as a natural effect, or they are not subject to us, but answer our labor according to their own wills. In the first sense the labor bestowed on the earth is called *culture;* and the education of children, a *culture* of their minds. In the second sense, where men's wills are to be wrought to our purpose, not by force but by complaisance, it signifies as much as courting—that is, a winning of favor by good offices, as by praises, by acknowledging their power, and by whatsoever is pleasing to them from whom we look for any benefit. And this is properly *worship,* in which sense *Publicola* [3] is understood for a worshiper of the people, and *cultus Dei* for the worship of God.

Several signs of honor. From internal honor, consisting in the opinion of power and goodness, arise three passions: *love,* which has reference to goodness, and *hope* and *fear,* that relate to power; and three parts of external worship: *praise, magnifying,* and *blessing,* the subject of praise being goodness, the subject of magnifying and blessing being power, and the effect thereof felicity. Praise and magnifying are signified both by words and actions: by words, when we say a man is good or great; by actions, when we thank him for his bounty and obey his power. The opinion of the happiness of another can only be expressed by words.

[3] [Also *"poplicula":* a friend of the people.]

There be some signs of honor, both in attri-
Worship natural and arbitrary. butes and actions, that be naturally so: as among attributes *good, just, liberal,* and the like; and among actions *prayers, thanks,* and *obedience.* Others are so by institution or custom of men, and in some times and places are honorable, in others dishonorable, in others indifferent: such as are the gestures in salutation, prayer, and thanksgiving, in different times and places, differently used. The former is *natural,* the latter *arbitrary* worship.

And of arbitrary worship, there be two dif-
Worship commanded and free. ferences, for sometimes it is a *commanded,* sometimes *voluntary* worship: commanded, when it is such as he requires who is worshiped; free, when it is such as the worshiper thinks fit. When it is commanded, not the words or gesture, but the obedience is the worship. But when free, the worship consists in the opinion of the beholders: for if to them the words or actions by which we intend honor seem ridiculous and tending to contumely, they are no worship because no signs of honor; and no signs of honor because a sign is not a sign to him that gives it but to him to whom it is made, that is, to the spectator.

Again, there is a *public* and a *private* worship.
Worship public and private. Public is the worship that a commonwealth performs as one person. Private is that which a private person exhibits. Public, in respect of the whole commonwealth, is free; but in respect of particular men, it is not so. Private, is in secret free; but in the sight of the multitude, it is never without some restraint, either from the laws or from the opinion of men, which is contrary to the nature of liberty.

The end of worship among men is power. For
The end of worship. where a man sees another worshiped, he supposes him powerful and is the readier to obey him, which makes his power greater. But God has no ends; the worship we do him proceeds from our duty and is directed according to our capacity by those rules of honor that reason dictates to be done by the weak to the more potent men in hope of benefit, for fear of damage, or in thankfulness for good already received from them.

Attributes of divine honor.

That we may know what worship of God is taught us by the light of nature, I will begin with his attributes. Where, first, it is manifest, we ought to attribute to him *existence.* For no man can have the will to honor that which he thinks not to have any being.

Secondly, that those philosophers who said the world or the soul of the world was God spoke unworthily of him and denied his existence. For by God is understood the cause of the world, and to say the world is God is to say there is no cause of it—that is, no God.

Thirdly, to say the world was not created but eternal, seeing that which is eternal has no cause, is to deny there is a God.

Fourthly, that they who attributing, as they think, ease to God, take from him the care of mankind, take from him his honor; for it takes away men's love and fear of him, which is the root of honor.

Fifthly, in those things that signify greatness and power, to say he is *finite* is not to honor him; for it is not a sign of the will to honor God to attribute to him less than we can, and finite is less than we can, because to finite it is easy to add more.

Therefore, to attribute *figure* to him is not honor, for all figure is finite;

Nor to say we conceive and imagine or have an *idea* of him in our mind, for whatsoever we conceive is finite;

Nor to attribute to him *parts* or *totality,* which are the attributes only of things finite;

Nor to say he is in this or that *place,* for whatsoever is in place is bounded and finite;

Nor that he is *moved* or *rests,* for both these attributes ascribe to him place;

Nor that there be more Gods than one, because it implies them all finite, for there cannot be more than one infinite;

Nor to ascribe to him (unless metaphorically, meaning not the passion but the effect) passions that partake of grief, as *repentance, anger, mercy,* or of want, as *appetite, hope, desire,* or of any passive faculty, for passion is power limited by somewhat else.

And therefore when we ascribe to God a *will,* it is not to be understood, as that of man, for a *rational appetite,* but as the power by which he effects every thing.

Likewise, when we attribute to him *sight* and other acts of sense, as also *knowledge* and *understanding,* which in us is nothing else but a tumult of the mind raised by external things that press the organical parts of man's body; for there is no such thing in God and, being things that depend on natural causes, cannot be attributed to him.

He that will attribute to God nothing but what is warranted by natural reason must either use such negative attributes as *infinite, eternal, incomprehensible,* or superlatives as *most high, most great,* and the like, or indefinite as *good, just, holy, creator;* and in such sense as if he meant not to declare what he is (for that were to circumscribe him within the limits of our fancy) but how much we admire him and how ready we would be to obey him, which is a sign of humility and of a will to honor him as much as we can. For there is but one name to signify our conception of his nature, and that is I AM; and but one name of his relation to us, and that is *God,* in which is contained Father, King, and Lord.

Actions that are signs of divine honor. Concerning the actions of divine worship, it is a most general precept of reason that they be signs of the intention to honor God, such as are, first, *prayers.* For not the carvers, when they made images, were thought to make them gods; but the people that *prayed* to them.

Secondly, *thanksgiving,* which differs from prayer in divine worship no otherwise than that prayers precede and thanks succeed the benefit, the end, both of the one and the other, being to acknowledge God for author of all benefits, as well past as future.

Thirdly, *gifts*—that is to say, *sacrifices* and *oblations*—if they be of the best, are signs of honor, for they are thanksgivings.

Fourthly, *not to swear by any but God* is naturally a sign of honor, for it is a confession that God only knows the heart, and that no man's wit or strength can protect a man against God's vengeance on the perjured.

Fifthly, it is a part of rational worship to speak considerately of God, for it argues a fear of him, and fear is a confession of his power. Hence follows, that the name of God is not to be used rashly and to no purpose, for that is as much as in vain; and it is to no purpose, unless it be by way of oath, and by order of the commonwealth, to make judgments certain, or between commonwealths, to avoid war. And that disputing of God's nature is contrary to his honor, for it is supposed that in this natural kingdom of God there is no other way to know anything but by natural reason—that is, from the principles of natural science, which are so far from teaching us anything of God's nature, as they cannot teach us our own nature nor the nature of the smallest creature living. And therefore when men, out of the principles of natural reason, dispute of the attributes of God, they but dishonor him, for in the attributes which we give to God we are not to consider the signification of philosophical truth but the signification of pious intention to do him the greatest honor we are able. From the want of which consideration have proceeded the volumes of disputation about the nature of God that tend not to his honor but to the honor of our own wits and learning, and are nothing else but inconsiderate and vain abuses of his sacred name.

Sixthly, in *prayers, thanksgivings, offerings,* and *sacrifices,* it is a dictate of natural reason that they be every one in his kind the best and most significant of honor. As, for example, that prayers and thanksgiving be made in words and phrases not sudden nor light nor plebeian, but beautiful and well composed. For else we do not God as much honor as we can. And therefore the heathens did absurdly to worship images for gods, but their doing it in verse and with music, both of voice and instruments, was reasonable. Also that the beasts they offered in sacrifice, and the gifts they offered, and their actions in worshiping, were full of submission and commemorative of benefits received was according to reason, as proceeding from an intention to honor him.

Seventhly, reason directs not only to worship God in secret but also, and especially, in public and in the sight of men. For without that, that which in honor is most acceptable, the procuring others to honor him, is lost.

Lastly, obedience to his laws—that is, in this case to the laws of nature—is the greatest worship of all. For as obedience is more acceptable to God than sacrifice, so also to set light by his commandments is the greatest of all contumelies. And these are the laws of that divine worship which natural reason dictates to private men.

Public worship consists in uniformity. But seeing a commonwealth is but one person, it ought also to exhibit to God but one worship; which then it does when it commands it to be exhibited by private men publicly. And this is public worship, the property whereof is to be *uniform,* for those actions that are done differently by different men cannot be said to be a public worship. And therefore, where many sorts of worship be allowed, proceeding from the different religions of private men, it cannot be said there is any public worship, nor that the commonwealth is of any religion at all.

All attributes depend on the laws civil. And because words, and consequently the attributes of God, have their signification by agreement and constitution of men, those attributes are to be held significative of honor that men intend shall so be; and whatsoever may be done by the wills of particular men, where there is no law but reason, may be done by the will of the commonwealth by laws civil. And because a commonwealth has no will nor makes no laws but those that are made by the will of him or them that have the sovereign power, it follows that those attributes which the sovereign ordains in the worship of God for signs of honor ought to be taken and used for such by private men in their public worship.

Not all actions. But because not all actions are signs by constitution, but some are naturally signs of honor, others of contumely, these latter, which are those that men are ashamed to do in the sight of them they reverence, cannot be made by human power a part of Divine worship, nor the former, such as are decent, modest, humble behavior, ever be separated from it. But whereas there be an infinite number of actions and gestures of an indifferent nature, such of them as the commonwealth shall ordain to be publicly and universally in use as signs of honor and part of God's worship are to be taken and used for such by the subjects. And that which is said in the Scripture, *It is better to obey God than man,*[4] has place in the kingdom of God by pact, and not by nature.

4 [Acts 5:29.]

Having thus briefly spoken of the natural king-
Natural punish-
ments.
dom of God and his natural laws, I will add
only to this chapter a short declaration of his
natural punishments. There is no action of man in this life that
is not the beginning of so long a chain of consequences as no
human providence is high enough to give a man a prospect to
the end. And in this chain there are linked together both pleasing and unpleasing events, in such manner as he that will do
anything for his pleasure must engage himself to suffer all the
pains annexed to it; and these pains are the natural punishments of those actions which are the beginning of more harm
than good. And hereby it comes to pass that intemperance is
naturally punished with diseases, rashness with mischances, injustice with the violence of enemies, pride with ruin, cowardice
with oppression, negligent government of princes with rebellion, and rebellion with slaughter. For seeing punishments are
consequent to the breach of laws, natural punishments must be
naturally consequent to the breach of the laws of nature, and
therefore follow them as their natural, not arbitrary, effects.

And thus far concerning the constitution, na-
The conclusion of
the second part.
ture, and right of sovereigns, and concerning
the duty of subjects, derived from the princi-
ples of natural reason. And now, considering how different this
doctrine is from the practice of the greatest part of the world,
especially of these western parts that have received their moral
learning from Rome and Athens, and how much depth of moral
philosophy is required in them that have the administration of
the sovereign power, I am at the point of believing this my labor
as useless as the commonwealth of Plato. For he also is of opinion that it is impossible for the disorders of state and change of
governments by civil war ever to be taken away till sovereigns
be philosophers. But when I consider again that the science of
natural justice is the only science necessary for sovereigns and
their principal ministers; and that they need not be charged
with the sciences mathematical, as by Plato they are, farther
than by good laws to encourage men to the study of them; and
that neither Plato nor any other philosopher hitherto has put
into order and sufficiently or probably proved all the theorems
of moral doctrine that men may learn thereby both how to
govern and how to obey—I recover some hope that one time or

other this writing of mine may fall into the hands of a sovereign who will consider it himself (for it is short, and I think clear) without the help of any interested or envious interpreter, and by the exercise of entire sovereignty, in protecting the public teaching of it, convert this truth of speculation into the utility of practice.

A REVIEW AND CONCLUSION [1]

From the contrariety of some of the natural faculties of the mind, one to another, as also of one passion to another, and from their reference to conversation, there has been an argument taken to infer an impossibility that any one man should be sufficiently disposed to all sorts of civil duty. The severity of judgment, they say, makes men censorious and unapt to pardon the errors and infirmities of other men; and on the other side, celerity of fancy makes the thoughts less steady than is necessary to discern exactly between right and wrong. Again, in all deliberations and in all pleadings, the faculty of solid reasoning is necessary, for without it the resolutions of men are rash and their sentences unjust; and yet if there be not powerful eloquence, which procures attention and consent, the effect of reason will be little. But these are contrary faculties, the former being grounded upon principles of truth, the other upon opinions already received, true or false, and upon the passions and interests of men, which are different and mutable.

And among the passions, *courage* (by which I mean the contempt of wounds and violent death) inclines men to private revenges and sometimes to endeavor the unsettling of the public peace; and *timorousness* many times disposes to the desertion of the public defense. Both these, they say, cannot stand together in the same person.

And to consider the contrariety of men's opinions and manners in general, it is, they say, impossible to entertain a constant civil amity with all those with whom the business of the world constrains us to converse, which business consists almost in nothing else but a perpetual contention for honor, riches, and authority.

[1] [This is the final chapter of the work, following Part IV, "Of the Kingdom of Darkness."]

To which I answer that these are indeed great difficulties, but not impossibilities, for by education and discipline they may be and are sometimes reconciled. Judgment and fancy may have place in the same man but by turns, as the end which he aims at requires. As the Israelites in Egypt were sometimes fastened to their labor of making bricks and other times were ranging abroad to gather straw, so also may the judgment sometimes be fixed upon one certain consideration and the fancy at another time wandering about the world. So also reason and eloquence, though not perhaps in the natural sciences, yet in the moral may stand very well together. For wheresoever there is place for adorning and preferring of error, there is much more place for adorning and preferring of truth, if they have it to adorn. Nor is there any repugnancy between fearing the laws and not fearing a public enemy, nor between abstaining from injury and pardoning it in others. There is therefore no such inconsistence of human nature with civil duties as some think. I have known clearness of judgment and largeness of fancy, strength of reason and graceful elocution, a courage for the war and a fear for the laws, and all eminently in one man; and that was my most noble and honored friend, Mr. Sidney Godolphin, who, hating no man nor hated of any, was unfortunately slain in the beginning of the late civil war, in the public quarrel, by an undiscerned and an undiscerning hand.

To the Laws of Nature, declared in Chapter xv, I would have this added, *that every man is bound by nature, as much as in him lies, to protect in war the authority by which he is himself protected in time of peace.* For he that pretends a right of nature to preserve his own body cannot pretend a right of nature to destroy him by whose strength he is preserved; it is a manifest contradiction of himself. And though this law may be drawn by consequence from some of those that are there already mentioned, yet the times require to have it inculcated and remembered.

And because I find by divers English books lately printed that the civil wars have not yet sufficiently taught men in what point of time it is that a subject becomes obliged to the conqueror, nor what is conquest, nor how it comes about that it obliges men to obey his laws, therefore for further satisfaction of men therein I say the point of time wherein a man becomes subject to a conqueror is that point wherein, having liberty to submit to him, he consents either by express words or by other sufficient sign to be his subject. When it is that a man has the liberty to submit, I have showed before in the end of Chapter XXI —namely, that for him that has no obligation to his former sovereign but that of an ordinary subject, it is then when the means of his life are within the guards and garrisons of the enemy, for it is then that he has no longer protection from him but is protected by the adverse party for his contribution. Seeing therefore such contribution is everywhere as a thing inevitable, notwithstanding it be an assistance to the enemy, esteemed lawful, a total submission which is but an assistance to the enemy cannot be esteemed unlawful. Besides, if a man consider that they who submit assist the enemy but with part of their estates whereas they that refuse assist him with the whole, there is no reason to call their submission or composition an assistance, but rather a detriment to the enemy. But if a man, besides the obligation of a subject, has taken upon him a new obligation of a soldier, then he has not the liberty to submit to a new power as long as the old one keeps the field and gives him means of subsistence either in his armies or garrisons, for in this case, he cannot complain of want of protection and means to live as a soldier. But when that also fails, a soldier also may seek his protection wheresoever he has most hope to have it, and may lawfully submit himself to his new master. And so much for the time when he may do it lawfully if he will. If therefore he do it, he is undoubtedly bound to be a true subject, for a contract lawfully made cannot lawfully be broken.

By this also a man may understand when it is that men may be said to be conquered and in what the nature of conquest and the right of a conqueror consists, for his submission in itself implies them all. Conquest is not the victory itself but the acquisition, by victory, of a right over the persons of men. He therefore that is slain is overcome but not conquered; he that is taken and put into prison or chains is not conquered though overcome, for he is still an enemy and may save himself if he can; but he that upon promise of obedience has his life and liberty allowed him is then conquered and a subject, and not before. The

Romans used to say that their general had *pacified* such a *province*—that is to say, in English, *conquered* it—and that the country was *pacified* by victory when the people of it had promised *imperata facere*—that is, *to do what the Roman people commanded them;* this was to be conquered. But this promise may be either express or tacit: express, by promise; tacit, by other signs. As for example, a man that has not been called to make such an express promise because he is one whose power perhaps is not considerable, yet if he live under their protection openly he is understood to submit himself to the government; but if he live there secretly, he is liable to anything that may be done to a spy and enemy of the state. I say not he does any injustice, for acts of open hostility bear not that name, but that he may be justly put to death. Likewise, if a man when his country is conquered be out of it, he is not conquered nor subject; but if at his return he submit to the government, he is bound to obey it. So that *conquest,* to define it, is the acquiring of the right of sovereignty by victory. Which right is acquired in the people's submission, by which they contract with the victor, promising obedience for life and liberty.

In Chapter XXIX, I have set down for one of the causes of the dissolutions of commonwealths their imperfect generation, consisting in the want of an absolute and arbitrary legislative power; for want whereof, the civil sovereign is fain to handle the sword of justice unconstantly and as if it were too hot for him to hold. One reason whereof, which I have not there mentioned, is this, that they will all of them justify the war by which their power was at first gotten and whereon, as they think, their right depends, and not on the possession. As if, for example, the right of the kings of England did depend on the goodness of the cause of William the Conqueror and upon their lineal and directest descent from him, by which means there would perhaps be no tie of the subjects' obedience to their sovereign at this day in all the world; wherein while they needlessly think to justify themselves, they justify all the successful rebellions that ambition shall at any time raise against them and their successors. Therefore I put down for one of the most effectual seeds of the death of any state that the conquerors require not only a submission of men's actions to them for the future but also an approbation of all their actions past, when there is scarce a commonwealth in the world whose beginnings can in conscience be justified.

And because the name of tyranny signifies nothing more nor less than the name of sovereignty, be it in one or many men, saving that they that use the former word are understood to be angry with them they call tyrants, I think the toleration of a professed hatred of tyranny is a toleration of hatred to commonwealth in general, and another evil seed not differing much from the former. For to the justification of the cause of a conqueror, the reproach of the cause of the conquered is for the most part necessary, but neither of them necessary for the obligation of the conquered. And thus much I have thought fit to say upon the review of the first and second part of this discourse.

In Chapter xxxv, I have sufficiently declared out of the Scripture that in the commonwealth of the Jews God himself was made the sovereign by pact with the people, who were therefore called his *peculiar people* to distinguish them from the rest of the world over whom God reigned not by their consent but by his own power; and that in this kingdom Moses was God's lieutenant on earth, and that it was he that told them what laws God appointed them to be ruled by. But I have omitted to set down who were the officers appointed to do execution, especially in capital punishments, not then thinking it a matter of so necessary consideration as I find it since. We know that generally in all commonwealths, the execution of corporal punishments was either put upon the guards or other soldiers of the sovereign power or given to those in whom want of means, contempt of honor, and hardness of heart concurred to make them sue for such an office. But among the Israelites it was a positive law of God their sovereign that he that was convicted of a capital crime should be stoned to death by the people, and that the witnesses should cast the first stone, and after the witnesses then the rest of the people. This was a law that designed who were to be the executioners, but not that anyone should throw a stone at him before conviction and sentence, where the congregation was judge. The witnesses were nevertheless to be heard before they proceeded to execution, unless the fact were committed in the presence of the congregation itself or in sight of the lawful judges, for then there needed no other witnesses but the judges themselves. Nevertheless, this manner of proceeding, being not thoroughly understood, has given occasion to a dangerous opinion that any man may kill another in some cases by a right of zeal, as if the executions done upon offenders in the kingdom of God in old time proceeded not from the sovereign command but from the authority of private zeal; which, if we consider the texts that seem to favor it, is quite contrary.

First, where the Levites fell upon the people that had made and worshiped the Golden Calf and slew three thousand of them, it was by the commandment of Moses from the mouth of God, as is manifest, Exod. 32:27. And when the son of a woman of Israel had blasphemed God, they that heard it did not kill him but brought him before Moses, who put him under custody till God should give sentence against him; as appears Levit. 24: 11-12. Again (Num. 25:6-7), when Phinehas killed Zimri and Cozbi, it was not by right of private zeal: their crime was committed in the sight of the assembly; there needed no witness; the law was known and he the heir apparent to the sovereignty; and, which is the principal point, the lawfulness of his act depended wholly upon a subsequent ratification by Moses, whereof he had no cause to doubt. And this presumption of a future ratification is sometimes necessary to the safety of a commonwealth, as in a sudden rebellion any man that can suppress it by his own power in the country where it begins, without express law or commission, may lawfully do it and provide to have it ratified or pardoned while it is in doing or after it is done. Also Num. 35:30, it is expressly said, *Whosoever shall kill the murderer, shall kill him upon the word of witnesses;* but witnesses suppose a formal judicature, and consequently condemn that pretense of *jus zelotarum.* The law of Moses concerning him that entices to idolatry—that is to say, in the kingdom of God to a renouncing of his allegiance (Deut. 13:8-9)—forbids to conceal him, and commands the accuser to cause him to be put to death and to cast the first stone at him, but not to kill him before he be condemned. And (Deut. 17:4-7) the process against idolatry is exactly set down: for God there speaks to the people as judge and commands them, when a man is accused of idolatry, to inquire diligently of the fact and finding it true then to stone him, but still the hand of the witness throws the first stone. This is not private zeal but public condemnation. In like manner when a father has a rebellious son, the law is (Deut. 21: 18-21) that he shall bring him before the judges of the town and all the people of the town shall stone him. Lastly, by pretense of these laws it was that St. Stephen was stoned, and not by pretense of private zeal; for before he was carried away to execution, he had pleaded his cause before the high priest.[2] There is nothing in all this, nor in any other part of the Bible, to countenance executions by private zeal, which, being oftentimes but a conjunction of ignorance and passion, is against both the justice and peace of a commonwealth.

In Chapter xxxvi, I have said that it is not declared in what manner God spoke supernaturally to Moses, nor that he spoke not to him sometimes by dreams and visions and by a supernatural voice as to other prophets, for the manner how he spoke unto him from the mercy seat is expressly set down, Num. 7:89, in these words: *From that time forward, when Moses entered into the Tabernacle of the congregation to speak with God, he heard a voice which spake unto him from over the mercy-seat, which is over the Ark of the testimony; from between the cherubim he spake unto him.* But it is not declared in what consists the pre-eminence of the manner of God's speaking to Moses above that of his speaking to other prophets, as to Samuel and to Abraham, to whom he also spoke by a voice (that is, by vision), unless the difference consist in the clearness of the vision. For *face to face* and *mouth to mouth* cannot be literally understood of the infiniteness and incomprehensibility of the Divine nature.

And as to the whole doctrine, I see not yet but the principles of it are true and proper and the ratiocination solid. For I ground the civil right of sovereigns, and both the duty and liberty of subjects, upon the known natural inclinations of mankind and upon the articles of the law of nature, of which no man that pretends but reason enough to govern his private family ought to be ignorant. And for the power ecclesiastical of the same sovereigns, I ground it on such texts as are both evident in themselves and consonant to the scope of the whole Scripture. And therefore am persuaded that he that shall read

2 [Acts 7.]

it with a purpose only to be informed shall be informed by it. But for those that by writing or public discourse or by their eminent actions have already engaged themselves to the maintaining of contrary opinions, they will not be so easily satisfied. For in such cases it is natural for men at one and the same time both to proceed in reading and to lose their attention in the search of objections to that they had read before. Of which, in a time wherein the interests of men are changed (seeing much of that doctrine which serves to the establishing of a new government must needs be contrary to that which conduced to the dissolution of the old), there cannot choose but be very many.

In that part which treats of a Christian commonwealth, there are some new doctrines which, it may be, in a state where the contrary were already fully determined, were a fault for a subject without leave to divulge, as being an usurpation of the place of a teacher. But in this time that men call not only for peace but also for truth, to offer such doctrines as I think true, and that manifestly tend to peace and loyalty, to the consideration of those that are yet in deliberation is no more but to offer new wine to be put into new casks, that both may be preserved together. And I suppose that then, when novelty can breed no trouble nor disorder in a state, men are not generally so much inclined to the reverence of antiquity as to prefer ancient errors before new and well-proved truth.

There is nothing I distrust more than my elocution, which nevertheless I am confident, excepting the mischances of the press, is not obscure. That I have neglected the ornament of quoting ancient poets, orators, and philosophers, contrary to the custom of late time, whether I have done well or ill in it, proceeds from my judgment, grounded on many reasons. For first, all truth of doctrine depends either upon *reason* or upon *Scripture,* both which give credit to many but never receive it from any writer. Secondly, the matters in question are not of *fact* but of *right,* wherein there is no place for *witnesses.* There is scarce any of those old writers that contradicts not sometimes both himself and others, which makes their testimonies insufficient. Fourthly, such opinions as are taken only upon credit of antiquity are not intrinsically the judgment of those that cite them, but words that pass, like gaping, from mouth to mouth.

Fifthly, it is many times with a fraudulent design that men stick their corrupt doctrine with the cloves of other men's wit. Sixthly, I find not that the ancients they cite took it for an ornament to do the like with those that wrote before them. Seventhly, it is an argument of indigestion, when Greek and Latin sentences unchewed come up again, as they use to do, unchanged. Lastly, though I reverence those men of ancient time that either have written truth perspicuously or set us in a better way to find it out ourselves, yet to the antiquity itself I think nothing due. For if we will reverence the age, the present is the oldest. If the antiquity of the writer, I am not sure that generally they to whom such honor is given were more ancient when they wrote than I am that am writing. But if it be well considered, the praise of ancient authors proceeds not from the reverence of the dead but from the competition and mutual envy of the living.

To conclude, there is nothing in this whole discourse, nor in that I wrote before of the same subject in Latin, as far as I can perceive, contrary either to the Word of God or to good manners, or to the disturbance of the public tranquillity. Therefore I think it may be profitably printed, and more profitably taught in the Universities, in case they also think so to whom the judgment of the same belongs. For seeing the Universities are the fountains of civil and moral doctrine, from whence the preachers and the gentry, drawing such water as they find, use to sprinkle the same (both from the pulpit and in their conversation) upon the people, there ought certainly to be great care taken to have it pure, both from the venom of heathen politicians and from the incantation of deceiving spirits. And by that means the most men, knowing their duties, will be the less subject to serve the ambition of a few discontented persons in their purposes against the state, and be the less grieved with the contributions necessary for their peace and defense; and the governors themselves have the less cause to maintain at the common charge any greater army than is necessary to make good the public liberty against the invasions and encroachments of foreign enemies.

And thus I have brought to an end my Discourse of Civil and Ecclesiastical Government, occasioned by the disorders of the present time, without partiality, without application, and without other design than to set before men's eyes the mutual relation between protection and obedience, of which the condition of human nature and the laws divine, both natural and positive, require an inviolable observation. And though in the revolution of states there can be no very good constellation for truths of this nature to be born under (as having an angry aspect from the dissolvers of an old government, and seeing but the backs of them that erect a new), yet I cannot think it will be condemned at this time either by the public judge of doctrine or by any that desires the continuance of public peace. And in this hope I return to my interrupted speculation of bodies natural; wherein, if God give me health to finish it, I hope the novelty will as much please as in the doctrine of this artificial body it uses to offend. For such truth as opposes no man's profit nor pleasure is to all men welcome.